T0361186

Routledge Revivals

Economic Growth and Development in Jordan

First Published in 1979 *Economic Growth and Development in Jordan* is a comprehensive analysis of the economies of pre-1967 Jordan and the post-1967 East Bank. Part I includes statistical data that measures the growth performance of Jordan's prewar economy and presents the first quantitative explanation of its concentration in the service sector. Part II surveys the postwar East Bank economy, including a critical analysis of statistical data. The third section of the book covers Jordan's development policies and experiences in the areas of agriculture, industry, and planning. Dr Mazur concludes with speculations on the future of the Jordanian economy with and without a Middle East peace settlement. This is an interesting read for students and researchers of economics, Middle East studies and Middle East economics.

Economic Growth and Development in Jordan

Michael P. Mazur

First published in 1979
by Westview Press

This edition first published in 2022 by Routledge
4 Park Square, Milton Park, Abingdon, Oxon, OX14 4RN

and by Routledge
605 Third Avenue, New York, NY 10017

Routledge is an imprint of the Taylor & Francis Group, an informa business

© 1979 Westview Press, Inc.

Publisher's Note
The publisher has gone to great lengths to ensure the quality of this reprint but points out that some imperfections in the original copies may be apparent.

Disclaimer
The publisher has made every effort to trace copyright holders and welcomes correspondence from those they have been unable to contact.

A Library of Congress record exists under ISBN:

ISBN: 978-1-032-40880-4 (hbk)
ISBN: 978-1-003-35512-0 (ebk)
ISBN: 978-1-032-40883-5 (pbk)

Book DOI 10.4324/9781003355120

Economic Growth and Development in Jordan

Michael P. Mazur

Westview Press / Boulder, Colorado

Westview Special Studies on the Middle East

Copyright © 1979 by Westview Press, Inc.

Published in 1979 in the United States of America by
    Westview Press, Inc.
    5500 Central Avenue
    Boulder, Colorado 80301
    Frederick A. Praeger, Publisher

Library of Congress Catalog Card Number: 78-22518
ISBN: 0-89158-455-2

Composition for this book was provided by the author.
Printed and bound in the United States of America.

Contents

Tables

xi

Preface

This study draws upon the results of two research trips to the Middle East, in 1969 and 1976.
The latter trip, upon which the greater part of
this study is based, was assisted by a grant awarded by the Joint Committee on the Near and Middle
East of the Social Science Research Council and
the American Council of Learned Societies.

The results of my research trip in 1969 are
embodied in my thesis, "The Economic Development of
Jordan," unpublished Ph.D. thesis, Department of
Economics, Massachusetts Institute of Technology,
Cambridge, Mass., 1972 (hereafter referred to as
"Mazur thesis"). Part 1 of the present study draws
heavily upon material in the thesis. The reader
interested in further methodological detail of the
material presented in Part 1 here is advised to
consult that thesis.

I owe a special debt of gratitude to two per-
sons whose lavish help during my first research
trip to Jordan in 1969 was invaluable: Jacob L.
Crane and Wasef Y. Azar. I am grateful for the help
of many others, including Evsey D. Domar, Sidney S.
Alexander, Everett E. Hagen, Hashem Debbas, Abdul
Wahhab Jamil Awwad, Gordon Pierson, Ghalib Arafat,
Mohamed Haitham El-Hurani, Lloyd George, John
Hyslop, Salem O. Ghawi, Shawki Barghouti, Said
Nabulsi, Carl Gotsch, Jawad Salah, Tayseer Abdel-
Jaber, Rima Kamal, Nureddin Taquieddin, Jawad Anani,
and Yahya Sheqwara.

I also wish to thank Nijmeddin Dajani, Najati
al-Bukhari, Ziyad Innab, Tawfiq Battarsi, Adnan
Hindi, Ali Dajani, Adnan Dabbas, Munthar Masri,
Tony Babb, Fuad Qushair, Barry Hudson, Taher H.

Kanaan, Richard J. Ward, Frederick C. Thomas, George
Soussou, Arthur M. Handly, Marwan Dodin, Hanna Odeh,
Shuja al-Asad, Kamel Abu Jaber, Farhi Obeid, Fuad
Ayoub, Burhan Abu Howayej,Duncan Muir, Amin Abu
Sha'er, Munir Abu Ghazzala, Abdul Moneim Abu Nuwar,
Abdullah Hamadneh, Malek el-Bukhari, Mohammad
Hassan Ismail, Zaki Takrouri, Wadi Halasa, and
Abdul Moneim Melhas.

Economic Growth and
Development in Jordan

1
Introduction

The nation of Jordan is the creation of recent
political events. Prior to the twentieth century,
no such entity existed. The major division of the
area was between the East Bank and the West Bank,
neither of which ever had constituted a distinct
unit and between which there were few contacts. This
division was dictated by geography and is of long
standing. The deep geological rift formed by the
Jordan River Valley, Lake Tiberias and the Dead Sea
was long an obstacle to contacts between the two
banks.

The West Bank (comprising chiefly the Palestine
hills) usually was oriented toward the remainder of
Palestine, primarily the coastal plain. In times of
prosperity, when the Mediterranean commerce of Palestine coastal towns flourished, the Palestine hills
to a modest degree constituted a hinterland to these
urban areas. For the most part, however, the communities of the Palestine hills were localized, both
in their commerce and in their loyalties. In part,
this was the result of geography. Most of the West
Bank inhabitants farmed the long, narrow valleys of
the westward slopes of the Palestine hills. Thus,
the natural unit dictated by geography was a small
one. Historically, when political unification existed, it was generally imposed from outside by the
incorporation of the area into a larger empire, and
such unification was frequently only a thin overlay
on a basically localized region.

For the East Bank the overwhelming historical
factor has always been the level and extent of security. Transjordan was almost invariably the front
line in the continuing conflict between the nomad
and the settled farmer. In times of security new
towns would be built and the cultivated area extended eastward, not only by the migration of farmers,

1

but also by the settlement of nomads. When security deteriorated, the settled area would recede and the easternmost lands revert to pastoralism. During most of its history Transjordan's position on important trade routes was more important than the area itself. Even in ancient times, caravan routes between Mesopotamia and both Egypt and Arabia passed through the East Bank. After the coming of Islam in the seventh century, it was also important as a pilgrimage route from Syria to the Islamic holy cities of Arabia. And as trade between Europe and the Orient expanded, Transjordan shared in the gains.

The area that ultimately became Jordan reached its highest development prior to the twentieth century in the first centuries of the Christian era, when it was part of the Roman Empire. Under the Romans the settled area expanded and agricultural products were exported to Rome. Transjordan was connected with Palestine by numerous roads across the Jordan Valley and the whole area was oriented toward Mediterranean commerce. Irrigation was developed under the Romans to a degree perhaps not even achieved today. Wells were dug and springs cleaned and improved. Bridges, aqueducts, dams, irrigation canals and cisterns were constructed.

The decline from the heights achieved under the Romans was neither precipitous nor continuous. It was not, as sometimes suggested, the immediate consequence of the Arabic-Islamic conquest of the seventh century. Many of the Roman constructions decayed and fell into disuse in the later years of Byzantine rule over the area, a time of greatly decreased security. The early years of Islam in fact restored some measure of prosperity to the area because of the proximity of Damascus, for a time the capital of the Islamic Empire. However, after the center of authority was shifted to Baghdad in the mid-eighth century, the region reverted to its status as something of a backwater. Its fortunes fluctuated somewhat in subsequent years, partly depending on the status of local potentates in Syria. But even two centuries of Crusades (eleventh through thirteenth centuries) did not produce very great and lasting changes.

Early in the sixteenth century the area was incorporated into the Turkish Ottoman Empire, but Ottoman rule was quite loose and had limited effect on indigenous society. The Ottoman garrisons provided only modest security from bedouin attack. For the most part, the Turks could not control the bedouins and dealt with them mainly by paying subsidies for the safe passage of pilgrims to Mecca. Security deteriorated greatly in the eighteenth century, partly as the result of new tribal movements out of Arabia and partly from the decline of the Ottoman state. As always, the effect of decreased security was greatest on Transjordan, as settlements disappeared and most of the area reverted to pasture for the flocks of nomads. The isolation and backwardness of Transjordan was exacerbated by European discovery of the water route around Africa, greatly reducing Transjordan's role as a caravan route.

For a variety of reasons the Ottoman Empire began to decline early and lingered on as the "sick man of Europe" for centuries. From the viewpoint of the outlying provinces, such as the area that was to become Jordan, the most important manifestation of Ottoman decline was the virtual disappearance of central authority. The Ottoman government acquiesced in the growing power of local potentates and sometimes even promoted it by such measures as the granting of tax-farming privileges. The pernicious system of tax farming, by which the tax farmer could in effect squeeze as much as possible out of the peasantry in return for a lump-sum payment to the central government, began to take hold in the seventeenth century and was an important factor in the spread of feudalism and large absentee landholdings in the Arab provinces of the Ottoman Empire, although the problem was not as serious in the areas that became Jordan as in such regions as present-day Syria and Iraq.

An important interlude in the reign of Ottoman feudalism occurred during 1830-41, when Egyptian forces of Mohammed Ali, under his son, Ibrahim Pasha, conquered and unified most of geographical Syria (present-day Lebanon, Syria, Jordan and Israel). Mohammed Ali had largely destroyed the feudal, tax-farming land system in Egypt and a beginning was made in Syria as well. While the restoration of the Ottomans in Syria brought some reversion, the old feudal relationships had been dislocated and were not to be fully restored.

Another important consequence of the Egyptian invasion was greatly increased contact with Europeans. European contacts had existed previously: Along with increasing French cultural influence, purchases by French merchants of tobacco, olive oil, soap, and cotton cloth had contributed to an improvement in economic conditions in Palestine during the eighteenth century. European missionary activity in the Middle East increased significantly in the nine-

3

teenth century and made a particularly important contribution in education. Another important group of European arrivals was made up of Jewish settlers, who began the first wave of Jewish immigration to Palestine around 1880. Up to World War I, however, their numbers were not large enough significantly to affect the indigenous culture; most of the influence went the other way, from the native culture of Oriental Jews onto the European Jews.

In the nineteenth century the Ottoman Empire underwent a halfhearted revival, insufficient to prevent its ultimate demise. The most important effect in the Jordan area was the gradual reassertion of Turkish control in Transjordan. Turkish troops, equipped with modern rifles, managed to restore a modest measure of security against bedouin raids. This, together with increased European demand for grain, brought about a significant expansion in settled agricultural cultivation on the East Bank, as peasant immigrants were attracted from Palestine and elsewhere in the area. Despite these developments, Transjordan at the end of the nineteenth century remained much more backward and insecure than the rest of the area. In the words of two turn-of-the-century travellers: "On the western bank is comparative safety, while just over the narrow stream is no man's land where theft, bloodshed and murder are the commonest everyday occurrence."[1]

Under the British Mandate over Palestine established after World War I, the Arabs of Palestine experienced considerable cultural, social, and economic change. The Mandate government provided improved security and administration and introduced fiscal reforms, particularly in the system of land taxation. Some progress, albeit modest, was achieved in the settlement of private claims to land which had previously been held in village communal tenure. By present-day standards for government promotion of economic development, the Mandate government was not very active, but by the standards of the time for less developed countries (LDCs) or in comparison with the prewar period in most of the Middle East, the Palestine Mandate authorities played a significant role. Education and health services were expanded. The road network was augmented significantly. Agricultural services, such as veterinary, research, and demonstration services were introduced, although they did not attain a high level of development during the Mandate period.

It is difficult to separate the effects of the various sources of Western influence on the Arabs of Palestine--the British Mandate, the worldwide improvement in communications, increased tourist and other Western interest in the Holy Land, and the expansion of the Jewish population and economy in Palestine. The Arab and Jewish economies in Palestine were essentially two separate economies with only a limited amount of contact between them.[2] Jews and Arabs lived separately, and Jewish and Arab employers endeavored to hire members of their own groups. In 1936-37 hostility between the two communities broke out into the open and was followed by an Arab boycott of Jewish manufactures.

It does not require a great deal of direct contact between West and East to bring about significant modernization and industrialization. The Jews of Palestine, whose numbers rose from 10% to 30% of the Palestine population during the interwar years, must have had a significant effect on the Arab economy, even in areas (such as that which became the West Bank of Jordan) where few Jews resided.

Jewish land purchases bid up the price of land greatly, and Arab land sales probably provided the capital for modernization of Arab agriculture and industry, although they may also have reduced agricultural employment opportunities for Arab peasants. Palestine Arab industry, producing almost solely for consumption by the Palestine Arab community, apparently was expanded and modernized under the Mandate. It is not known by precisely how much Arab manufacturing expanded, but it was doubtless not nearly as great as the rapid expansion of Jewish manufactures, particularly during World War II. Wealth accumulated through land sales helped to provide the nucleus of a growing Arab middle class.

Expanded Arab employment in the Mandate government service also added to the Arab middle class. Although Jewish industrial employers attempted to employ only Jewish labor, the scarcity of Jewish labor and low cost of Arab labor impelled them to employ numerous Arabs. Thus, the expansion of both Jewish and Arab industry led to the development of an Arab urban working class. As a result of these various factors, there was a significant trend toward urbanization of the Palestine Arab population during the Mandate.

Besides the stimulus provided by investment of receipts from Arab land sales, Arab agricultural productivity was enhanced in other ways. Particularly in citriculture, Arabs borrowed improved agricultural techniques applied on Jewish farms. The Jewish settlers, concentrated in the cities of the Pales-

5

tine coastal plain, were far from self-sufficient in agricultural products. The coastal region provided an important market for the surplus agricultural output (mainly wheat and barley) of Arab farms in the Palestine hills. Even then, Palestine as a whole imported substantial amounts of foodstuffs. When the Mandate authorities reduced food imports greatly during World War II, the prices of food-stuffs, particularly of the sort produced by Palestine Arab agriculture, rose to extremely high levels, and many Arab farmers were able to extinguish their debts and make capital improvements.

The post-World War I British Mandate extended to Transjordan. Politically, Transjordan, nominally ruled by the Amir Abdullah under British tutelage, was in some ways tied to Palestine, but essentially it was separate from the Palestine Mandate adminis-tration. The government of Transjordan was support-ed by subsidies from Great Britain and the civil ad-ministration of Palestine. Most of the British aid was intended for the upkeep of the British-commanded Arab Legion and for the execution of public works projects, many of which served a military function. Almost all of Transjordan's government budget expen-ditures went to defense and administration. Very little expenditure was undertaken to promote econo-mic development directly. There was, for instance, only very modest expansion in educational facilities.

Yet in spite of the government's very limited participation in development activities of the usual kind, striking progress was made in economic and social development during the Mandate years. Trans-jordan was so backward and insecure at the close of World War I that measures taken for granted elsewhere achieved significant results. One of the most im-portant actions of the interwar period was the es-tablishment of security against bedouin raids. The Arab Legion, created in the early 1920s, was almost immediately successful, and by the early 1930s the bedouins were no longer a threat to the settled areas. Perhaps an equally important achievement of the interwar period was the settlement of land claims and individual ownership in most of the country. Previously, the communal village system of mushaa tenure had been widespread. Under this system vil-lage lands were periodically reallocated among mem-bers of the village, an obvious deterrent to land improvement by a single individual. By the 1940s this system had largely been replaced by individual ownership and Transjordan's landholding system was "perhaps the best system in the Arab Middle East."[3]

6

Also under the Mandate, the confused and inequitable Ottoman tax system was reformed.

Improved security resulted in eastward expansion of the settled area.[4] Numerous bedouins, motivated by a deteriorating nomad economy, became settled farmers, or at least seminomadic. The improvement of security had deprived bedouins of protection money paid by villagers. Expansion of the cultivated area deprived them of some of their grazing lands. The introduction of the automobile drove down the price of camels and reduced bedouin employment in supplying and guiding caravans. Increased commercial contacts in the Middle East had introduced the nomad to new commodities such as sugar and tea, to which he had become habituated, so that the loss of earning power from nomadic activity was strongly felt.

In view of the subsidies received, it is not surprising the Transjordan continually ran deficits in its balance of trade. However, Transjordan apparently ran a surplus in its trade with Palestine, its most important customer, to which it sold mainly agricultural products.[5] In addition, some Transjordanians found seasonal employment in Palestine, especially on public construction projects. A large share of Transjordan's imports came by way of Palestine, but most were re-exports of goods produced elsewhere (except during World War II, when other supplies were cut off and Transjordan's purchases of Palestine manufactures rose greatly).

In Transjordan under the Mandate, manufacturing industry was almost nonexistent. What little there was consisted largely of small-scale processing of agricultural products (especially flour milling). Most industries were carried on at home or in small workshops and even these activities were relatively rare. Only one industry--the two British-owned cigarette companies--operated on even a moderately large scale using modern methods. In view of Transjordan's history the low level of manufacturing development is not surprising. Only a century earlier Transjordan had been little more than a large pasture. In addition, the free trade enforced by the Mandate authorities and the small size of the local market hampered industrial development. A lack of electricity was an additional barrier.[6] Partly as a consequence of the absence of industry, less than a quarter of Transjordan's 1943 population lived in towns of 10,000 or more and many of the nominally urban population were more rural than urban. The largest town, Amman, numbered only about 30,000 in 1943.[7]

Prior to the introduction of the automobile during World War I, beasts of burden were almost the sole means of transport. Even the animal-drawn cart was unknown, except to the small communities of Circassians. Only modest progress was made in road building, with the best communication being between Transjordan and Palestine. Very little development occurred in other modes of transport. Transjordan was important for the transit trade of neighboring countries. Goods passing between Iraq and the Mediterranean often went by way of Palestine and Transjordan, and in addition the Iraq Petroleum Company pipeline from Iraq to Haifa passed through Transjordan. These transit activities had little economic effect on Transjordan, however. [8]

World War II brought greater prosperity to Transjordan. As an exporter of cereals to Palestine, Transjordan benefited greatly from the very high level of grain prices existing there during the war. In addition, the war stimulated commercial activity in Transjordan, particularly Amman. Because import restrictions were less stringent in Transjordan than in nearby countries, Amman became a sort of commercial center, re-exporting (and smuggling) imported goods to neighboring countries and especially to Palestine. Although many of the merchants engaged in this activity were from other countries, the effect on Transjordan, and particularly Amman, was probably substantial. [9]

The preceding should make clear the great gap in modernization between Transjordan and the Palestine Arabs. The Palestinian Arabs were more urban, more cosmopolitan, and more educated than the Arabs of Transjordan. While the gap may have widened during the Mandate, it was of long standing, apparently dating at least as far back as the eighteenth century.

After the 1948-49 Arab-Israeli war, the flight of the Palestine refugees, the partition of Palestine, and Transjordan's annexation of the West Bank, the new state of Jordan came into existence with a population three times as great as that of the former Transjordan but with total arable land increased by only about a third. The citizens of the new state numbered about 1,185,000: 375,000 Transjordanians, 460,000 West Bank Palestinians and 350,000 refugees. [10]

The frontier between Jordan and Israel essentially marked the positions of the opposing armies at the time of the cease-fire in 1949. In some areas the electricity and water supplies were cut off. More important, many West Bank border villages lost large parts of their farmlands, which were on the other side of the border. Estimates of the number of people seriously affected in this way run around 100,000. In the early 1950s about half of these migrated elsewhere.[11] Although not technically refugees, since they had not lost their homes, the situation of many of these people differed little from that of the refugees. Loss of employment was suffered by others of the original West Bank inhabitants, who previously were employed in the area of Palestine that became Israel, often on the Palestine railroad or in seasonal labor on the citrus plantations of the coastal plain.

Besides the inevitable fall in wages and greatly increased unemployment, the influx of the refugees and the expenditure of funds transferred by them to Jordan touched off an import boom, thus expanding and enriching the commercial community, mainly in Amman.[12] The arrival of the refugees also set into motion a round of frenetic residential construction, whose demands for labor somewhat mitigated the extreme over-supply in the labor market. Particularly on the West Bank, where most of the refugees were located, the distress was great and only slightly alleviated by the provision of assistance from the United Nations Relief and Works Agency for Palestine Refugees in the Near East (UNRWA), which itself provided employment to a modest number of refugees.

In the early 1950s Jordan's economic development prospects appeared anything but promising. The West and East Banks were not so much economically complementary with each other as they were both complementary with that part of Palestine which became Israel, in which were located the region's major commercial and industrial centers and which provided a key market for the agricultural output of the two banks. The transport network of the East and West Banks was directed to the west, particularly the port of Haifa. When the establishment of Israel closed off this traffic, Jordan was faced with high transport costs and the necessity of developing a new transport system along north-south lines.

Jordan's natural resource endowment was meager, limited principally to high-grade phosphate deposits in Transjordan and to mineral salts in the Dead Sea. Water resources were poor. Only in the northern hills of the East and West Banks did average annual rainfall exceed 24 inches. In a sizable part of the cultivated area the average was below 16 inches, making the area unsuitable for regular rotation of winter and summer crops or for the cultivation of fruit trees and vineyards. In addition, Jordan's

agricultural production, almost completely rainfed
in the early 1950s, was subject to extreme instability as a result of rainfall fluctuations.

Of the small area of land suitable for cultivation (about 10% of the total land area) a large part
was eroded and of low quality. In particular, the
land in the West Bank, which was some of the worst
farmland in Palestine, was especially poor and eroded. There was very little opportunity for expansion
of the sown area, except by the costly method of ir-
rigation--and even here the possibilities were limited. There were no perennial surface water sources
other than the Jordan River and its tributaries.
The Jordan River, despite its prominence in religious
literature and folklore, is actually quite small.
Since most cultivable land in Jordan is on hills or
plateaus, the potential for irrigation from low-
lying rivers is restricted by the cost of pumping.
Ground water resources are also quite limited. Even
the principal cities, Amman and Jerusalem, were without adequate water supplies and suffered seasonal
shortages.

The percentage of the Jordanian population that
was employed in the early 1950s was substantially
lower than in many other countries because the influx of refugees resulted in high unemployment, because a high population growth rate caused a large
percentage of children in the population, and because the prevailing attitude discouraged female employment in most occupations. A small number of
workers accordingly had to support a large consuming
population. The unemployed labor did, however, represent a potential asset that could be utilized if
Jordan mobilized cooperating factors of production.

The continuing state of tension between Israel
and the neighboring Arab states, the volatility of in-
tra-Arab politics since the Arab setback in 1948-49,
and internal tensions in Jordan all required the
maintenance of security forces that were large relative to Jordan's small size and low per capita income. Had these not been externally financed, they
would have reduced resources available for capital
formation. These tensions and recurrent crises also
might have hindered potential entrepreneurs from
otherwise profitable investments--a factor of particular importance in a country relying on private
enterprise as much as Jordan does.

At its birth Jordan inherited very little manufacturing industry, as Transjordan's manufacturing
was almost nonexistent and that of Palestine had
mainly been located in the area that became Israel.[13]

With its small population and low per capita income,
Jordan offered only a limited market for domestically
produced goods, thus handicapping the establishment
of industries operating under economies of scale.
Industrialization was also hindered by the high cost
of power, Jordan having very little hydroelectric
potential and being unable to take full advantage of
economies of scale in thermal electric generation.
Furthermore, Jordan lacked industrial raw materials,
other than olive oil, tobacco, and hides.

In this situation Jordan had to rely heavily on
imports for consumer goods, investment goods, and
inputs into domestic industries. But Jordan was pen-
alized--both as importer and exporter--by the high
costs of transport. In its early years almost all
Jordan's trade passed by way of Beirut and Damascus
--a costly trip. The port of Aqaba became progressively more important, but this too was expensive.

Against this catalogue of handicaps, there were
few offsetting advantages. Jordan possessed the
rather negative advantage of beginning from a low
level of development. Per capita national income in
1953 was probably not much more than $100, broadly
comparable to the levels attained at the same time
by countries such as Egypt, India, and Pakistan.
With domestic industry in its infancy, it might be
comparatively easy to achieve rapid industrial growth
via import substitution in such industries as food
processing, building materials, household furnish-
ings, textiles, clothing, and footwear.

Jordan possessed an undeniable economic asset in
the tourist potential entailed by its sovereignty
over the principal shrines of the Holy Land. In addition, Jordan had added significantly to its educated merchant, civil service, and professional groups
as a result of the flight of educated Palestinians
from Israeli-occupied territory and from the annexation of the West Bank. These provided a fairly high
level of sophisticated leadership in government and
private economic activity.

Land tenure in Jordan was more satisfactory than
in many other developing countries. Most land was in
small and medium-sized holdings, mainly owner-operated. However, many owners had extremely small holdings, and most holdings were divided into a number of
scattered plots.[14]

In the 1950s Jordan's economic prospects were
regarded almost universally as dismal. The World
Bank mission that visited Jordan in 1955 estimated
that gross domestic product (GDP) in current prices
had grown at an average annual rate of about 10% from

1952 to 1954, but it did not believe that such a high rate could be sustained in the future. The mission set 4% as an attainable annual growth rate for gross national product (GNP), but suggested that it would not be easy to achieve. It would require a capital-output ratio of 4, which the mission suggested might also be difficult to attain.[15]

The performance of the Jordanian economy apparently ran completely counter to such pessimistic expectations. According to official and unofficial estimates, the growth rate of GDP at current prices continued to average over 10% per year between 1954 and 1966. While no respectable constant-price GDP estimates had ever been presented, many observers contended that it must have grown at an average annual rate of 8% or more.

Other indicators, such as the number of motor vehicles or production indices of major industrial and mineral products, also suggested rapid growth. The population of Amman, the leading industrial and commercial city, as well as the capital, grew spectacularly: 60 thousand in 1945, 108 thousand in 1966.[16]

As its first task, this study takes up the story of the economic development of Jordan during the period between the unification of the two banks and the 1967 Middle East war. The analysis, which is presented in Part 1 below, is primarily statistical. Its fundamental objective is to assess quantitatively Jordan's prewar economic structure and development performance. Published and unpublished economic statistics of Jordan are reasonably abundant and reliable for the prewar years, particularly for the period 1959-66, though some attention must be given to their limitations.

Part 2 takes up the economic developments in Jordan since the 1967 war. It is concerned with the developments only in the East Bank, the sole area under the effective control of the national government in Amman since 1967. The omission of the West Bank from the analysis is for practical reasons--to keep the study to manageable proportions--and no implications about the future political status of the West Bank should be attributed to it.

The statistical analysis of the postwar period in Part 2 is less extensive than that in Part 1 for the prewar period. The reasons are both practical and conceptual. First, the quality of economic data for the 1967-75 period is substantially worse than that for the 1959-66 period. Second, the period since the 1967 war has been so abnormal and so much affected by fortuitous and transitory shocks to the economy (such as the shelling of the Jordan Valley by Israel, the 1970-71 civil conflict, the closing of the Suez Canal, and border closings by neighboring states) that even if postwar economic statistics were perfect, it would be difficult to draw conclusions from them about fundamental long-run economic trends. This difficulty is compounded by the sudden impact on Jordan of the 1973 Middle East war and especially of the subsequent revolution in oil prices.

In Part 3 the focus shifts from overall statistical assessment of the economy and its performance to examination of the most important policies to promote development. Three vital policy spheres have been selected for analysis: agricultural development policy, industrial development policy, and development planning, with special emphasis on the Five Year Development Plan for 1976-80. The study concludes with a review of Jordan's development experience and speculations on some possibilities for the future.

NOTES

1. William Libbey and Franklin E. Hoskins, The Jordan Valley and Petra, London, 1905, vol. I, p. 152, quoted in Benjamin Shwadran, Jordan: A State of Tension, New York: Council for Middle Eastern Affairs Press, 1959, p. 99.

2. Total trade in both intermediate and final goods and services between the Arab and Jewish sectors has been estimated at only about 7% of Palestine's national income for 1936. This figure may be uncharacteristically low, since 1936 was a year of open conflict between the two communities. Nadav Halevi and Ruth Klinov-Malul, The Economic Development of Israel, New York: Praeger, 1968, p. 38. One reason for the low percentage is the high degree of self-sufficiency of much of Arab agriculture; probably at least two-thirds of Arab agricultural production was consumed on the farm.

3. Shwadran, p. 165.

4. The extension of security was not without its drawbacks, however. The destruction of trees and bushes by peasants seeking fuel and by overgrazing of livestock was accelerated when the improved security allowed peasants and their flocks to range further from the village area.

5. The supporting data for this statement are poor, primarily because there were no customs barriers between Transjordan and Palestine. Furthermore, it is not known what proportion of Transjordan's exports to Palestine were re-exported.

6. Proposals for electrification of the country by the Jewish Palestine Electric Corporation met widespread opposition. As a result, Transjordan lacked a grid covering any sizable area, although small power plants provided high-cost

electricity in some localities.

7. Small though Amman's 1943 population was, it represented a rapid rate of increase over its population of 5,000 in 1920, when it was little more than a village.

8. No pipeline transit royalties were paid. Presumably because of British interests in the Iraq Petroleum Company, the British Mandate officials brought about this very favorable (for the company) arrangement. Local benefits were thus limited to employment during the two years of the pipeline's construction.

9. The population of Amman grew phenomenally during the war, from about 20,000 in 1938 to about 60,000 in 1945.

10. The International Bank for Reconstruction and Development (IBRD), The Economic Development of Jordan, Baltimore: Johns Hopkins, 1975, p. 41. The refugees and the original inhabitants of the West Bank were granted full Jordanian citizenship.

11. Paul Grounds Phillips, The Hashemite Kingdom of Jordan: Prolegomena to a Technical Assistance Program, Chicago: University of Chicago, 1954, p. 83.

12. The commercial sector in Amman had expanded during the war years and had prospered in the immediate postwar years as well, as expenditures on previously unobtainable imported consumer goods expanded.

13. In 1954 value added in mining, manufacturing and electricity combined was less than $10 per capita.

14. See especially Gabriel Baer, "Land Tenure in the Hashemite Kingdom of Jordan," Land Economics, 33 (August 1957), 187-97.

15. IBRD, pp. 10, 66-68. A similarly pessimistic view was expressed by James Baster in "The Economic Problems of Jordan," International Affairs, 31 (January 1955), 26-35.

16. "Report on the Social Survey of Amman, Jordan, 1966," in United Nations Economic and Social Office in Beirut (UNESOB), Studies on Social Development in the Middle East, 1969, New York: United Nations, 1970, p. 19.

BIBLIOGRAPHICAL NOTE

In addition to the sources cited in the footnotes to Chapter 1, the following materials have been used in the preparation of this chapter.

Great Britain Naval Intelligence Division, Palestine and Transjordan, Geographical Handbook Series, London: Oxford University Press, 1943.

Z. Y. Hershlag, Introduction to the Modern Economic History of the Middle East, Leiden: E. J. Brill, 1964, especially parts I, II, VI, and IX.

Sa'id B. Himadeh, ed., Economic Organization of Palestine,

Beirut: American University of Beirut, 1938.

P.M. Holt, Egypt and the Fertile Crescent, 1516-1922: A Political History, Ithaca, N.Y.: Cornell University Press, 1966.

David Horowitz and Rita Hinden, Economic Survey of Palestine, Tel Aviv: Economic Research Institute of the Jewish Agency for Palestine, 1946.

A. Konikoff, Transjordan: An Economic Survey, Jerusalem: Economic Research Institute of the Jewish Agency for Palestine, 1946.

Robert R. Nathan, Oscar Gass and Daniel Creamer, Palestine: Problem and Promise, Washington: Public Affairs Press, 1946.

Raphael Patai, "On Culture Contact and Its Working in Modern Palestine," American Anthropological Association Memoir Series no. 67, American Anthropologist, n.s., 49 (October 1947).

_____, The Kingdom of Jordan, Princeton: Princeton University Press, 1958.

R. S. Porter, "Economic Survey of Jordan," Beirut: British Middle East Office, 1953 (mimeographed).

_____, "The Movement of Palestine Funds to Jordan 1948-1952," Beirut: British Middle East Office, n.d. (mimeographed).

Yusif A. Sayigh, "Economic Implications of UNRWA Operations in Jordan, Syria and Lebanon," unpublished M.A. thesis, Department of Economics, American University of Beirut, Beirut, 1952.

Systems Research Corporation, Area Handbook for the Hashemite Kingdom of Jordan, Washington: U.S. Government Printing Office, 1969, Chapters 1-3.

United Nations Conciliation Commission for Palestine, Final Report of the United Nations Economic Survey Mission for the Middle East, 2 vols., Lake Success, N.Y., 1949.

Part 1
Prewar Development Performance:
A Statistical Analysis

2
The Record of Growth

By a fortunate chance, the time period for
which the best economic data on Jordan exist is also
the one period of comparative tranquility in Jordan's
turbulent political history.[1] This interval, from
1959 to 1966, is the one period when good economic
data could be most informative, for they can give
some indication of the structure and performance of
the economy under comparatively normal circumstances
not distorted by war, political turmoil and other
disturbances. It is this coincidence of superior
statistics and political normality that leads to the
emphasis on the 1959-66 period in the three chapters
of Part 1.

1. THE GROWTH OF REAL INCOME

The analysis will deal primarily with trends in
gross domestic product (GDP), rather than net product or national product. Gross product is preferred over net because of the difficulty of accurately estimating depreciation, not only in Jordan,
but even in the most developed countries. National
and domestic product differ by the amount of net
factor income from abroad, which in Jordan consisted
mainly of emigrants' remittances (the largest component), pipeline royalties, and interest on official holdings of foreign reserves. Emigrants' remittances to Jordan have been impossible to measure
accurately and it is generally acknowledged that
published estimates are highly unreliable. The
other reason for focusing on domestic product is
that domestic product is the better measure of the
effect of a country's development efforts. Net
factor income from abroad is affected most by developments abroad and to a much lesser degree by
domestic events.

The quality of Jordanian national accounts statistics for the prewar period probably is about average for a country at its level of economic development. The best estimates are for 1959-66; the estimates for 1954-58 are acceptable, and estimates for earlier years are of almost no value. The available estimates are surveyed in the Appendix.

a. Deflation of 1959-66 GDP

A persistent problem in assessing economic growth in Jordan is that all GDP estimates were in current prices. They were never adequately corrected for inflation, although several unsuccessful attempts at deflation were made. Here an attempt is made to deflate the 1959-66 GDP estimates of the Jordan Department of Statistics (JDS) from the production side, i.e., to deflate value added for different production sectors.

There are several reasons why this approach is preferable to the commonly used alternative of deflating different expenditure categories. First, numbers on the production side of Jordan's national accounts are more reliable. Second, for certain sectors (livestock, transport, and construction), the JDS estimates of value added have been based upon certain assumptions about prices. This means that we can deflate these sectors by adjusting for year-to-year changes in the prices assumed by the JDS. We do not need to know the actual price changes that occurred. In fact, if we did know the actual prices in these sectors, it would be incorrect to use them to deflate the JDS estimates (unless, by chance, they happened to be identical to the prices assumed by the JDS).

Partially deflated estimates of 1959-66 GDP are presented in Table II.1. Available information is sufficient to permit virtually complete deflation of value added in agriculture. The deflation of the trade sector should also be considered quite satisfactory. In the mining and manufacturing sector it was possible to deflate only eight industries and the deflations must be considered very crude approximations.

That part of total construction value added which is "private construction," (one-third to one-half of the total) is expressed in constant prices in Table II.1. For the transport sector current-price estimates of value added are taken to represent constant-price value added, since the JDS estimates deviate from constant-price assumptions only

18

in a few minor and partially offsetting instances with negligible net effect. In the sectors of public administration and defense and of services, that part of value added which represents payment by the central government of wages and salaries to civilian employees may be considered to be at constant prices, since civil service pay scales remained unchanged throughout the 1959-66 period.

In Table II.1 roughly 60-68% of GDP (depending on the year) is expressed in constant prices. In row 12 of Table II.1 is presented the implicit GDP deflator that results when current-price GDP is divided by the partially deflated GDP shown in row 11. This would be the true implicit deflator if there were zero inflation in those parts of GDP not deflated in Table II.1. In this case the average rate of inflation embodied in the national accounts would be 0.6% per year over the 1959-66 period. A slightly different GDP deflator is presented in row 13 of Table II.1. This is the implicit deflator calculated for a fraction of GDP only, viz., that fraction which is successfully deflated in Table II.1, rows 1-11. This would be the true implicit deflator if inflation in the undeflated sectors were at the same rate as in the deflated sectors. On this assumption the average rate of inflation embodied in the national accounts would be 1.1% per year between 1959 and 1966.

Of the 32-40% of GDP which has not been deflated, about half is scattered among a wide variety of activities: various mining and manufacturing activities, government and UNRWA construction, electricity and water supply, banking and finance and various nongovernmental services. From the small price changes assumed by the JDS for private construction, we may infer that price changes in government and UNRWA construction were also small over the period. Of the rest of these activities, no single one is very important and there is little reason to expect exceptional rates of price change in total. It is most likely that price change in all these activities together was close to that of the economy as a whole. This leaves two major undeflated sectors, defense and ownership of dwellings, in which there is the possibility of exceptionally large price changes during the 1959-66 period. Together they comprise 17-23% of GDP (depending on the year).

Value added in defense and public security, as estimated by the JDS, grew at an average annual rate of 3.8% between 1959 and 1966.[2] Data on the 1959-66 growth of military employment are unavailable, but

TABLE II.1. PARTIALLY DEFLATED GROSS DOMESTIC PRODUCT BY INDUSTRIAL SECTOR, 1959-66 (J.D. million)

	1959	1960	1961	1962	1963	1964	1965	1966
1. Agriculture	15.76	14.17	23.94	21.35	21.99	34.17	34.11	25.42
2. Mining & Manufacturing*	6.62	7.38	9.48	8.06	11.29	12.53	15.65	17.43
3. Construction*	4.66	4.50	4.50	6.15	6.12	5.45	7.87	9.15
4. Electricity**	.66	.69	.67	.74	.93	1.03	1.16	1.47
5. Transport	10.70	11.12	12.64	12.53	12.77	12.03	12.60	14.42
6. Wholesale & Retail Trade	17.99	18.94	23.50	24.80	26.12	28.01	30.48	26.24
7. Banking & Finance**	.80	.87	1.27	1.46	1.35	1.51	2.11	2.77
8. Ownership of Dwellings**	6.30	7.13	8.01	8.58	9.39	9.93	10.69	11.20
9. Public Administration & Defense*	14.95	15.79	16.74	17.06	17.61	19.70	21.93	22.53
10. Services*	7.78	8.26	8.63	9.51	10.37	11.19	12.83	14.10
11. Total GDP at Factor Cost	86.22	88.85	109.38	110.24	117.94	135.55	149.43	144.73
12. Implicit Deflator for Total GDP (1964 = 100)	98.8	100.7	101.4	98.5	99.8	100.0	101.0	103.4
13. Implicit Deflator for that Portion of GDP Converted to 1964 Prices in this Table (1964 = 100)	98.0	101.1	102.1	97.6	99.6	100.0	101.6	105.5

NOTES

No asterisk denotes sector 100% or virtually 100% deflated. One asterisk denotes sector partially deflated. Two asterisks denote sector undeflated. All deflated values are in 1964 Jordan dinars (J.D.).

The source for current-price GDP and sectoral value added is JDS, The National Accounts, 1959-1967, Amman, n.d., p. 10. For full details of the deflation see Mazur thesis, pp. 62-72, 103-15.

Row 2: Because of the unavailability of necessary data, the year 1962 is undeflated. In the remaining years from 31% to 49% (depending on the year) of current-price value added has been deflated. The deflations must be considered quite rough: Some involve deflation by less-than-perfect price indices; others involve extrapolation of 1964 value added according to some index of production, which assumes that intermediate costs measured in constant prices were a constant proportion of the constant-price value of production.

Row 6: To deflate current-price value added, I constructed an index of prices of goods traded, weighted by the 1966 distribution of trade revenue among different goods categories. Since agricultural products made by far the most important contribution to trade revenue and since my price indices for agricultural products are relatively good, the deflation of the trade sector should be considered relatively satisfactory.

Row 12: Derived by dividing current-price GDP (from JDS, The National Accounts, 1959-1967, p. 10) by row 11 of the present table.

Row 13: Derived by dividing current-price value added for that portion of total GDP deflated here by my constant-price estimate of value added for that same portion.

21

the limited information available suggests that
some, and perhaps most, of this increase in value
added was attributable to increase in numbers,
rather than to increases in wages.[3]

It is widely believed that Jordan, and particularly Amman, experienced considerable inflation in
residential rents prior to the June War. However,
the only available statistical evidence contradicts
this belief, for it implies that rents paid by civil
servants (most of whom lived in Amman) increased at
an average annual rate of only 1.8% between 1958 and
1967.[4] The most likely explanation of this difference between the widely held view of rapid rental
inflation and the published estimate suggesting slow
inflation lies in the existence of a form of rent
control in Jordan. Rent cannot legally be increased
unless there is a new tenant. If rental inflation
were high, renters' mobility would be low and the
rental inflation would be reflected only in that
small fraction of the stock of dwellings newly rented each year. Thus, rapid inflation in the rent for
new tenants may coincide with slow average inflation
for all dwellings.

In view of all the foregoing considerations, it
seems most reasonable to put at about 2% the average
annual rate of price increase between 1959 and 1966
in that fraction of GDP at factor cost not deflated
in Table II.1. This would give an overall GDP deflator increasing at an average 1.5% per year. Even
if we were to be extremely conservative and use a
figure of 3-1/2% per year for inflation in the sectors not deflated in Table II.1, this would still
give an average annual rate of inflation overall of
only 2% per year. In sum, we can state with a fair
degree of confidence that the rate of price increase
embodied in the official current-price GDP estimates
for 1959-66 is 1-2% per year.

b. Rates of Growth in Real Income, 1959-66

Determination of longer-term growth trends in
GDP is complicated by the extremely large year-to-
year fluctuations occurring in agriculture as a result of variations in rainfall. If one measures
growth between a good crop year and a bad one, or
vice versa, the result will be a very misleading indicator of underlying trends. I have therefore run
regressions for crop and livestock output, mainly on
time and an index of rainfall, using data for the 14
years 1953-66. By then assuming rainfall in every
year to be constant at its average 1953-66 level, I

have obtained series for the value of production in various agricultural sectors which largely remove the influence of rainfall fluctuations and random influences. The resulting figures have been used in the calculation of average annual growth rates of agricultural value added and GDP in Table II.2. To reduce the effect of rainfall-induced fluctuations in nonagricultural sectors and other random occurrences, I have calculated the growth rates between the averages of the two-year periods 1959/60 and 1965/66.[5]

The preceding discussions have dealt mainly with GDP at factor cost. However, GDP at market prices, which exceeds GDP at factor cost by the amount of indirect taxes less subsidies to business, is frequently preferred because it values goods and services at the prices consumers actually pay for them. There were no subsidies to business during 1959-66, at least according to the national accounts. Since indirect tax revenues grew much faster than GDP, the growth rate of GDP at market prices was significantly above that of GDP at factor cost. At least part of the rise in indirect tax receipts reflects inflation, as a result of legislated increases in tax rates and of inflation in the prices of goods taxed on an ad valorem basis. Consequently, in Table II.2 the growth of GDP at factor cost probably gives a truer picture of real growth than the growth of GDP at market prices.

The growth rates presented in column (1) of Table II.2 represent a mixed bag of deflated, partially deflated and undeflated sectors. The average annual growth rate of 7.9% in GDP at factor cost does not correct for inflation in those sectors not deflated in Table II.1. In the light of the discussion at the end of section (a) above, the growth rate of real GDP between 1959/60 and 1965/66 may be placed at a round figure of 7%, or perhaps very slightly higher. While not as spectacular as the figures sometimes quoted, this growth rate ranks very high in comparison with those of other LDCs.

Column (1) of Table II.2 suggests that growth during this period was propelled forward by a very rapid rate of industrialization. While agriculture had one of the lowest rates of growth, its performance can by no means be judged poor. Rapid growth in agriculture is generally very difficult in LDCs-- more difficult to achieve than an equally rapid growth rate in the industrial sector--and 6% represents a high rate in comparison with other LDCs.

Sectoral growth rates alone do not give an

23

TABLE II.2. AVERAGE ANNUAL GROWTH RATE OF GDP BY SECTORS AND
SECTORAL SHARES IN GDP GROWTH, 1959/60-1965/66

	Growth Rate (percent per year) (1)	Share in GDP Growth (percent) (2)
1. Agriculture	6.0	15.3
2. Mining & Manufacturing*	15.4 } 15.1	18.1 } 19.3
3. Electricity**	11.8	1.2
4. Construction*	10.9	7.4
5. Transport	3.6	4.9
6. Wholesale & Retail Trade	7.4 } 8.1	18.7 } 21.7
7. Banking & Finance**	19.6	3.0
8. Ownership of Dwellings**	8.5	8.0
9. Public Administration & Defense*	6.3	13.0
10. Services*	9.0	10.3
11. GDP at Factor Cost	7.9	100.0
12. Indirect Taxes	13.9	-
13. GDP at Market Prices	8.4	-

NOTES

Asterisks refer to the degree of deflation of the respective sectors as described in the notes to Table II.1. The
figures for the combined rows 2 and 3 and the combined rows 6
and 7 are for later use, to facilitate comparisons with the
1954/55-1959/60 period in Table II.3.

Column (1) represents average annual growth rates between
the average for the two years 1959/60 and the average for the
two years 1965/66. Column (2) was calculated in the following
way: For each sector, the absolute increase in annual value
added in that sector (measured by the difference between average value added for the two years 1965/66 and the average value added for the two years 1959/60) was divided by the absolute
increase in annual GDP at factor cost measured in the same way
over the same period.

Row 1: Derived from smoothed, constant-price estimates of crop
and livestock production.

Rows 2-10: Calculated from figures in Table II.1

Row 12: Calculated from JDS, The National Accounts, 1959-1967,
p. 10.

adequate picture of the role of different sectors in economic development. A fast-growing sector may be of little importance if it contributes only a very small fraction of total production in the economy. Column (2) of Table II.2 shows the proportion of total absolute growth in GDP contributed by each of the major sectors. This table indicates clearly that growth in GDP was not the result of growth in only a few sectors, but rather growth in many sectors made sizable contributions to the overall level of growth. The fastest growing sectors--mining and manufacturing, construction, electricity, banking, and finance--were relatively small ones, while the largest sectors--agriculture, commerce, and government--were among the slower growing sectors. Thus, growth during 1959/60-1965/66 was along a fairly wide front.

c. Estimates of Pre-1959 National Income

A 1961 paper by Robert Porter presented current-price GNP estimates for 1954-59.[6] While not as reliable as the JDS estimates for 1959-66, they are acceptable for many purposes. Although the Porter estimates have never been revised, they can fairly readily be reconciled with the JDS estimates because of the overlapping year, 1959, and because the Porter estimates are essentially an extrapolation from the benchmark year of 1959. The Porter estimates are surveyed briefly in the Appendix.

Adjustments of Porter's estimates were used to derive sectoral growth rates and sectoral contributions to GDP growth for 1954/59-1959/60 and 1954/59-1965/66, as shown in Table II.3. The 1954/55-1959/60 growth rate for GDP at factor cost shown in Table II.3 is 11.6%--considerably higher than that estimated for the 1959/60-1965/66 period. However, the 11.6% rate is undoubtedly an overstatement for several reasons: (1) Except for crop output, the estimates from which the 1954/55-1959/60 growth rate was derived were in current prices; if the other sectors had been deflated, the growth rate might be several percentage points less. (2) As noted in the Appendix, the growth in the transport sector probably is substantially overstated. (Note the large difference in the transport sector between the earlier period shown in Table II.3 and the later period shown in Table II.2. Much of this difference may be spurious, due to the bias in the estimates for the earlier period.)

Besides the possibly spurious decrease in the

TABLE II.3. AVERAGE ANNUAL GROWTH RATE OF GDP BY SECTORS AND SECTORAL SHARES IN GDP GROWTH 1954/55-1959/60 AND 1954/55-1965/66

	Growth Rate (percent per year) (1)		Share in GDP Growth (percent) (2)	
	1954/55-1959/60	1954/55-1965/66	1954/55-1959/60	1954/55-1965/66
1. Agriculture	6.8	6.3	14.1	14.8
2. Mining, Manufacturing & Electricity	10.5	13.0	7.8	15.0
3. Construction	22.0	15.8	7.4	7.4
4. Transport	15.5	8.9	14.4	9.0
5. Trade & Banking	12.1	9.9	21.6	21.7
6. Ownership of Dwellings	13.9	10.9	8.3	8.1
7. Public Administration & Defense	11.9	8.9	17.0	14.1
8. Services	13.0	10.8	9.4	9.9
9. GDP at Factor Cost	11.6	9.5	100.0	100.0
10. Indirect Taxes	16.6	15.1		
11. GDP at Market Prices	12.0	10.0		

NOTES

Columns (1) and (2) have the same meanings as in Table II.2. The underlying data for 1959-66 are the same as used in Table II.2.

Row 1:   Derived from smoothed, constant-price estimates of crop production and smoothed, current-price estimates for 1954-58 livestock production

Rows 2-8, 10:   Data from R. S. Porter, Economic Trends in Jordan, 1954-1959, were adjusted to make them comparable in coverage to data from JDS, The National Accounts, 1959-1967.

growth rate for the transport sector, comparison of Tables II.2 and II.3 reveals some important differences in the pattern of growth for the two periods. Growth in the sector of mining, manufacturing, and electricity was not as important a driving force behind the growth of GDP in the earlier years as it was in the later period. On the other hand, construction, government and other services were more important as leading sectors in the earlier period.

For Jordan the 1950s were years of adjustment to the establishment of Israel, the annexation of the West Bank, and the influx of Palestinian refugees. This shows up in the different sectoral growth patterns of our two periods. As the rapid growth in the construction sector suggests, these were years of building infrastructure, particularly housing for the refugees and roads to reorient the country's transport network to the new political boundaries in the region. Foreign aid to Jordan was stepped up during the 1950s, helping to finance the expansion of physical infrastructure and of the government and service sectors. By the end of the 1950s, when a substantial expansion of infrastructure had been provided and political security seemed more assured, the industrial sector could become the leader in the growth process.

Two estimates of 1952-54 GDP have been made, but they rest on a very inadequate data base and are inconsistent with each other and with other sources.[7] They should be used with extreme caution, and then only to reach very general and limited conclusions. Little more than the following may be concluded: (1) There was significant growth in GDP between 1952 and 1954, although the magnitude cannot be specified. (2) The year 1953 was a poor crop year, during which GDP was markedly depressed. (3) During the 1952-54 period the largest sectors in terms of value added were agriculture, government and commerce.

2. POPULATION GROWTH AND INTERNAL MIGRATION

Birth and death statistics in Jordan have never been very reliable. Official records have underrecorded births slightly and grossly underrecorded deaths. A study which attempted to correct for these inadequacies placed the natural growth rate of population during 1959-63 at a relatively high 3.1% per year--the result of a crude birth rate of 4.7% and a crude death rate of 1.6%.[8] Between 1952 and 1961 the number of residents in Jordan, as recorded by the censuses of those two years, grew at

an average annual rate of 2.8%--probably a slight
overestimate because under-registration was greater
in the earlier census.[9] The difference between
these two rates probably is due to emigration,
rather than to any acceleration in the natural
growth rate.[10]

The 1961 population of Jordan was relatively
urbanized compared to other LDCs. In 1961 36.1% of
the population inhabited localities over 20,000 persons.[11] The comparable 1960 figures were 15% for
the world population of LDCs and 46% for the population of developed countries.[12] However, except for
Amman (administration and commerce), Zarqa (industry), and Jerusalem (tourism), most Jordanian towns
were medium-sized (50,000 inhabitants or less) agricultural centers, presumably still quite rurally
oriented in both economic activity and social attitudes. Hence, such statistics exaggerate the degree
of true urbanization in Jordan, but in a similar
manner they probably exaggerate that of other LDCs
as well.

As in other LDCs, there was large and continuous migration from rural to urban areas. Between
1952 and 1961, while the total population grew at
an average annual rate of 2.8%, the rural population
averaged 1.4% annual growth and the urban population
5.0%.[13] Most of the migration was directed toward
Amman and Zarqa, which also received migrants from
other urban areas, particularly on the West Bank.[14]

Most of the net internal migration between 1952
and 1961 was from the West Bank to the East Bank,
with the result that the West Bank population grew
at an average annual rate of less than one percent
over the period. The rate of migration was even
higher from West Bank urban areas than from West
Bank rural areas.[15] It seems certain that the migration resulted from the crowding of the refugees
from the 1948 war with Israel onto the West Bank,
which could not support such numbers. Even in 1961,
after a very large population shift from the West
Bank to the East Bank, the West Bank remained considerably more densely populated than the East Bank.[16]
Refugees from that part of Palestine which became
Israel in 1948 almost certainly comprised the major
component of the East-West migration.[17]

There is some incomplete evidence suggesting
that migration from the West Bank to the East Bank
and from rural to urban areas was at a lower rate
from 1961 to the outbreak of the 1967 war than between 1952 and 1961. The evidence is from a JDS
study of six cities in early 1967.[18] Mazen Dajani

noticed an inconsistency in this study and recalcu-
lated the in-migration rate. For the five East Bank
towns together (i.e., all except Jerusalem, which
experienced net out-migration between 1961 and 1967)
his re-estimates show average annual in-migration
between 1961 and 1967 40% less than between 1952 and
1961.[19] If the in-migration estimates of the 1967
JDS study are used rather than Dajani's re-estimates,
the decline in in-migration would be even greater.

3. LABOR FORCE AND EMPLOYMENT

     According to the 1961 census, only 22.9% of the
total population was economically active, a very low
rate.[20] One cause of this is the large proportion
of children in the population, combined with low
labor force participation rates among children. To
abstract from the effect of the large proportion of
children and the statistical problems of female
labor force data in LDCs, we might consider the
group of males 15-64 years old. For them the participation rate was 81.4%, still rather low for that
population group.[21]
     The 1961 census reported an unemployment rate
of 7.0%, but there are several possible sources of
error in these estimates. Some adult males not in
the labor force may have been "discouraged workers"
--unemployed, but not seeking work because they did
not expect to find employment. On the other hand,
the 1961 census enumeration was made at a time of
the year when seasonal demand for agricultural labor
was exceptionally low.[22] My highly conjectural estimates suggest that when allowance is made for
these two factors, the true 1961 unemployment rate
appears to be around 7-10%. This must be qualified
by the recognition that many employed workers were
employed only seasonally or otherwise part time.
     The widespread existence of part-time and
seasonal employment greatly reduces the significance
of any quantitative employment estimates. Although
the precise extent of part-time employment is not
known, it is clear that it was widespread in both
rural and urban areas. The survey of employment in
crop production during the first three months of
1967 reported that on average "permanent" workers
were employed for about 41% of the working days of
the season and "temporary" workers for 24%.[23] Data
reported from the social survey of Amman in 1960
suggested that about 22% of those working had part-
time employment.[24] In developed economies the dura-
tion of work has been standardized for a large frac-

tion of the jobs in the economy--much larger than
in LDCs. Thus, while the dividing line between employment and unemployment tends to be fairly sharply defined in developed economies, there is much
more of a continuum between full employment and no
employment in LDCs. The use of an arbitrarily defined demarcation between employed and unemployed
is thus much more likely to be misleading in a less
developed than in a developed economy.

Because of this and other factors, the concept
and definition of the labor force is much more amor-
phous in LDCs than in developed countries. The
problem of defining the labor force is especially
acute with respect to unpaid family workers, mainly
women and children. For this reason comparative
studies of labor force and employment frequently exclude unpaid family workers; where possible and appropriate, this approach will also be taken here.

The World Bank mission which visited Jordan in
1955 estimated unemployment for that year at 16.5%.[25]
The estimate is a very speculative one, but it more
probably understates than overstates unemployment,
since it embodies the assumption that all nonrefugees were employed, which is certainly untrue. Although there is a sizable margin of error in both
the 1955 and 1961 unemployment estimates, there is
little doubt that economic growth in Jordan during
the period produced a substantial increase in employment. This is hardly surprising in view of the
rapid growth in GDP which occurred in the late
1950s, particularly in construction, generally a
relatively labor-intensive activity. Any estimate
of the rate of increase of employment between 1955
and 1961 must be highly conjectural. Given this
qualification, we may place the rate of increase in
the area of 5% per year.[26]

Direct evidence on the change in employment and
unemployment between 1961 and the June War is even
less adequate than for the 1955-61 period. Data
gathered for Amman suggest a declining rate of unemployment there.[27] However, changes in unemployment in the capital and largest city of Jordan may
be a poor indicator of trends in the country as a
whole. Another indicator of diminishing unemployment during the 1961-66 period is the marked rise
in the wage of unskilled labor which took place.[28]

My extremely conjectural estimation of the increase in labor force and employment between 1961
and 1966 was published in 1972.[29] It suggested that
the number employed grew at an average annual rate
of about 4% between 1961 and 1966. This represents

a decline in the rate of labor absorption when compared with the estimate of 5% for 1955-61, but was sufficiently rapid to reduce the unemployment rate significantly--perhaps from the 7-8% range in 1961 to 4-5% in 1966. The decline in the growth rate of employment is derived from very speculative estimates, but it is certainly plausible in view of the fact that GDP apparently grew more rapidly in the earlier part of the 1955-66 period and that growth in the earlier period was more concentrated in labor-intensive sectors (construction, public administration and defense) as opposed to the importance of manufacturing in the later period.

Unemployment in Jordan is frequently viewed in terms of the problems of Palestinian refugees, but employment has prevailed among refugees and nonrefugees alike, if not to the same degree. Nonetheless, the situation of the refugees, as an important and distinct group, is of separate interest. Unfortunately, very little information has ever been collected on the refugees in Jordan separate from the rest of the population.

UNRWA has compiled some information on refugees, but for most purposes it cannot be relied upon. It is impossible to derive from UNRWA data an accurate estimate of the number of refugees in Jordan, the number of refugees actually receiving rations from UNRWA or the number of refugees actually residing in camps. The majority of refugees were registered with UNRWA for receipt of rations. From the beginning of refugee relief operations there were false and duplicate registrations. The passage of time aggravated the problem, as the ration cards of refugees who had died, left the country or become self-supporting were not turned in to UNRWA but retained by family members or sold. Some effort to rectify the relief rolls was made by UNRWA, but--particularly in Jordan--success was limited.[30] The problem has its favorable side, however. The inability of UNRWA to enforce in Jordan a means test for receipt of rations or services has meant the virtual absence of any disincentive to refugee employment from the prospect of loss of benefits.[31]

A sizable number of refugees found employment in the years immediately following the partition of Palestine. UNRWA, most of whose employees were refugees, itself provided employment. Other refugees found opportunities for farming in the underdeveloped Jordan Valley area.[32] An UNRWA survey placed the number of refugees employed in 1953 at about 77 thousand, of whom only 13.5% were employed full

31

time.[33] If we accept this figure, the percentage
of the male refugee labor force 15-65 without employment of any kind in 1953 may be placed at very
roughly 40-50%. Surprisingly, unemployment rates
among residents of refugee camps were lower than
among non-camp refugees. Possible errors are many
and large, however, and the most likely bias involves overstatement of non-camp unemployment.
These qualifications notwithstanding, the evidence
appears to be against the commonly held expectation
that employment rates were much lower among camp
dwellers than among non-camp refugees. This conclusion is confirmed by the results for the occupied
West Bank of the 1967 Israeli census.[34]

In the 1960 sample survey of Amman data were
collected for residents of Amman refugee camps
separate from the rest of the population. These
suggest an unemployment rate of 10% among adult
males not resident in camps and 15% among the same
group living in camps.[35] Although these figures
are not strictly comparable with the preceding ones,
they do suggest the unsurprising conclusion that the
rapid economic growth experienced by Jordan in the
1950s made substantial inroads into refugee unemployment.

NOTES

1. The years up to 1958 in Jordan were years of political turbulence and uncertainty, which must have diverted
government efforts from economic development and deterred private investment, especially in industry. The assassination
of Abdullah in 1951 was followed by the one-year reign of
Talal, who was deranged. After a brief regency Hussein succeeded to the throne in 1953 at the age of 18. After the
formation of the Baghdad Pact in 1955 Jordan experienced riots
and political instability, as Egypt and other Arab states
mounted pressures on Jordan to remain outside the Pact. The
growing prestige of Nasser in the Arab world increased pro-
Egyptian sentiment within Jordan. In 1957 Jordan experienced
political crises and an attempted coup. When in 1958 the
United Arab Republic was formed and the Hashemite monarch in
Iraq, with which Jordan had been allied, was overthrown, Jordan found itself largely isolated in the Arab world. British
troops were sent to Jordan for several weeks, coinciding with
the landing of U.S. troops in Lebanon. The year 1958 appears
to mark a turning point; the succeeding years until the 1967
Middle East war were, at least comparatively, placid ones for
Jordan.
    2. From unpublished worksheets, JDS Economic Section.

3. Between 1956 and 1966 the number in the armed forces grew at an average annual rate of about 3.7%. Number for 1956 from P. J. Vatikiotis, Politics and the Military in Jordan: A Study of the Arab Legion, 1921-1957, London: Frank Cass, 1967, p. 81. Number for 1966 from Lawrence L. Ewing and Robert C. Sellers, The Reference Handbook of the Armed Forces of the World, 1966, Washington, 1966. Satisfactory data on intermediate years are unavailable.

4. An index of civil servants' rental costs for 1958 and 1968 is available from JDS, Family Expenditures and Cost of Living Index for Civil Servants, 1968, Amman, 1968. This cannot be considered very accurate, since it is derived by inquiry in 1968 as to what rents were in 1958. This index gives a 1958-68 average annual growth rate of 1.95%. To obtain the 1958-67 average annual growth rate, I used the 1967 and 1968 indices of rental costs used in calculating the consumer price index for Amman in JDS, Amman and Zarka Consumer Price Index and Civil Servants Price Index, Amman, October 1969, p. 4. Unfortunately, 1967 is the first year for which these price indices were calculated.

5. Throughout this study the slash sign between two consecutive years will represent an average for those two years.

6. R. S. Porter, "Economic Trends in Jordan, 1954-1959," Middle East Development Division, British Embassy, Beirut, Lebanon, 1961 (mimeographed). Porter was the principal figure in the establishment of official national income statistics in Jordan. The first official national income estimate published by the JDS--for 1959--was identical to that for 1959 in Porter's 1961 paper.

7. IBRD, pp. 58-60, 64, 437-40; and "The National Income of Jordan, 1952-1954," prepared by the Economic Research Institute of the American University of Beirut under the direction of Albert Y. Badre with the cooperation of the JDS, n.d., (typescript).

8. JDS, Analysis of the Population Statistics of Jordan, prepared by the demographic section under the direction of Dr. Hilde Wander, vol. I, Amman, 1966, First Report.

9. JDS, First Census of Population and Housing, 18 November 1961, Amman, 1964, vol. I, pp. 3, 29, and vol. IV, pp. 66-67.

10. There is no acceptable direct information on emigration during this period, but the 1961 census does give a figure for the number of Jordanians abroad in 1961--not a very reliable one since it was derived from reports of relatives or neighbors in Jordan. If the figure is approximately correct, somewhat conjectural reasoning suggests that emigration alone could account for the difference between a 3.1% natural growth rate and a 2.8% growth rate of the resident population.

11. JDS, First Census, vol. I, p. 29.

12. United Nations Department of Economic and Social Affairs, World Economic Survey, 1967, New York, 1968, p. 37.

13. JDS, *First Census*, vol. I, p. 29.

14. The 1952 and 1961 censuses do not give the actual migratory movements within Jordan between 1952 and 1961. It is only possible to examine changes in population in different areas and to deduce net migration by making assumptions about the natural growth of population in different areas. This is done in JDS, *Analysis of the Population Statistics*, Third Report, pp. 6-7, using the assumption that the natural rate of population growth was the same in all regions.

15. Net migration from West Bank urban areas during 1952-61 was 21.5% of the West Bank urban population in 1952. Net migration from West Bank rural areas was 19.0% of the West Bank rural population in 1952. Ibid., Third Report, p. 6.

16. Population density in 1961 was more than twice as high on the West Bank as on the East Bank, whether it is measured by population per square kilometer of nondesert land, population per square kilometer of cultivated land or rural population per square kilometer of cultivated land. Ibid., Third Report, p. 4.

17. The 1960 social survey of Amman recorded that 30.5% of the population of Amman had been born in the part of Palestine which became Israel. Ministry of Social Affairs, *Social Survey of Amman, 1960*, Amman, n.d., p. 53. Some may have migrated before 1948 and hence may not be truly refugees, but these are undoubtedly few.

18. JDS, *Population Census and Internal Migration for Amman, Jerusalem, Zarqa, Ruseifa, Irbid and Aqaba, 1967*, Amman, n.d.

19. Mazen Dajani, "Economic Development with Unlimited Supplies of Labour: The Jordanian Case, 1948-1967," unpublished M.A. thesis, Graduate Program of Development Administration, American University of Beirut, 1969, pp. 24-30.

20. JDS, *Analysis of the Population Statistics*, Third Report, p. 33. Comparable figures are given for six Middle Eastern and four developed countries. Only in Syria is the participation rate as low as that for Jordan.

From a larger sample of countries the average labor force participation rate for a country at Jordan's level of per capita income is about 40%. Simon Kuznets, *Modern Economic Growth: Rate, Structure, and Spread*, New Haven: Yale University Press, 1966, p. 402.

21. Calculated from JDS, *First Census*, vol. II, p. 3. Comparable figures for other Arab countries are: Iraq (1957), 91.6%; Syria (1960), 87.9%; UAR (1960), 90.5%, and Tunisia (1956), 85.3%. Calculated from International Labour Office, *Yearbook of Labour Statistics*, Geneva, 1966, Table I.

22. Some evidence is supplied by a 1967 sample survey of the agricultural labor force in crop production, conducted at a time of high--but not peak--seasonal demand for farm labor. (JDS, *Population and Labor Force in the Agriculture Sector, 1967*, Amman, 1968.) Compared to the 1961 census, the 1967

survey showed a significantly larger share in the farm work force to be female and wage workers, who are predominantly seasonal workers.

23. Ibid., Tables 6, 7.

24. Ministry of Social Affairs, p. 89. I define part-time employment as employment for 1-20 days in the month. Almost 90% of those working part-time worked 11-20 days in the month. The percentage of part-time employment was substantially higher for residents of refugee camps than for others.

25. IBRD, pp. 10, 441-44. Another 11% of the labor force was reported only partially employed. Employment and labor force figures used to make the unemployment rate calculation exclude women employed in agriculture.

26. I calculated the rate of increase using the World Bank estimates for 1955 and my estimates for 1961, derived from the 1961 census as described in Appendix A to Chapter III of Mazur thesis. Women employed in agriculture were omitted from the calculation. I assumed that 10% of nonrefugees were unemployed in 1955, in contrast to the World Bank estimate of full employment among nonrefugees

27. The unemployment rate among males in Amman was reported at 8.1% for 1960, 7.2% for 1961 and 5.1% for 1966. The unemployment rates for females behaved much more irregularly. For males and females together, the rates were 9.0% for 1960, 7.0% for 1961 and 5.9% for 1966.

The unemployment rates were calculated from data in Ministry of Social Affairs, pp. 89, 95, 97, 103; JDS, First Census, vol. II, p. 19; and "Report on the Social Survey of Amman, Jordan, 1966," p. 66. The methodology and definitions of the three studies appear to be reasonably similar.

28. FAO Mediterranean Development Project, p. 6.

29. Michael P. Mazur, "Economic Development of Jordan," in Charles A. Cooper and Sidney S. Alexander, eds., Economic Development and Population Growth in the Middle East, New York: American Elsevier, 1972, pp. 232-36. For subsequent, slightly revised estimates, see Mazur thesis, pp. 141-48.

30. UNRWA, "The Problem of the Rectification of the UNRWA Relief Rolls (1950-1962)," UNRWA Reviews, Information Paper No. 6, Beirut, 1962, and United Nations, Report of the Commissioner General of the United Nations Relief and Works Agency for Palestine Refugees in the Near East, 1 July 1965-30 June 1966, New York, 1966, pp. 8-9.

31. It might be thought that the existence of refugee camps reduced the willingness of camp residents to seek employment at a significant distance from the camps, and especially abroad. This is largely untrue, however, because a camp resident was able to rent out his camp dwelling and could sell his UNRWA ration entitlement card (although without UNRWA's approval).

32. JDS, The East Jordan Valley: A Social and Economic Survey, 1961, Amman, 1961, p. 138.

33. N. Dajani, "Employment, Occupations and Income of Palestinian Refugees in Jordan," n.p. [1954], mimeographed.

34. Yoram Ben-Porath and Emanuel Marx, "Some Sociological and Economic Aspects of Refugee Camps on the West Bank," The Rand Corporation, Santa Monica, California, Report R-835-FF, August 1971, pp. 39-40.

35. Calculated from figures in Ministry of Social Affairs, pp. 89, 95, 97, 103. The figures cover males 15-60 (plus a few males over 60 actively seeking work). The unemployed are here taken to be both those actively seeking work and those reporting that they did not wish to work.

3
Investment and its Finance: Sources of Growth

   During the prewar period the share of GDP devoted to investment by Jordan probably was about
average for a country at Jordan's level of economic
development. For 1959-66 gross domestic investment
averaged 17.1% of GDP.[1] The official national accounts estimates of investment omitted capital expenditure on imported aircraft by the national airline. If this were included, the proportion would
be raised, probably to around 18%.

1. THE SECTORAL ALLOCATION OF INVESTMENT

   It is important to know not only the level of
total investment, but also the distribution of investment among different sectors, such as agriculture, industry, and transportation. Such data may
provide some indication of the government's development strategy, and when combined with data on sectoral growth rates, they assist in the assessment
of the development performance of different sectors.
   Available published and unpublished data are
sufficient to permit reasonably reliable estimates
of gross fixed investment during 1959-66 in three
major using sectors--agriculture, transport, and
dwellings--which together received over 60% of
gross fixed investment during that period. Data
exist on investment in mining and manufacturing, but
they are poor. These data provide estimates of
mining and manufacturing investment by two alternative methods. Regrettably, the results of the two
different approaches are so far apart as to cast
doubt on both estimates.
   The results of these estimates were used to
prepare Table III.1, which shows the percentage
distribution of total gross fixed investment among
sectors. Two alternative sets of estimates are

TABLE III.1. SHARE OF USING SECTORS IN GROSS FIXED INVESTMENT, 1959-66 (percent)

	Unadjusted (1)	Adjusted for Unrecorded Investment in Aircraft (2)
Agriculture	9.6	9.1
Mining & Manufacturing	9.7-17.0 ?	9.2-16.1 ?
Transport	22.6	26.6
Dwellings	31.4	29.7
All Other Sectors	19.4-26.7 ?	22.5-29.4 ?
Gross Fixed Investment	100.0	100.0

NOTES

All ratios represent the sum of sectoral gross fixed investment over the eight years 1959 to 1966 divided by the sum of total gross fixed investment over the same period, both in current prices. For details of the estimates, which partly draw upon unpublished materials of the JDS, see Mazur thesis, pp. 204-6, 255-61.

---

shown there: one including and the other excluding a rough adjustment to correct for the omission of expenditure on commercial aircraft. This adjustment is partly conjectural, as it is based on incomplete information.

In Table III.1 the estimates for mining and manufacturing must be considered highly conjectural, hence the question mark. The range of estimates for that sector represents the two alternative approaches to estimating the sectoral investment, and there can be no guarantee that the truth lies between them. The ratio for "all other sectors" is simply a residual, arrived at by subtracting the sum of the percentages for the first four sectors in Table III.1 from 100%. Therefore, the estimate for "all other sectors" has a range reflecting that in the mining and manufacturing sector, and any error in the estimate for mining and manufacturing will produce a corresponding error in "all other sectors."

Comparison of the shares shown in Table III.1 with those of other countries is made difficult by scarcity of comparable data. However, it seems fairly clear that an unusually large percentage of Jordan's investment went into construction of dwellings: around 30% compared with the 20% typical of countries at a low level of per capita income.[2] Perhaps the most likely explanation is that investment in housing was large because it was making up a deficit in housing arising from the influx of refugees after the partition of Palestine. Presumably, the deficit was made up slowly because the high rate of economic growth experienced by Jordan produced a rapid rise in the demand for housing.

The share of transportation in gross fixed investment was also well above the average, which is about 15%. It is very probable that the share of transportation was even greater in the years prior to 1959, as Jordan reoriented its highway network along north-south lines after the partition of Palestine. Most transport investment went into road transport, very little into railways. The development of Aqaba port and of the national airline also were of some importance.

Agriculture's share in Jordan's gross fixed investment appears somewhat low in comparison with other LDCs. If true, it may simply be due to the fact that the agricultural sector in Jordan is relatively less important than in other countries at a similar level of income per head (see Chapter 4 below). Of the 1959-66 agricultural investment recorded here, a large share (at least 43%) was devoted to a single project--the East Ghor Canal irrigation project. It is not possible to determine whether the shares of mining and manufacturing or of "all other sectors" in gross fixed investment are unusual or not. The range of possible values is too great to draw any conclusions.

The percentages shown in Table III.1 contrast strikingly with those implied by the projections of Jordan's Seven Year Plan for 1964-70. According to the plan, only 3% of investment was to be allocated to manufacturing and 12% to investment in dwellings.[3] It seems undeniable that both of these projections were completely unrealistic.[4] The plan put the share of agriculture in total 1964-70 investment at 25.7%, compared with an actual 9-10% during 1959-66. About two-thirds of this difference is accounted for by projected investments in the Yarmouk irrigation project, which was cut short by the 1967 war.[5] The projected 1964-70 share of mining in domestic investment was high compared to the 1959-66 experience due to the inclusion of one very large project--the proposed potash plant, which also was not carried out.

2. THE INCREMENTAL CAPITAL-OUTPUT RATIO

A frequently used, although not entirely satisfactory, measure of the effectiveness of a country's use of available capital is the incremental capital-output ratio (ICOR), measured as investment divided by the subsequent change in output. Other things equal, a low value for the ICOR generally would be interpreted as indicating effective use of capital. A measure of this type is especially desirable for analysis of a country, like Jordan, which has received relatively large amounts of foreign aid. If a country receiving much aid experiences a rapid growth in GDP, how can we know whether its rapid growth was not simply the consequence of its large aid receipts? The ICOR may help to answer this question, although at best it provides only part of the answer.

In Table III.2 are estimates of the aggregate gross ICOR in Jordan for various periods and under several assumptions. The estimates in row 1.a are derived from the GDP growth rates in Tables II.2 and II.3 above and from official investment estimates. They are "hard" figures in the sense that they do not include any important conjectural adjustments on my part. Rows 1.b and 2.b incorporate a rough estimate of unrecorded 1959-66 investment in aircraft. It is likely that the GDP growth rates in Tables II.2 and II.3 are exaggerated by the failure to eliminate entirely the effect of price inflation. This would bias the ICOR below the value of the true (constant-price) ICOR. The estimates of rows 2.a and 2.b have therefore been made using growth rates incorporating a very rough adjustment for price rises.

The figures in row 2.b are the "softest," in that they contain several conjectural adjustments, but they are probably most comparable to constant-price ICOR estimates of other countries. Whichever figures are used, it appears that the ICOR may have risen over time. We cannot be certain of this because of the much poorer quality of the data for the earlier years. The most probable biases in the earlier data would tend to understate the ICOR for that period. A rise in the ICOR is not implausible, however. It could be due to the fact that the

40

TABLE III.2. GROSS INCREMENTAL CAPITAL-OUTPUT RATIOS,
1954/55-1959/60-1965/66

	1954/55- 1959/60	1959/60- 1965/66	1954/55- 1965/66
1. Partially deflated			
a. Based on official investment statistics	1.2	2.0	1.6
b. Adjusted for unrecorded investment in aircraft	1.2	2.1	1.7
2. Fully deflated (approximate)			
a. Based on official investment statistics	1.7	2.4	2.05
b. Adjusted for unrecorded investment in aircraft	1.7	2.6	2.15

NOTES

In all cases the gross incremental capital-output ratio is calculated as the ratio of the gross domestic investment (GDI) proportion to the average annual growth rate of GDP at market prices. The GDI proportion is the ratio of GDI to GDP at market prices, both measured in current prices. Both the numerator and the denominator of the GDI proportion apply to the same years, implying a one-year lag between investment and the consequent increase in output. The GDI proportion is calculated as the ratio of the sum of GDI over the relevant years to the sum of GDP over the same period.

Row 1.a: GDI is adjusted from official JDS estimates as described in the Appendix. The average annual GDP growth rates (partially deflated and smoothed) are from Tables II.2 and II.3.

Row 1.b: GDI for 1959-66 was increased by 5% to account for unrecorded investment in aircraft. GDP and its rate of growth are the same as in row 1.a.

Row 2.a: GDI proportions are the same as in row 1.a. The average annual GDP growth rate was assumed to be 9.0% for 1954/55-1959/60, 7.0% for 1959/60-1965/66 and 8.0% for 1954/55-1965/66.

Row 2.b: The GDI proportion is the same as in row 1.b. The growth rate of GDP is the same as in row 2.a.

41

period of the 1950s was a period of recovery and re-adjustment after the dislocations of the Palestine partition. Employment appears to have expanded more rapidly during the 1950s than during the 1960s. As economic growth absorbed the unemployed, shortages of labor, at least of certain types, probably appeared and contributed to the higher ICOR of the 1960s.

Whichever of the alternative ICOR estimates in Table III.2 is used, Jordan's ICOR compares very favorably with the level of around 3-4 typical of a country at Jordan's level of per capita income.[6] This is particularly unexpected in view of the large share of Jordan's investment allocated to the housing sector, which has a high ICOR. If Jordan had had a "normal" share of housing in total investment (about 20%), its ICOR for the 1959/60-1965/66 period would have been 2.4, rather than 2.6.[7]

The estimates of the sectoral distribution of investment used to derive Table III.1 above also can be used to derive sectoral ICORs, which are shown in column (1) of Table III.3.[8] For purposes of comparison column (2) of Table III.3 gives sectoral fixed ICORs for the average of 18 countries, all (except possibly one, Israel) LDCs. Data on sectoral ICORs are very scanty and these should be viewed with caution. The period covered is very short--only three years. Furthermore, the countries represented are unlikely to constitute a random sample, as the few LDCs that possess adequate data for the construction of sectoral ICORs are unlikely to be typical of LDCs in general.

The figures of Table III.3 do not lead to very strong conclusions. ICORs in the agriculture sector of LDCs display wide variability from country to country. Hence, Jordan's agriculture ICOR, while low in comparison to the average, is by no means unique. Such a high degree of uncertainty is attached to my estimates of the ICORs in mining and manufacturing that it is foolhardy to draw any conclusions about this sector from the comparison of Table III.3.

Jordan's relatively high ICOR in transport, even excluding investment in aircraft, is a surprise. Most of Jordan's investment in this sector has been in road transport. Jordan's high transport ICOR casts suspicion upon the estimates of transport value added. The JDS estimates of value added in road passenger transport (which constituted a little over half of value added in road transport during the 1959-66 period) essentially assume

42

TABLE III.3. GROSS FIXED INCREMENTAL CAPITAL-OUTPUT RATIOS BY
SECTORS: JORDAN, 1959/60-1965/66, AND 18-COUNTRY
AVERAGE, 1966/67/68

	Jordan, 1959/60- 1965/66 (1)	18-Country Average, 1966/67/68 (2)
Agriculture	1.4	3.2
Mining & Manufacturing	1.2-2.1?	3.0
Transport:		
a. Unadjusted	10.5	6.4
b. Adjusted for unrecorded investment in aircraft	13.0	
Dwellings	8.5 ⎫ 1.8-2.1?	3.0
All Other Sectors	0.8-1.1? ⎭	

NOTES

The methodology of the ICOR calculation in column (1) is
the same as used in Table III.2, except that the investment
proportion used is the ratio of sectoral gross fixed investment to sectoral value added at factor cost. The sectoral
gross fixed investment estimates are the same as those used
to obtain Table III.1. Average annual growth rates of value
added in agriculture, transport and dwellings are from Table
II.2.

Column (2) presents the arithmetic average of all positive sectoral ICORs for a sample of 18 LDCs, from United
Nations Department of Economic and Social Affairs, World Economic Survey, 1969-1970, New York, 1971, p. 81. I have combined the ICORs for mining and manufacturing and also combined the ICOR for power with that of "other sectors" by the
appropriate weighted average (the reciprocal of the weighted
output-capital ratios), using as weights the sectoral investment shares of the same countries, from ibid., p. 80.

---

constant productivity per vehicle over the 1959-66
period. Yet since this was a period of considerable
road construction, one might expect some rise in productivity per vehicle over time. This suggests that
the recorded growth of value added in transport may
have been understated, but it is difficult even to
guess by how much. If the transport ICOR in Table
III.3 is correct, it implies that the large share of
the transport sector in total fixed investment shown

in Table III.1 is due to the high level of the
transport ICOR, which required especially large
transport investment to achieve only a normal increase in transport output.

Data for international comparison of ICORs in
ownership of dwellings is too scanty to be of much
use. What little there is does not suggest that
Jordan's ICOR in dwellings is greatly out of the
ordinary. This means that--in contrast to the
transport sector--the relatively large share of
housing in total investment was associated with a
relatively large increase in housing services; i.e.,
investment in housing was large because the demand
for housing was great, not because the housing sector used capital relatively inefficiently or intensively. Assuming that the housing ICOR was about
average, then the data in Table III.3 imply that
the ICOR for "all other sectors" was exceptionally
low in Jordan. Since a substantial part of Jordan's
value added in "all other sectors" could not be deflated, the low ICOR may be partly due to uncorrect-
ed inflation.

3. SOURCES OF GROWTH: LABOR AND CAPITAL

The concept of the ICOR singles out investment
as a determinant of income growth to the exclusion
of other factors, the most important of which is
obviously labor. If the marginal product of labor
were zero, the omission of labor would be easily
justified, but such a phenomenon can apply to few,
if any, LDCs. A more acceptable justification for
the neglect of labor implicit in the use of the ICOR
for international comparisons would be that labor
force growth rates are pretty much the same in most
LDCs, so that differences in labor force growth
rates are not a significant influence upon country-
to-country differences in ICORs.

According to the estimates cited in Chapter 2
the rate of growth of employment in Jordan averaged
about 4% per year during the 1961-66 period and
about 5% annually during the preceding six-year
period. These rates significantly exceed the rate
of labor force growth in the average LDC, which was
probably about 2.5% annually.[9] This more rapid expansion of employment in Jordan than in the average
LDC may partly account for Jordan's unusually high
rate of growth and low ICOR. Using two alternative
values for the elasticity of output with respect to
labor input,[10] we find that if employment in Jordan
had grown at 2.5% per year between 1959/60 and

1965/66, instead of at about 4.0% annually, the gross ICOR would have been 2.9-2.95, instead of 2.6. For the 1954/55-1959/60 period, if employment had grown at 2.5% annually instead of at about 5.0%, the gross ICOR would have been 1.9-2.0, instead of the 1.7 actually recorded.

The foregoing is a crude way of relating labor and capital to the growth of output. Conceptually more satisfactory is the estimation of sources of growth or total factor productivity based upon an aggregate production function.[11] However, such an approach requires information that either is not available or is unreliable in most LDCs, while the ICOR possesses the great practical advantage that it permits cross-country comparisons with a fairly large sample of LDCs. Jordanian statistics are inadequate for a really respectable sources-of-growth analysis, but some very speculative numerical estimates will be presented in this format. Given the commonly used assumptions of this analysis, the contribution to growth made by a factor equals the average annual rate of growth of that factor times the elasticity of output with respect to that factor. The reason that sources-of-growth analysis is rarely conducted for LDCs is that estimates of the capital stock are generally lacking, and hence the growth rate of the capital stock cannot be estimated. Capital stock estimates are nonexistent in Jordan. Hence, a sources-of-growth analysis for Jordan can be carried out only by using an extremely speculative estimate of the capital stock growth rate.[12]

In Table III.4 are presented four alternative sources-of-growth estimates for Jordan, based on two alternative estimates of the elasticity of output with respect to labor input and two alternative estimates of the return to capital. For comparison Table III.5 presents estimates of the absolute and relative contribution of the residual to growth in ten other countries, all of lower per capita income than the developed countries of northwest Europe. All the countries have per capita incomes significantly higher than Jordan's. Postwar recovery may be responsible for the large residual contributions to growth in Japan, the Philippines (1947-55 and 1947-65), Yugoslavia and Greece.

Comparisons based upon either column (2) or column (3) can be justified. If technical change embodied in new inputs (improved machines or better-educated labor) is considered very important, it seems more appropriate to emphasize column (3)

45

TABLE III.4. SOURCES OF NDP GROWTH IN JORDAN, 1959/60-1965/66

	Growth Rate (percent per year) (1)	Contribution to Growth (percent per year) (2)	Relative Contribution to Growth (percent) (3)
Net Domestic Product	7.0		
I. Labor Elasticity = .6			
Employed Labor	4.0	2.4	34
A. r = .15			
Capital	6.0	2.4	34
Residual		2.2	31
B. r = .20			
Capital	7.6	3.1	43
Residual		1.6	22
II. Labor Elasticity = .5			
Employed Labor	4.0	2.0	29
A. r = .15			
Capital	6.0	3.0	43
Residual		2.0	29
B. r = .20			
Capital	7.6	3.8	54
Residual		1.2	17

NOTES   Column (2) for employed labor or capital gives the average annual growth rate of NDP attributable to the growth of the particular factor alone. It equals the growth rate of the factor times its elasticity. (The elasticity of capital is equal to one minus the labor elasticity.) The residual in column (2) is the growth of NDP not attributed to labor or capital and here equals 7% minus the contributions to growth of labor and capital. Column (3) shows the share of each of these contributions in the growth of NDP; that is, here column (3) is column (2) divided by 7%. For the growth rate of NDP I used the 7% annual rate which makes some subjective allowance for failure to fully deflate the GDP estimates used in deriving the growth rates of Table II.2.

comparisons. If embodiment is important, a country may find rapid growth in total productivity easier when inputs are growing rapidly; the measure in column (3) makes an allowance for this in a rough way. On the other hand, one might de-emphasize embodiment and stress the organizational problems involved in the rapid increase of inputs, thus suggesting that the difficulty of achieving rapid growth in total productivity is no less when inputs grow rapidly. On the latter assumptions, comparison of the figures in column (2) would be more appropriate. Compared with the most successful countries in Table III.5 (Brazil, Mexico, Greece, Japan, Yugoslavia, and Israel), the contribution of the residual, both absolute and relative, is slightly lower in Jordan. However, all of these countries are considered to have developed exceptionally rapidly. "Success stories," at least in terms of rapid economic growth, seem to be over-represented in Table III.5. In this light, it seems likely that the residual for Jordan probably exceeds that of the average LDC, both absolutely and (to a lesser degree) relatively. However, the wide margins of error associated with this analysis should again be stressed.

4. SOURCES OF GROWTH: EDUCATION

School enrollments increased rapidly from very low levels from the early 1950s to the eve of the 1967 Middle East War.[13] By the early 1960s Jordan's enrollment ratios (enrollments at a given level as a percentage of total numbers in the age group normally attending that level), in comparison with those of other LDCs at comparable income levels at the same time, were about average at the primary level and substantially above average at higher levels, including the university level.[14]

School enrollment ratios are only a partial indicator of a country's investment in education, for they do not reveal the level of resources devoted to each student. It is difficult to compare investment in education internationally because published figures on educational expenditure often exclude expenditures by local government authorities or private schools, sometimes include expenditures on students' room and board, and usually do not distinguish between current and capital expenditures. My very rough estimate of total 1961 Jordanian investment in education, including the costs of earnings foregone by secondary and university students, puts

47

TABLE III.5. CONTRIBUTION OF THE RESIDUAL TO OUTPUT GROWTH IN VARIOUS DEVELOPING COUNTRIES

	Growth Rate (percent per year) (1)	Contribution to Growth (percent per year) (2)	Relative Contribution to Growth (percent) (3)
Argentina: 1955-59	1.7	-.6	-35
1960-64	1.2	-.6	-50
Brazil: 1955-59	5.6	1.7	30
1960-63	5.0	1.2	24
Chile: 1955-59	3.0	.1	3
1960-64	4.0	.9	23
Colombia: 1955-59	4.0	.4	10
1960-64	4.5	1.5	33
Mexico: 1955-59	5.7	2.0	35
1960-64	6.2	2.8	45
Greece: 1951-61	5.3	2.4	45
Philippines: 1947-55	7.3	4.0-4.1	55-56
1955-65	4.5	0.5-0.7	12-15
1947-65	5.7	2.1	37
Japan: 1950-58	7.9	3.0	38
Yugoslavia: 1949-59	5.5	3.2	56
Israel: 1950-65	11.0	1.9-3.4	17-31
Jordan: 1959/60-1965/66	7.0	1.2-2.2	17-31

NOTES

The meaning of each of the three columns is the same as in Table III.4, except that the output concept whose growth rate is presented in column (1) varies among GDP, NDP and NNP.

Argentina, Brazil, Chile, Colombia and Mexico are from Henry J. Bruton, "Productivity Growth in Latin America," American Economic Review, 57 (December 1967), 1099-1116. Greece is from Samuel Bowles, "Sources of Growth in the Greek Economy, 1951-1961," Economic Development Report No. 27, Project for Quantitative Research in Economic Development and Development Advisory Service, Center for International Affairs, Harvard University, Cambridge, Massachusetts, 1967 (revision, mimeographed). The source for the Philippines is Jeffrey G. Williamson, "Dimensions of Postwar Philippines Economic Progress," Quarterly Journal of Economics, 83 (February 1969), 93-109; the different values correspond to alternative assumptions about the elasticities of output with respect to capital and labor. Japan is from Odd Aukrust, "Factors of Economic Development: A Review of Recent Research," Productivity Measurement Review, 40 (February 1965), 6-22. The figures for Yugoslavia are from UN Economic Commission for Europe, Economic Survey of Europe in 1961: Part 2. Some Factors in Economic Growth in Europe in the 1950s, Geneva, 1964, p. 36. Estimates for Israel are presented in A. L. Gaathon, Economic Productivity in Israel, New York: Praeger, 1971, p. 79. The Gaathon estimates use as weights actual factor shares of about 70% for labor and 30% for capital. I calculated alternative estimates using weights of 50% for each factor, as suggested by Halevi and Klinov-Malul, p. 128, and in an earlier draft by Gaathon.

In some of these studies the contribution to growth of improved labor quality is calculated. In the interest of compatibility with the estimates for Jordan, the effect of changes in labor force quality are omitted here. Any changes in average quality of the labor force are thus recorded as part of the residual.

The figures for Jordan represent the extremes of the alternative estimates in Table III.4.

49

it at 7½-9½% of GNP. This compares with estimates made on a similar basis of around 10% for the United States and 9% for India.[15] Classroom size, teachers' pay in proportion to GNP per capita, and the educational level of teachers appeared to be all comparable to the levels of LDCs at a similar level of development.

It thus appears that after a decade of rapid expansion in education, Jordan by the beginning of the 1960s had reached ratios of enrollment and educational expenditure that were at least equal to those of the average LDC at a similar level of income per head and were at the higher educational levels probably greater. Could this extra educational effort explain the more rapid growth of GDP in Jordan compared to other LDCs? Probably not, for two reasons. First, Jordan's relatively high enrollment levels were not achieved until at least the late 1950s. Since education affects economic output only after a time lag, and perhaps a long one, high levels of schooling in the late 1950s and early 1960s may have had little effect on economic growth during the prewar period. Second, many educated Jordanians were employed outside Jordan, particularly in Arab oil-producing countries such as Kuwait.[16] While they may have contributed to Jordan's gross national product through remittance of earnings, they did not contribute directly to gross domestic product.

5. FINANCING OF INVESTMENT

Table III.6 indicates Jordan's dependence upon foreign-supplied resources in the years preceding the 1967 war. During the 1959-66 period Jordan maintained a large import surplus relative to total resources available (GNP plus imports). Jordan used domestically for consumption or investment (row 1) resources considerably in excess of its own output (row 5). Reliance upon foreign-supplied resources was being reduced in relative terms, as the decline in the share of the import surplus in total resources indicates. While the size of the import surplus increased in absolute terms, the rate of increase was negligibly small.

Jordan's relatively large import surplus was made possible by large receipts of foreign aid.[17] While there are difficulties in defining, valuing and gathering complete information on foreign aid flows, there can be little doubt that Jordan's per capita receipts of foreign aid have been among the

50

TABLE III.6. GROWTH RATES AND SHARE IN TOTAL RESOURCES OF DOMESTIC AND FOREIGN
SOURCES AND USES, 1959-66

	Share in Total Resources (percent)			Average Annual Growth Rate (percent per year)
	1959-62 (1)	1963-66 (2)	1959-66 (3)	1959/60-1965/66 (4)
1. Domestic Uses	86.7	83.9	85.1	8.3
2. Exports	7.1	9.4	8.5	18.5
3. Net Factor Income from Abroad	5.0	5.4	5.3	14.0
4. Total Uses	98.9	98.8	98.8	9.4
5. GNP	71.0	72.1	71.7	9.8
6. Imports	29.0	27.9	28.3	7.4
7. Import Surplus (6-2-3)	16.9	13.1	14.5	0.3

NOTES

Source: JDS, The National Accounts, 1959-1967. All underlying data are in current prices. Two adjustments have been made, as discussed in the Appendix: (1) The "statistical discrepancy" is not included in gross domestic investment, but (in effect) in private saving; (2) the erroneous JDS treatment of payments to Jordanians employed in Jordan by UNRWA, other UN agencies, and other charitable institutions has been corrected.

Domestic uses is defined as the sum of expenditures on private and government consumption and gross domestic capital formation. Total resources is defined as the sum of GNP and imports. Total uses is defined as the sum of domestic uses, exports and net factor income from abroad. According to national income accounting identities, total uses should be identically equal to total resources. Because of the adjustments mentioned in the preceding paragraph, this accounting identity is not precisely satisfied here. Therefore, row 4 is not identically equal to 100.0. Except for rounding error, row 4 equals the sum of rows 1, 2, and 3 for columns (1)-(3). Also for columns (1)-(3) and excluding rounding error, the sum of rows 5 and 6 must equal 100.0

51

highest in the world.[18]   From 1958 until the 1967
war most of Jordan's foreign aid receipts came from
the United States in the form of "budget support,"
simply an outright grant not associated with any
specific projects.   Prior to 1958, most aid came
from the United Kingdom under similar arrangements.
As a result, after years of large aid inflows Jordan's anticipated debt burden remained low.   Except
for aid in kind of UNRWA, other UN agencies, other
charitable institutions, and the U.S. Food for Peace
program (and for a brief, unsuccessful attempt by
the United States from February 1961 to January
1962[19]), aid was not tied to particular commodities
or suppliers.   Since most aid thus was in the form
of untied grants, Jordan apparently ranked even
higher in terms of the per capita real "grant equivalent" of foreign aid than in terms simply of receipts per head.[20]

Table III.7 presents the contribution of domestic private and government saving and foreign resources to the financing of domestic investment.   It
suggests that the foreign current account deficit
financed virtually all of investment.   Domestic saving was relatively small and sometimes negative.
The government was always a large net dis-saver, but
this was at least partially offset by positive private saving.   Between the 1959-62 period and the
1963-66 period, domestic saving rose and the foreign
deficit fell in relative importance.   Both an increase in private saving and a relative decline in
the government deficit contributed to this result,
the latter contribution being more important.

Table III.7 presents the relative contributions of government, the private sector, and the
foreign account to the financing of investment, on
the conventional assumptions that foreign aid to
government only financed investment and that foreign aid to households (such as UNRWA assistance)
only financed consumption.   Although customarily
used, these assumptions, and particularly the former, are unrealistic.   For example, foreign aid to
government can increase consumption directly
through increasing government consumption expenditure and indirectly through allowing the recipient
government to reduce tax collections.   It can also
increase investment directly through increasing
government investment expenditure and indirectly
through reducing the recipient government's domestic borrowing and thereby releasing loanable funds
for private investment.   Typically, in LDCs both
consumption and investment have significant shares

TABLE III.7. SHARE IN GROSS DOMESTIC INVESTMENT OF CURRENT
ACCOUNT FOREIGN DEFICIT, GROSS DOMESTIC SAVING,
AND COMPONENTS, 1959-66 (percent)

	Deficit On Foreign Current Account (1)	Gross Domestic Saving (2)	Gross Government Saving (3)	Gross Private Saving (4)
1959-62	107.5	-7.5	-60.2	52.7
1963-66	79.9	20.3	-38.9	59.3
1959-66	91.3	8.7	-47.8	56.5

NOTES

Source: JDS, The National Accounts, 1959-1967, revised
as described in the notes to Table III.6 and in the Appendix.
For each period and except for rounding error (1)+(2) =
100.0, and (3)+(4) = (2).

in the incremental spending permitted by foreign
aid.[21]

The conventional treatment of foreign aid and
saving in national accounts estimates can lead to
results that if not wrong, are at least easily mis-
interpreted. The large negative saving rates shown
in Table III.7 may give the impression of a profli-
gate government, not only unable to save, but requiring large amounts of foreign support to pay for
its consumption expenditure. This interpretation
ignores the likelihood that an increase in consumption expenditure may be a desirable consequence of
an increase in foreign aid. Indeed, it is often
the intention of the aid donor that consumption expenditure should be increased. This may be because
the donor wishes to promote the social and cultural,
as well as economic, development of the recipient.
To promote economic development, the donor may also
desire increased consumption expenditure because
some expenditures customerily classified as consumption by national income accounts (e.g., government expenditures on the salaries of teachers, extension agents, and agricultural research workers)

53

may contribute to development fully as much as investment expenditures.[22]

a. Private Saving

Table III.7 indicates that during the years preceding the 1967 war Jordan was becoming relatively less dependent on foreign resources and more reliant on domestic saving for the finance of investment. Table III.8 shows the various developments contributing to this result. Private consumption expenditure fell from 82.3% of GNP for 1959-62 to 79.4% for 1963-66. Of this 2.9 percentage point decline, about 2.1 (or 70%) is due to a decline in the share of private disposable income in GNP and the remaining .8 is attributable to a fall in the average share of private consumption in private disposable income.[23] However, the decline in the share of private consumption should not obscure the fact that private consumption in current prices grew at an average annual rate of 8.6% over the 1959/60-1965/66 period. With 3% per year population growth and roughly 2% inflation per year, this implies a rise in real per capita consumption of about 3-4% a year-- a rapid rate of increase, but hardly surprising in view of the rapid growth of incomes.

Instead of examining changes in the share of consumption in GNP and disposable income, we can look at changes in the private saving rate, which give a similar picture.[24] Gross private saving averaged 10.2% of private disposable income over the 1959-66 period. There was a modest rise in the ratio from 9.5% for 1959-62 to 10.7% for 1963-66. However, the year-to-year variations are sufficiently large (the ratio ranges from 5.4% in 1963 to 16.2% in 1964) that little, if any, significance should be attached to the slight trend observed in the saving rate.

The private saving rate in Jordan might be expected to be either above or below average, since there were different forces acting in opposite directions. Jordan's high GNP growth rate should have produced a higher personal saving rate, according to the permanent-income or life-cycle theories of consumption. On the other hand, Jordan's liberal import system may have encouraged higher consumption rates than a system in which foreign travel and many imports, particularly luxury goods, are sharply restricted. The share of private disposable income saved in Jordan during 1959-66 appears somewhat below average in comparison with other countries.[25]

TABLE III.8: GROWTH RATES AND SHARE IN GNP OF CONSUMPTION, INVESTMENT, SAVING, AND RELATED ITEMS, 1959-66

| | Share in GNP (percent) | | | Average Annual Growth Rate (percent per year) |
	1959-62 (1)	1963-66 (2)	1959-66 (3)	1959/60-1965/66 (4)
1. GNP	100.0	100.0	100.0	10.2
2. Private Disposable Income	89.5	87.2	88.1	9.3
3. Private Consumption	82.3	79.4	80.5	8.6
4. Private Saving	8.5	9.3	9.0	15.9
5. Government Domestic Revenue	14.4	15.9	15.3	13.7
6. Government Consumption Expenditure	23.7	21.2	22.2	6.4
a. Government Defense Expenditure	14.1	11.2	12.4	3.3
b. Government Nondefense Expenditure	9.6	10.1	9.9	10.5
7. Government Dissaving	9.7	6.1	7.6	-6.2
8. Gross Domestic Investment	16.1	15.7	15.9	9.3
9. Gross Domestic Saving	-1.2	3.2	1.4	-
10. Deficit on Foreign Current Account	17.4	12.5	14.5	-0.9

NOTES   Source: JDS, The National Accounts, 1959-1967, revised as described in the notes to Table III.6 and the Appendix.

In columns (1)-(3) we expect rows 3+4=2, but the equality does not hold here because of my adjustments to the original data.

"Government domestic revenue" equals "total current revenue" less "current transfers from abroad" and "budget support loan from abroad." Hence, it includes transfer payments from households to government.

Government consumption expenditure does not include government transfer payments. Therefore, government dis-saving equals government consumption expenditure plus government transfer payments less government domestic revenue. Thus, in columns (1)-(3), row 5 plus row 7 slightly exceeds row 6.

However, the margin of error in private saving estimates, for Jordan and other LDCs, is so great that little significance should be attached to this finding.

b. Government Saving

As previously observed, most (70%) of the decline in the share of consumption in GNP was due to a fall in the share of private disposable income in GNP, rather than to the rise in the proportion of private disposable income saved. The share of government consumption in GNP also fell significantly, by 2.5 percentage points between 1959-62 and 1963-66 (Table III.8, row 6). Of the total decline in the relative share of private and government consumption in GNP (5.4 percentage points), only about 15% (0.8 percentage points) was due to an increase in private saving as a proportion of disposable income. Therefore, it is to the government budget, rather than to private saving behavior, that we must look for the major source of the rise in the relative importance of domestic saving.

Government current domestic revenue was 15.3% of GNP for the 1959-66 period, about average for a country of Jordan's per capita income.[26] However, Jordan's economy was exceptionally open, in the sense that foreign trade was relatively important. Among LDCs the governments of open economies are generally able to raise a higher share of GNP in taxes than those of more closed economies, largely because of the administrative ease of taxing foreign trade. When the effect of the openness of Jordan's economy is taken into account, we find that its "tax effort" was markedly below the average level of 20% typical of an LDC with an equally open economy.[27]

One is tempted to interpret this comparatively low level of "tax effort" for Jordan as an indicator of failure on the part of the government, but the issue merits further examination. The difference in "tax effort" between Jordan and the typical comparable LDC was primarily due to a difference in revenue from taxes on foreign trade. Several factors other than inadequate performance by the Jordan government may explain the difference. In Jordan a significant fraction of imports was direct contributions by foreign aid and charitable agencies and hence not subject to import duties. Also, many LDCs have become increasingly disenchanted with policies of high tariff protection. Thus, the higher "tax effort" of the typical LDC to some degree may represent consistently inferior policies. Perhaps the most significant justification of Jordan's liberal import policy is the practical difficulty of successfully enforcing a highly restrictive system. The likely result of a high-tariff regime in Jordan would be extensive smuggling of goods from low-tariff countries such as Saudi Arabia, Kuwait,and Lebanon. Elimination of smuggling would be very difficult to achieve, not only because Jordan's borders are difficult to control, but because there is so much trade and travel between Jordan and these low-tariff countries.

Revenue from personal and corporate income taxes was a small fraction of GNP in Jordan, but this is characteristic of other LDCs as well. In Jordan all agricultural income[28] and all capital gains have been exempt from income taxation, while dividends have been exempt from personal, but not corporate, income taxes. Similar exemptions are widespread elsewhere, sometimes for political reasons, sometimes--in the case of agricultural income and capital gains--because of the administrative difficulty of identifying and measuring the income. Like many other LDCs, the low level of income tax revenue collected in Jordan was as much attributable to failure to collect all taxes legally due as to the exemption of certain income from tax liability. Jordan's income tax administration suffered from understaffing, poor training and low pay and morale of assessors, excessive discretionary authority granted to assessors, a multiplicity of appeal procedures, and inadequate or ineffective penalties on delays in payment.[29]

The sharp reduction shown in row 6 of Table III.8 for the share of total government consumption expenditure in GNP was entirely due to a decline in the share of government defense expenditure in GNP. The share of government nondefense consumption expenditure in GNP rose slightly between 1959-62 and 1963-66--a typical phenomenon as average income per capita rises. The share of government nondefense consumption expenditure was roughly average for a country at Jordan's level of per capita income.[30]

Although the absolute level of defense expenditure increased during the 1959-66 period, the defense burden relative to GNP declined significantly, as row 6.a of Table III.8 shows. This decline accounts for most of the reduction in the ratio of the government deficit to GNP. Jordan's Seven Year Plan for 1964-70 had forecast a sharp decline in the relative defense burden as an essential precondition for its forecast of a substantial reduction in Jordan's dependence on foreign aid by 1970.[31] The reduction in defense expenditure forecast for 1966 by the plan was not achieved in absolute terms but the projected decline in the ratio of defense expenditures to GNP was achieved, as both GNP and defense expenditure grew faster than forecast.

Jordan's exceptionally heavy defense burden accounted for much of the country's large government deficit, low domestic saving, and heavy reliance upon foreign aid. Over the 1959-66 period government defense expenditure equalled 12.4% of GNP. In normal circumstances, defense expenditure probably need not have been more than 5% of GNP.[32] Thus, the extra military expenditure caused by Jordan's special political circumstances was probably 7-10% of GNP-- equal to a large part, but not all, of Jordan's deficit on foreign current account (14.5% of GNP during 1959-66).

NOTES

1. Calculated as the total of gross investment during 1959-66 divided by GDP at market prices for the same period, from data in JDS, The National Accounts, 1959-67, pp. 10, 13 (adjusted to remove the statistical discrepancy, as discussed in the Appendix). All figures are in current prices, as no constant-price estimates of investment in Jordan exist. For other LDCs see Hollis Chenery and Moises Syrquin, Patterns of Development, 1950-1970, London: Oxford University Press, 1975, pp. 20, 201.

2. Comparative data for other LDCs derived from Simon Kuznets, "Quantitative Aspects of the Economic Growth of Nations: V. Capital Formation Proportions: International Comparisons for Recent Years," Economic Development and Cultural Change, 8 (July 1960, Part II), 32-43, 80-83.

3. All figures given here for the plan's projected 1964-70 sectoral share in domestic investment are from FAO Mediterranean Development Project, Jordan Country Report, Rome: Food and Agriculture Organization of the United Nations, 1967, p. 133.

4. One apparent reason for the low estimate for manufacturing is that for new plants, only investment in projects specifically identified in the plan was included; there was no allowance for unforeseen investments. Equally important, the Seven Year Plan assumed a very pronounced, and probably unrealistic, reduction in the rate of growth of consumption. Consequently, the plan projected a low rate of growth of manu-

facturing production and a low level of investment in manufacturing. The apparent reason for the low forecast of dwelling investment is not that the projected trend in dwelling investment was implausible, but that the plan used as the base for its projections an estimate of actual 1963 investment in dwellings which was less than two-thirds of the actual 1963 figure.

5. If the Yarmouk project is excluded, the projected 1964-70 share of agriculture in total investment is about 15%.

6. Kuznets, "Quantitative Aspects V," pp. 50-53, and Hollis B. Chenery and Alan M. Strout, "Foreign Assistance and Economic Development," American Economic Review, 56 (September 1966, Part I), 706-7. In the former study the best estimate of the ICOR for the typical country at Jordan's level of development was 3.0. In the latter, for a sample of 30 LDCs (31 including Jordan), the unweighted mean of the ICOR was 4.06 (3.97 including Jordan) and the median was 3.52-3.54.

7. One possible reason for the low measured ICOR in Jordan might be the bias caused by the use of gross ICORs rather than the theoretically correct ICOR net of depreciation or replacement of capital. When two economies are compared, the use of gross ICORs will understate the ICOR for the more rapidly growing economy. But if allowance is made for this phenomenon, Jordan's ICOR remains below the LDC average, although the gap is significantly reduced. For details, see Mazur thesis, pp. 214-21, 265-66.

8. The methodology of these sectoral ICORs is not strictly comparable to that used to derive the aggregate ICORs in Table III.2. The aggregate gross fixed ICOR implied by these sectoral ICORs is 2.2 without adjustment for unrecorded aircraft expenditure, or 2.3 with such adjustment.

9. The average annual growth rate of population in LDCs was 2.5% during the first half of the 1960s (UN, World Economic Survey, 1967, p. 18). In most cross-section studies of growth, it is assumed that the labor force growth rate equals the population growth rate. The justification for this is that there does not appear to be any systematic relationship between labor force participation rates and the level of per capita income. See Kuznets, Modern Economic Growth, pp. 401-2.

10. The elasticity of output with respect to labor is commonly approximated by the share of labor in total income, which for Jordan was about .6. It is frequently suggested that market imperfections widespread in LDCs overprice labor and underprice capital. To deal with this and because the elasticity estimate of .6 may be biased upward for other reasons, an alternative estimate of .5 is also used here.

11. Among the seminal works in this area are Robert M. Solow, "Technical Change and the Aggregate Production Function," Review of Economics and Statistics, 39 (August 1957), 312-20; John W. Kendrick, Productivity Trends in the United States, Princeton, N.J.: Princeton University Press, 1961;

Edward F. Denison, The Sources of Economic Growth in the United States and the Alternatives Before Us, New York: Committee for Economic Development, 1962; and Evsey D. Domar, "On the Measurement of Technological Change," Economic Journal 71 (December 1961), 709-29.

12. If the rate of return to capital in the economy were known, an estimate of the capital stock could be made from the identity

$$b \equiv \frac{rK}{Y}$$

where $b \equiv$ the share of property income in net domestic product (NDP), $r \equiv$ the net (of depreciation) return on capital, $Y \equiv$ NDP, and $K \equiv$ the value of the stock of capital. Given estimates of b, r, and Y, one can then solve for K. I have estimated K assuming two alternative rates of return, $r = 15\%$ and $r = 20\%$, two figures that are plausible enough in the light of the experience of other countries, but that admittedly rest on no information derived from the Jordanian economy itself.

13. Total enrollments at the elementary (first six years), preparatory (grades seven through nine), and secondary levels increased at an average annual rate of 7.1% between 1952/53 and 1966/67 with the growth rate higher than the level of schooling. Calculated from Jordan Ministry of Education, Annual Report for School Year, 1959-1960 (Arabic), Amman, pp. 244-45; and idem, Yearbook of Educational Statistics for the Year, 1966-67, Amman, pp. 162-63.

The only serious estimate of post-secondary enrollments of Jordanian students (most of whom were enrolled in universities outside Jordan) appeared in JDS, Jordanian Students in the Third Level of Education, 1969/1970, Amman, 1971. The figures there must be adjusted to allow for the numbers missed by the survey.

14. Enrollment ratios for other countries are taken from Frederick Harbison and Charles A. Myers, Education, Manpower and Economic Growth: Strategies of Human Resource Development, New York: McGraw-Hill, 1964, p. 38.

15. See Samuel Bowles, Planning Educational Systems for Economic Growth, Cambridge, Mass.: Harvard University Press, 1969, p. 6, and the sources cited there.

16. According to the 1961 census, about 8% of all economically active Jordanians were in foreign countries. Among economically active persons abroad, 40% were in professional, administrative, clerical, or sales positions, compared with about 15% for the domestic labor force. (JDS, First Census, vol. I, pp. 316, 329-32; vol. II, pp. 50-55.)

17. During this period financial aid flows to Jordan exceeded the import surplus, primarily because Jordan was increasing its holdings of foreign exchange reserves.

18. See especially Jagdish N. Bhagwati, Amount and Sharing of Aid, Washington: Overseas Development Council, 1970, Chapter IV, Tables 2 and 6.

19. See Richard J. Ward, "Foreign Aid and the Moral of Compulsory Imports (The Case of Jordan)," Indian Journal of Economics, 45 (January 1965), 267-76. One reason for the failure of the attempt to tie certain imports to U.S. suppliers was that American exporters simply were not interested in the small Jordanian market.

20. The UN Conference on Trade and Development estimated the grant equivalent of the 1965-66 loans and grants per capita for 47 LDCs by discounting loans at 8%. Jordan ranked first with $36.50 per capita, and Israel second with $28.60 per capita. Of the 45 countries, only nine received more than $10 per capita. See Bhagwati, pp. 78-79.

21. Chenery and Syrquin, Chapter 5, and Peter S. Heller, "A Model of Public Fiscal Behavior in Developing Countries: Aid, Investment, and Taxation," American Economic Review, 65 (June 1975), 429-45.

22. I have carried out an extremely speculative exercise by calculating the financing of investment on the assumption that 90% of foreign aid to households was for the finance of consumption (since the marginal propensity to consume was about .9) and that 55% of foreign aid to government was for the finance of consumption (based on average behavior in LDCs, from Chenery and Syrquin, pp. 121, 123-27, 132). On these highly conjectural assumptions, the deficit on foreign account financed 40% of gross domestic investment, the remaining 60% coming from domestic saving. Of this 60%, private saving accounted for 53 percentage points and government saving for the remaining 7 percentage points.

23. Private disposable income for 1963-66 was multiplied by the 1959-62 ratio of private consumption to private disposable income and the result was divided by 1963-66 GNP, giving 80.2%. Thus, if the saving rate had not changed, private consumption would still have fallen from 82.3% of GNP to 80.2% of GNP between 1959-62 and 1963-66.

24. Ordinarily, looking at the shares of private consumption and private saving in disposable income is just looking at two sides of the same coin because of the accounting identity that private consumption plus private saving equal private disposable income. However, because of the adjustments I have made to the saving and investment estimates (discussed in the Appendix), this accounting identity does not hold precisely here.

25. Determined by use of regression equation (8), p. 219, of H. S. Houthakker, "On Some Determinants of Saving in Developed and Under-Developed Countries," in E. A. G. Robinson, ed., Problems in Economic Development, London: Macmillan, 1965. Net private saving per capita in Jordan was about 75% of that expected for the average country of equal net private disposable income per capita.

26. Simon Kuznets, "Quantitative Aspects of the Economic Growth of Nations: VII. The Share and Structure of Consump-

tion," Economic Development and Cultural Change, 10 (January 1962, Part II), 8.

27. Two cross-section studies provide the means of comparison. Both relate the share of government current domestic revenue in GNP to the level of GNP per capita and the "degree of openness" of the economy. The degree of openness is defined as the share of imports plus exports in GNP by Jorgen R. Lotz and Elliott R. Morss, "Measuring 'Tax Effort' of Developing Countries," International Monetary Fund Staff Papers, 14 (November 1967), 478-97. The degree of openness is defined as the share of imports plus exports in GNP by Harley H. Hinrichs, A General Theory of Tax Structure Change During Economic Development, Cambridge: Harvard University Law School, 1966.

28. Direct taxes on the agriculture sector were a land tax on irrigated land (varying with the use and quality of the land) and an animal head tax. Together they contributed less than 1% of total tax revenue during 1959-66.

29. Abdul Rahman S. Tukan, "The Implications of Achieving Fiscal Independence for Jordan," unpublished Ph.D. thesis, Department of Economics, Vanderbilt University, Nashville, Tennessee, 1967, pp. 118-21; and Hani Abu-Jabarah, "The Income Tax Law in Jordan," unpublished M.B.A. thesis, Department of Business Administration, American University of Beirut, Beirut, Lebanon, 1968.

31. For other countries see Kuznets, "Quantitative Aspects VII," p. 8.

31. Jordan Development Board (JDB), Seven Year Program for Economic Development, 1964-1970, Amman, n.d., pp. 34, 36.

32. For 37 LDCs in the early 1960s, government defense expenditures averaged 2.1% of GNP. Calculated from Joergen R. Lotz, "Patterns of Government Spending in Developing Countries," The Manchester School of Economic and Social Studies, 38 (June 1970), Table 2, 125.

4
The Orientation to Services

Compared with other economies at a similar level of development, Jordan's economic structure is unusual. An exceptionally large proportion of economic activity is in the services sector. This chapter examines the sectoral structure of the pre-war Jordanian economy and attempts to identify and quantify the causes of Jordan's atypical economic structure.

1. THE SECTORAL STRUCTURE

Kuznets, Chenery, and Taylor have carried out cross-country sectoral studies which determine the value added and labor force shares typical of countries at various levels of per capita income.[1] In Table IV.1 Jordan's sectoral shares for 1961/62 are compared with those typical of a country at Jordan's 1961/62 level of per capita income and, for some values, population. Compared to the "typical country," the share of the services sector, both in total value added and in the employed labor force, was exceptionally large in Jordan.[2] Corresponding to the large share of services are relatively small shares for agriculture and for manufacturing.

The technical failings of cross-country studies of sectoral structure are well known: inadequate specification of the model, errors and differences of definition in national accounts statistics, the bias introduced by conversion at official exchange rates. Thus, it is not surprising that regressions explaining sectoral shares in total product leave much variation unexplained.[3] The difference between Jordan and the typical country is so large, however, that it cannot plausibly be accounted for by inadequacies in the cross-country studies.[4]

Jordan's unusual sectoral structure was recognized, in an imperfect way, by Shorter.[5] For six Middle Eastern countries and Morocco he compared

63

TABLE IV.1. SHARE OF INDUSTRIAL SECTORS, 1961/62, JORDAN AND TYPICAL COUNTRY (percent)

	Value Added		Labor Force	
	Jordan 1961/62	Typical Country	Jordan 1961	Typical Country
I. Primary Production	22.2	36.6	38.6	57.5
A. Agriculture	21.0	35.2	35.7	56.4
B. Mining	1.1	1.4	2.8	1.1
II. Industry	11.4	17.2	22.2	15.5
A. Manufacturing	6.6	12.4	9.8	11.6
B. Construction	4.9	4.8	12.4	3.9
III. Services	66.4	42.3	39.3	26.0
A. Transport	11.5	5.8	3.7	3.4
B. Trade, Banking and Insurance	23.1	17.3	9.2	6.5
C. Public Administration and Defense	15.4	6.4}		
D. Other Services	16.5	15.7}	26.4	16.1

NOTES: Value Added

Data for Jordan are from JDS, The National Accounts, 1959-1967, p. 10. Each percentage is calculated as the ratio of current-price sectoral value added to current-price GDP at factor cost. The typical country ratio for transport includes value added in communications; for Jordan communications is included in "other services."

Items I, II, and III for the typical country were calculated from the B equations for small countries given in Chenery and Taylor, p. 396, and items I.A, I.B, II.A, II.B, and III.A from equations in Chenery, p. 634. All these equations provide estimates of sectoral share as a function of GNP per capita and population, for which I used average annual GNP per capita in Jordan for 1961 and 1962 (in 1960 U.S. dollars) and the end-1961 Jordanian population excluding those resident abroad. The ratios for III.B, III.C, and III.D are for group IV in Kuznets, Economic Growth of Nations, pp. 104-5.

Labor Force

The ratios for Jordan are derived from data in JDS, First Census, vol. 3, p. 10. From total active population in Jordan I subtracted unpaid family workers, those seeking work, those of unclassified economic status and those in "activities not adequately described." Kuznets classifies those in the armed forces as part of the services sector, whereas the Jordan census puts them under "activities not adequately described." There were roughly 30,000 persons in the Jordanian armed forces in 1961. Accordingly, I added 30,000 to the number employed in "public administration and defense."

Items I.A, III.B, III.C, and III.D of the typical country ratios are for the combined group V-VI-VII in Kuznets, "Quantitative Aspects II," pp. 23, 27. Unpaid family workers are excluded from the definition of the labor force. The typical country ratios for items I.B, II.A, II.B, and III.A are for group IV in Kuznets, Economic Growth of Nations, p. 200. The definition of the labor force differs somewhat for the different countries used in computing the averages, but generally unpaid family workers are included in the definition of the labor force. The typical country ratios in rows I, II, and III are the sums of their respective components.

Thus, ratios I.B, II.A, II.B, and III.A for the typical country differ from the ratios for other typical country sectors and for Jordan in that the former include unpaid family workers in the definition of the labor force. In general, it is preferable to exclude family workers from the definition of the labor force because statistics on them are generally unsatisfactory, and this is certainly true for Jordan. The use of some typical country ratios including unpaid family workers was dictated by the lack of satisfactory alternatives. The consequences should not be very serious, since the ratios for sectors in which unpaid family labor is most important (agriculture, commerce, some services) are calculated exclusive of unpaid family workers.

the shares of agricultural value added in GDP with shares derived from cross-section studies of Kuznets and Chenery. He found most of the seven countries to have below-average agricultural shares. However, this treatment lumps together some very dissimilar elements; for example, the small share of agriculture in Iraq obviously was due to its petroleum resources, an explanation not relevant for Jordan or Lebanon. Furthermore, by examining solely agriculture's share, Shorter failed to point out Israel's concentration in services, which is attributable to some of the same factors that explain Jordan's sectoral structure.[6]

The concentration of the 1961 labor force in nonagricultural sectors shown by Table IV.1 apparently did not prevail prior to the partition of Palestine. Although there are no statistical estimates of the Transjordan labor force, descriptions of the area strongly suggest that the population must have been heavily concentrated in agricultural activity, much of it pastoral. Of the 1936 non-Jewish labor force in Palestine, 62% were employed in agriculture, according to one estimate.[7] Since this included non-Arabs, who were mainly Britons employed in government service, the proportion of the Arab labor force in agriculture would be a bit larger. Some concentration of value added, as opposed to labor force, in nonagricultural sectors does appear to have existed in non-Jewish Palestine prior to partition. One estimate placed agriculture's share in 1936 value added at a relatively low 27%.[8] However, if the value added attributable to non-Jewish Europeans were excluded, the share of agriculture would be modestly higher (perhaps around 30%), but still somewhat below the average for a typical comparable country. On the other hand, similarly conjectural statistics suggest that the 1936 share of mining and manufacturing value added in total value added of the non-Jewish population of Palestine was significantly greater than the share that prevailed in Jordan during 1961/62.[9] If these estimates are correct, they imply that the partition of Palestine put the greater part of industry in Israel and may have left Jordan relatively underindustrialized at its creation.

These estimates suggest that the causes of Jordan's services concentration are not to be sought in historical phenomena of long standing, antedating the partition of Palestine. Although there may have been some services concentration in the Arab economy of Palestine, it evidently was considerably less than in Jordan after its creation in 1950. The causes of Jordan's concentration in services are best sought in events occurring with and following the partition of Palestine.

2. THE ROLE OF THE IMPORT SURPLUS

Relatively large receipts of foreign aid and factor income from abroad (especially emigrants' remittances) allowed Jordan to maintain an import surplus that was exceptionally large relative to the size of the economy. This section estimates the effect of this import surplus on Jordan's concentration in services.

The effect of the import surplus on the services share may occur because services do not constitute nearly as large a share of international trade as of production, since it is infeasible, or at least very expensive, to trade most services internationally. Thus, the import surplus must be composed mainly of goods. To restore a "normal" proportion between goods and services in the total resources (GDP plus the import surplus) available to the economy, the economy adjusts by producing a larger share of services.

A hypothetical example will illustrate the approach used here to estimate the size of the import surplus effect on sectoral shares. Assume an economy originally with no import surplus and GDP = $100, divided equally between goods and services. This situation is shown in row 1 of Table IV.2. Now imagine that foreign aid permits the country to run an import surplus of $30, divided 80% goods and 20% services (row 3 of Table IV.2). If the domestic economic structure did not adjust to the appearance of the import surplus, the distribution of GDP in row 2 would remain the same as before the import surplus (row 1). As a result of the import surplus, the share of goods in total resources (GDP plus the import surplus) would rise from 50% (row 1) to 57% (row 4). If the appearance of the import surplus does not change the desired division of total resources between goods and services, the domestic economy must adjust so that total resources are once again divided 50% goods and 50% services (row 7). Given rows 6 and 7, we can derive row 5, which shows that the proportion of services in GDP must rise to 59%. In this example, a nine percentage point increase in the share of services (from 50% to 59%) may be attributed to the import surplus. Thus, the basic approach will be to compare the

TABLE IV.2. HYPOTHETICAL EFFECT OF IMPORT SURPLUS ON SECTORAL DISTRIBUTION

	Goods		Services		Total Value
	Value	% of Total	Value	% of Total	
No Import Surplus					
1. GDP = Total Resources	$50	50	$50	50	$100
Import Surplus,					
No Domestic Adjustment					
2. GDP	$50	50	$50	50	$100
3. Import Surplus	$24	80	$ 6	20	$ 30
4. Total Resources	$74	57	$56	43	$130
Import Surplus,					
Domestic Adjustment					
5. GDP	$41	41	$59	59	$100
6. Import Surplus	$24	80	$ 6	20	$ 30
7. Total Resources	$65	50	$65	50	$130

share of services in total resources with the share in GDP. The observable data correspond to those in rows 5-7 of Table IV.2 for the hypothetical example.

In measuring the effect of the import surplus on Jordan's deviation from typical sectoral structure, it might seem natural to calculate the sectoral distribution of the import surplus as the sectoral distribution of Jordan's own exports and imports. However, this treatment mixes together two things which should be kept separate. In comparison with other countries, services constituted an exceptionally large share of exports and small share of imports in Jordan.[10] If we took Jordan's actual sectoral composition of exports and imports to measure the effect of the import surplus, we would be measuring the consequence not only of the import surplus, but also of Jordan's specialization in services, the latter in turn having several possible causes. Therefore, in measuring the composition of the import surplus, the composition of imports and exports for a typical country is used. The effect of the import surplus is thereby abstracted from the effect of Jordan's international specialization in services.

Using data from forty-five countries, Kuznets presents average shares of goods and of services in both exports and imports.[11] Ideally, the import surplus should be expressed in terms of the sectoral composition of value added. However, for imports and exports, only statistics of the sectoral distribution of gross value exist, and these will have to be used here.

In Kuznets' figures the share of services in exports is markedly larger than its share in imports. For the world as a whole with an ideal accounting system, the share of services in exports should equal its share in imports, since one country's export must be some other country's import. There are a number of possible reasons for the difference shown in the Kuznets figures.[12] It may be inferred that the correct figures would have sectoral shares the same in both exports and imports. I have therefore made an adjustment of Kuznets' figures and arrived at a sectoral composition of the import surplus of 83.5% goods and 16.5% services.[13] This approach has a certain practical convenience as well: It is not necessary to make any (necessarily arbitrary) decision on the degree to which the import surplus caused a rise

69

in imports versus a fall in exports. Since the sectoral composition of exports and imports is assumed the same, it makes no difference.

The import surplus presumably affects the sectoral structure only with a lag, of unknown magnitude. I arbitrarily used the import surplus for the three years, 1959-61.[14] Over this period Jordan's import surplus averaged 37% of GDP at factor cost. The average LDC maintained an import surplus of about 5% of GDP.[15] Thus, even in the typical country there must have been some concentration in the services sector as the result of an import surplus. This must be allowed for if we wish to estimate the degree to which Jordan's above-average import surplus (relative to GDP) contributed to the deviation of Jordan's sectoral shares from those of the average LDC. The simplest way to do this is to imagine that Jordan's import surplus is 32% (37% - 5%) of GDP and make no adjustment to the figures for the average LDC.

In calculating the effect of the import surplus on the industrial structure, the construction sector is more akin to the services sector than to the goods-producing sector, since--like services--only a small proportion of construction output is traded internationally, and since international trade in construction is generally recorded as a form of trade in services (e.g., when a contracting firm is employed on a construction project in a foreign country). For this calculation, therefore, the services sector is to be understood to include construction.

According to Table IV.1, 28.7% of 1961/62 GDP was in goods production, and 71.3% was in services (including construction). Using an import surplus of 32% of GDP, composed of 83.5% goods and 16.5% services, the sectoral distribution of total resources is calculated as 42.0% goods and 58.0% services.[16] Thus, compared with the typical country, the share of the services sector (including construction) in Jordan's GDP was increased by 13.3 percentage points (from 58.0% to 71.3%) as a result of the large degree by which Jordan's import surplus (relative to GDP) exceeded that of the typical country. This accounts for more than half of the 24.2 percentage-point difference between Jordan and the typical country in the value-added share of services (including construction). Clearly, these estimates give only rough orders of magnitude, but it seems reasonable to conclude that the effect of the import surplus accounted for very roughly half the difference in the services share between Jordan and the typical country at a comparable level of per capita income and population.

There is another way in which an import surplus may increase the share of services. The cross-country studies cited here all find that on average the services share increases as per capita income increases. The appearance of an import surplus may then increase the services share, since like an increase in income it places more resources at the disposal of the country. Ofer calls this the income effect of an import surplus and refers to the effect discussed in the first part of this section as the substitution effect.[17]

An income effect of this sort is questionable on several grounds. Increased income per capita may affect sectoral shares from both the demand side (particularly through differences in income elasticities of demand) and the supply side (particularly through changing comparative advantages as the capital-labor ratio rises). The appearance or increase of the import surplus may be expected to have only the former effect. Second, as Balassa has observed, a recorded increase in the services share as per capita income rises may result from changing relative prices as per capita income rises, because on balance technological change has the least effect on the services sector.[18] This is significant here because an increased import surplus by itself would not be expected to have such a relative price effect. Thus, if changing relative prices are the sole cause of the recorded rise in the services share as per capita income increases, there would be no income effect of an import surplus on the services share. In any case, it is presently impossible to disentangle the effect of relative price changes from other factors causing the services share to rise with increasing per capita income. In view of these two considerations, the income effect of the import surplus is expected to be relatively small. If an income effect does exist, the total effect of the import surplus on the services share is somewhat greater than that measured above.

3. THE EFFECT OF DEFENSE, TOURISM, AND EDUCATION

One of the most striking differences (see Table IV.1) between Jordan and the typical country lies in the sector of "public administration and defense." This difference is primarily attributable to the exceptionally large share of GDP Jordan devoted to defense. Jordan's 1961/62 share of government defense expenditures in GNP was roughly six times that of the typical country.[19] If we assume that this proportion was the same for defense value added as for defense expenditures, the effect of Jordan's large defense effort on the sectoral shares may be estimated by dividing Jordan's defense value added by six and calculating the new sectoral shares. This calculation reduces the share of services of 58.0% (adjusted for the effect of the import surplus) to 53.9%,[20] so that the fact that the share of defense was above average in Jordan accounted for 4.1 percentage points of the services share. This is 16.9% of the 24.2 percentage point difference in services share between Jordan and the typical country of comparable per capita income and population.

Possessing Jerusalem and other areas of religious significance, Jordan had a comparative advantage in tourist services, which probably contributed to its services concentration, but only modestly. Receipts from tourism were 4.3% of GDP during 1961/62.[21] If we accept the assumption of the Jordan Seven Year Plan that 32% of tourist expenditures went into imports,[22] then domestic value added (direct and indirect) into tourism was 2.9% of 1961/62 GDP. This does not mean that tourism increased the share of services in GDP by 2.9%. The true effect of tourism on the concentration in services must be considerably less than 2.9% because some tourist expenditures on domestic production are for goods, such as food, rather than just services, and because some of the resources directly or indirectly employed in tourism, if not engaged in production for tourists, would have been employed in services anyway. In addition, since we are comparing Jordan's services share with that of the typical country, it is only the excess of Jordan's tourism share over that of the typical country that matters, and there must be some tourism receipts on average in other LDCs. On plausible assumptions, the effect of Jordan's comparative advantage in tourism was to raise the 1961/62 share of services in GDP by 1-2 percentage points, accounting for around 5-10% of the disparity in the services share between Jordan and the typical country.

It might be thought that Jordan's exceptionally high level of school attendance, at least at higher levels, would lead to a large share of value added in education. However, offsetting this is the fact that in 1961/62 virtually all Jordanians in higher education were studying abroad. Some very rough computations suggest that when these two elements are combined, there is no significant effect of education on Jordan's services concentration.[23]

4. THE COMMERCE SECTOR

As Table IV.1 indicates, the sector of trade, banking, and insurance constituted a substantial part of GDP and of the excess of Jordan's services share over that of the average comparable LDC. By far the largest segment of this sector was wholesale and retail trade. Of total gross revenue in wholesale and retail trade, approximately 40-50% was derived from trade in domestically produced fruits and vegetables.[24] The remainder accrued from trade in a wide variety of imported and domestically produced products. Evidently, trade in domestically produced fruits and vegetables merits attention as a possible source of Jordan's concentration in services. While the JDS estimates of on-farm prices (and thereby the trade markups) for fruits and vegetables are rough ones based on limited and informal inquiries, informed observers outside the JDS generally agreed that the JDS markups were reasonably correct and, if anything, were conservative.

Conceivably, part of the large share of the commerce sector in GDP may have been due to the receipt of monopoly profits by traders. If monopoly profits were important in commerce, it is in wholesale trade in fruits and vegetables that they should be sought. The absence of import quotas and of government restrictions on the number of importers implies that importers' profits were unlikely to have been exceptionally large. Since in retail trade, entry was generally unrestricted, economies of scale negligible and sellers numerous, extensive monopoly power at the retail level was also unlikely. It is then primarily at the wholesale level and--because the trade is relatively so predominant--in fruits and vegetables that we should seek the possibility of monopoly power so extensive as to significantly affect the share of the commerce sector in GDP.

A 1971 study of the Amman organized wholesale fruit and vegetable market by Hamawi concluded that it was moderately to highly oligopolistic.[25] This conclusion was reached from consideration of the small number of sellers, the degree of concentration of sales within that small number, and the existence of supposed barriers to entry.[26] However, upon examination this characterization appears somewhat too strong. The total number of sellers was 37 in 1966/67 and 36 in 1968/69.[27] The four largest sellers accounted for 42-54% of total value of sales and the eight largest for 62-65%.[28] While not an atomistic market, this would certainly seem less than highly oligopolistic. If sellers were specialized in certain commodities, the market for any given product might be much more concentrated than the aggregative figures indicated. However, there was very little specialization, most firms dealing in 40 or more of the 69 commodities studied.[29] No really convincing reason for the existence of barriers to entry is given and the evidence presented is inconclusive.

The Hamawi study deals with fruit and vegetable wholesale merchants as potential monopolists in the sale of fruits and vegetables and does not deal with the merchants' potential monopsony power as buyers. Conceivably, they might lack monopoly power as sellers but possess monopsony power as buyers. This is plausible, since wholesale merchants may be geographically specialized so that the number of wholesalers competing as buyers in a single local market would be significantly smaller than the number selling in Amman, the biggest market. A 1961 survey of the East Jordan Valley suggested that the farmer generally had only a small number of wholesalers from which to choose and that these dealers colluded.[30] But a sample survey of the Jordan Valley conducted in 1966 reported that farmers believed there was keen competition among commission agents and had few complaints about them.[31] And the 1961 study indicated that trade margins in Jordan were not greatly different from those in other countries.[32] While this evidence is not very strong, the case that monopoly power was large in marketing of fruits and vegetables must be considered unproven, if not refuted.

Perhaps a better explanation than monopoly for the large share of commerce value added in Jordan is simply that Jordan had a comparative advantage in fruits and vegetables, which have a high services content. Actually, Jordan was not a net exporter of fruits and vegetables, but a small net importer, virtually self-sufficient by the immediate prewar years. However, per capita consumption of vegetables measured by weight, was unusually high in Jordan.[33] Furthermore, for an economy with an import surplus of around 30% of GDP and hence a net

74

importer of many goods, self-sufficiency in fruits and vegetables is an indicator of relative concentration, or comparative advantage, in them.

5. STRUCTURAL DISEQUILIBRIUM IN MANUFACTURING

The relatively small share of manufacturing in Jordan's GDP in part was the other side of the coin from factors already mentioned causing the share of services to be relatively large. But in addition the legacy of the partition of Palestine may have had an additional effect on the manufacturing sector in particular. It was suggested above (p. 66) that the partition of Palestine put most Palestinian Arab manufacturing industry inside Israel. Thus, a relatively underindustrialized West Bank was joined to a Transjordan in large part pacified only comparatively recently. This produced what might loosely be termed a "disequilibrium" in the economic structure of Jordan: a manufacturing sector that was relatively stunted compared to what it would have been if Jordan had had a more normal history.

Other things equal, such a disequilibrium probably sets up pressures toward self-correction, primarily in the form of exceptionally high returns to investment in the underdeveloped sector. However, partial evidence suggests that during the period of the 1950s no movement toward equilibrium occurred. This is suggested by the fact that the mining, manufacturing and electricity sector did not increase its share in total value added over the period 1954/55 to 1959/60.[34] In fact, since the share of manufacturing in total value added is normally expected to rise when per capita income rises, the failure of the share to rise in Jordan suggests that the disequilibrium may even have increased during this period.[35]

Perhaps one reason for the limited adjustment in early years is the political tension and uncertainty that prevailed in Jordan until about 1958 (see above, p. 32, n. 1). Anyone contemplating investment in manufacturing must have been greatly deterred by the prospect of political upheaval, to which investment in manufacturing is more vulnerable than many other kinds of investment. However, this explanation should not be overstressed. Even if a revolutionary regime had achieved control in the 1950s, it would probably not have been a socialist government, nor expropriated private capital investments. Socialism did not become an important

75

force in the Arab Middle East until the late 1950s and especially the early 1960s.

Another reason why this disequilibrium was not quickly eliminated lies in the inadequacy of transport facilities after the severing of transport lines through Israel to the Mediterranean. Not only did the lack of transport limit industrial development, but government efforts to remove this bottleneck probably tied up administrative, technical, and capital resources that would otherwise have been used to promote industrialization.

By around 1960 Jordan had achieved apparent political stability and had completed the most important transportation projects. From then until the 1967 war value added in manufacturing grew so much more rapidly than GDP that the disequilibrium represented by Jordan's share of manufacturing in GDP was substantially reduced, if not eliminated.[36]

NOTES

1. Hollis B. Chenery, "Patterns of Industrial Growth," American Economic Review, 50 (September 1960), 624-54; Hollis B. Chenery and Lance Taylor, "Development Patterns: Among Countries and Over Time," Review of Economics and Statistics, 50 (November 1968), 391-416; Simon Kuznets, "Quantitative Aspects of the Economic Growth of Nations: II. Industrial Distribution of National Product and Labor Force," Economic Development and Cultural Change, 5 (July 1957, supplement), and Simon Kuznets, Economic Growth of Nations: Total Output and Production Structure, Cambridge, Mass.: Harvard University Press, 1971.

2. Throughout, when reference is made to the typical country, it has a special meaning. If a sectoral share for the typical country is derived from the papers of Chenery or Chenery-Taylor, who estimated the relationship between sectoral shares and the independent variables of per capita income and population, it refers to a share computed from one of their regression equations by using Jordan's 1961/62 levels of per capita income and population. If a proportion for the typical country is derived from one of the studies by Kuznets, who computes averages for countries grouped by per capita income, it refers to the average for the group with per capita income closest to that of Jordan in 1961/62.

3. See especially Chenery and Taylor, Tables 1-5.

4. Compare Table IV.1 here with Kuznets, Economic Growth of Nations, Table 13, p. 108.

5. Frederic C. Shorter, "The Application of Development Hypotheses in Middle Eastern Studies," Economic Development and Cultural Change, 14 (April 1966), 340-54.

6. The causes of Israel's concentration in services are discussed in Gur Ofer, The Service Industries in a Developing Economy: Israel as a Case Study, New York: Praeger, 1967.

7. Calculated from Nathan et al., p. 150. Another estimate put the proportion of non-Jews in agriculture in 1939 at around 80% (ibid., p. 194). The two estimates are surely incompatible. The 80% estimate seems high, in light of some of the description of the non-Jewish Palestine economy. In any case the uncertainty of the estimates should be emphasized.

8. Calculated from ibid., p. 150.

9. For 1936 the share of mining and manufacturing in total value added of the non-Jewish sector of Palestine was 13.6% (calculated from ibid., p. 150), compared to 7.7% for Jordan in 1961/62 (from Table IV.1).

10. The comparison is made with figures computed from Table 1, pp. 4-5, of Simon Kuznets, "Quantitative Aspects of the Economic Growth of Nations: IX. Level and Structure of Foreign Trade: Comparisons of Recent Years," Economic Development and Cultural Change, 13 (October 1964, Part II).

11. Ibid., pp. 4-5.

12. The fact that goods exported are recorded f.o.b., while goods imported are recorded c.i.f., will cause recorded services exports to exceed recorded services imports and vice versa for goods. Also, Kuznets' sample does not include all countries; countries omitted might be net importers of services. In addition, the Kuznets proportions are unweighted averages of the ratios for individual countries; perhaps countries with a large share of world trade are net importers of services.

13. For countries at Jordan's level of per capita income services averaged 20.1% of exports and 12.8% of imports (Kuznets, "Quantitative Aspects IX," pp. 4-5, Table 1, column 5). To arrive at a single percentage for both exports and imports, as justified above, I simply used the unweighted arithmetic average of 16.5%.

14. The relative size of the import surplus changed slowly, so the choice of years does not make much difference.

15. Fanny Ginor, "The Impact of Capital Imports on the Structure of Developing Countries," Kyklos, 22 (1969-Fasc. 1), 104.

16. For example, the share of services is calculated as $(100.0 \times 71.3 + 32.0 \times 16.5)/132.0 = 58.0$.

17. Ofer, p. 40.

18. Bela Balassa, "Patterns of Industrial Growth: Comment," American Economic Review, 51 (June 1961), 394-97.

19. Over the two years, 1961-62, Jordan's government defense expenditure averaged 12.8% of GNP. JDS, The National Accounts, 1959-1967, p. 10. For 37 LDCs in the early 1960s, government defense expenditure averaged 2.1% of GNP (see footnote 32 of Chapter III above).

20. This approach implicitly assumes that if value added

77

in defense had been at a "typical" level in Jordan, the value added thereby released to other sectors would have been divided between goods production and services production in the proportion 42%-58%, the sectoral division of GDP adjusted for the effect of the import surplus.

21. JDS, The National Accounts, 1959-1967, pp. 10, 19.

22. JDB, Seven Year Program, p. 188.

23. I took the number of students in Jordan in excess of the average for LDCs of equal income per capita and multiplied by an estimate of current costs per student. For university students I multiplied the number of university students that would be normal for a country of Jordan's population and per capita income by an estimate of current costs per university student (not including opportunity costs, room and board, books, etc.).

24. Based upon data for three years only: 1963, 1965, and 1966. Data for 1965 and 1966 are from unpublished worksheets of the JDS Economic Section and for 1963 from JDS, The National Accounts, 1959-1963, p. 58.

25. Fahd Mahmud El-Hamawi, "Structure, Conduct and Performance of the Amman Organized Wholesale Fruit and Vegetable Market," unpublished M.S. thesis, Department of Agricultural Economics, American University of Beirut, Beirut, Lebanon, 1971. The market studied here physically came into existence only in 1966. The trade previously occurred in a different location and under somewhat different regulations. For the issues raised here, however, the thesis results should be reasonably representative of the earlier period.

26. Ibid., p. 37.

27. Ibid., p. 33. Hamawi works with market data for only these two years.

28. Ibid., p. 35. The ranges refer to the values in the two years, 1966/67 and 1968/69.

29. Only 4 of the 36 firms studied in 1968/69 dealt in less than 39 commodities of the 69 commodities studied. (Ibid., pp. 69-71. No figures on this are given for 1966/67.) No breakdown by commodities is given, but I would guess that the more important commodities were handled by virtually all sellers.

Hamawi emphasizes the fact that many sellers received a large proportion of their total sales volume from a few commodities. However, this is partly attributable to the fact that a few commodities predominated in total sales in the market. Furthermore, this measure of concentration is not a good measure of competitiveness.

30. JDS, The East Jordan Valley, pp. 200, 203.

31. Jordan River and Tributaries Regional Corporation, Jordan Valley Project: Agro- and Socio-Economic Study, Final Report, Dar al-Handasah, Beirut, and Netherlands Engineering Consultants, The Hague, 1969, Vol. III, Annex E, pp. 43-44.

32. JDS, The East Jordan Valley, p. 206.

78

33. Marion Clawson, Hans H. Landsberg, and Lyle T. Alexander, The Agricultural Potential of the Middle East, New York: American Elsevier, 1971, pp. 100-101.

34. Unfortunately, for the 1954/55-1959/60 period the available data do not give us the growth rate of value added in manufacturing separate from mining and electricity. According to Table II.3, current-price value added in mining, manufacturing, and electricity grew at an average annual rate of 10.5% between 1954/55 and 1959/60. This was less than the 11.6% average annual change in GDP at factor cost recorded for the same period (estimated at current prices, except for crop output, and smoothed for rainfall variations). Thus, the share of mining, manufacturing, and electricity appears to have fallen over the period, and it is reasonable to assume that manufacturing alone, the largest component, behaved in a not too dissimilar way.

35. In the range of Jordan's per capita income the typical elasticity of manufacturing value added per capita with respect to GDP per capita, as estimated from cross-section data on a number of countries, was 1.53 (Kuznets, Economic Growth of Nations, p. 111). For mining, manufacturing, and electricity in Jordan during 1954/55-1959/60 the elasticity was approximately 0.86.

36. During 1959/60-1965/66 the elasticity of manufacturing value added per capita with respect to GDP was roughly 2.44 for Jordan, compared with 1.53 typical of LDCs at Jordan's level of development (see preceding footnote). In 1966 the value added share of manufacturing in Jordan was less than that of the typical comparable LDC, but the gap was less than in 1959.

Part 2
The Postwar Economy:
A Survey

5
Postwar Growth: An Overview

1. THE SETTING

The 1967 war in the Middle East struck Jordan with a seemingly staggering host of problems. Most important were the Israeli occupation of the West Bank--an area especially important for agriculture and tourism--and an inflow of about 300,000 persons from the West Bank and Gaza into the East Bank, increasing the East Bank population by about a quarter in one year. Jordan's trade relations, especially the sale of phosphates to Turkey and Europe, were hindered by the 1967 closure of the Suez Canal. The postwar rise of the Palestine resistance movement threatened the internal stability of the country and led to Israeli shelling of the East Jordan Valley, including the East Ghor Canal irrigation area, the country's major development project. The physical damage to the project area, while not insignificant, was not as important as the loss of production and the delay in the further development of the area. By 1970 most of the inhabitants had fled the East Jordan Valley.

Despite these very serious problems, the Jordanian economy, after a sharp recession in activity immediately following the war, emerged into a pronounced, but quite artificial, recovery from 1968 through the first half of 1970. The recovery was partly sustained by expansion of the armed forces first to restore prewar levels and then beyond. The expansion, both in equipment and manpower, was financed by large grants from Kuwait, Saudi Arabia, and Libya, agreed upon at the Khartoum Arab summit meeting of September 1967.

The grants from the oil-rich Arab countries reputedly were intended for financing military activities only, but since substantial domestic resources would otherwise have been directed to defense, they had the effect of releasing funds for more directly productive activities. The funds were used not only for the importation of military equipment but to meet domestic military requirements, thus financing nonmilitary imports and the accumulation of foreign exchange reserves.

Over the three years 1967-69 foreign grants to the government of Jordan, more than three-fourths of which came from the Khartoum grants, averaged annually over $90 per capita.[1] This is a remarkably high figure in comparison with a $270 GNP per capita in 1966 (a typical rainfall year). It was generally acknowledged that in addition to published figures on foreign aid, there were substantial additional grants for the purchase of military equipment that went unrecorded.

During 1967 and 1968 Jordan increased its already large foreign reserves by over 50% and the Jordan dinar became quite strong on the exchange market. This was largely the consequence of the huge Arab aid payments, plus sizable foreign payments to commando groups in Jordan, local expenditures by Iraqi and Saudi Arabian troops stationed in Jordan, and a reduction in the imports of capital goods caused by the continuing stagnation of industrial investment. These more than offset such negative factors in the balance of payments as the decline in tourist earnings and in remittances, increased purchases of military equipment, and possibly some capital flight.

By 1969 industry had largely recovered from the serious slump of the immediate postwar period, although industrial investment remained stagnant. Favorable tariff reductions in neighboring Arab states permitted the expansion of manufactured exports, particularly cigarettes. The loss of the petroleum refinery's market in the West Bank was compensated by increased demand from an expanded Jordanian army, from commando groups, and from the Saudi Arabian and Iraqi troops stationed in the country. The cement plant was fully occupied in supplying the domestic market, which experienced a boom in housing construction, a persistent phenomenon in Jordan's economic history further stimulated by a new wave of refugees.

Although no complete data on employment for the period were ever compiled, it was widely believed that unemployment was even lower by 1969 and early 1970 than before the 1967 war despite the new refugee influx to the East Bank. One incomplete

indicator of this was a marked increase in the
level of wages for unskilled labor. Primarily responsible for the low unemployment rate were the
expansion of the army and of civilian government
employment, recruitment of commandoes by the Palestinian resistance movement, and the boom in housing
construction. Between mid-1967 and mid-1970 the
armed forces expanded by about 28,000.[2] By itself
this equals about 35-40% of the increase in the labor force attributable to the influx of refugees
from the West Bank and Gaza after the 1967 war.[3]

The steadily mounting tensions between the
Palestinian resistance forces in Jordan and the
Jordanian government exploded into civil war in
mid-September 1970. By late September the forces
of the government had defeated the Palestinian
commando forces and repulsed a Syrian invasion
force. During the following nine months the government increased its effective control over the country, culminating in a brief military action in mid-
July 1971 that eliminated the last pockets of Palestinian commando resistance.

The civil war and its aftermath produced a
severe, but temporary, setback to the economy.
Besides physical damages caused by the conflict,[4]
economic activity was cut back sharply. The economic slowdown had begun even before the civil war
broke out. Some hostilities took place during
June. Subsequently, politically motivated wildcat
strikes and absenteeism disrupted production in
industries such as petroleum refining and phosphates. In the weeks immediately preceding the
civil war many shops and offices in Amman were
closed and a number of people left Jordan for
neighboring countries. The civil war itself
caused power failure for several weeks in some
areas and brought industrial production nearly to
a standstill for more than a month. Shortages of
fodder resulted in substantial losses in livestock
and poultry production.

In reaction to the government's military
actions against the guerrillas, Libya and Kuwait,
but not Saudi Arabia, suspended further payments
of the aid which had been agreed to at Khartoum in
1967. However, financial assistance from the
United States, which had been reduced to very low
levels during 1968-70, was stepped up in 1971, so
that despite the loss of aid payments from Libya
and Kuwait, foreign aid in total continued at about
the same level in 1971 as in 1970. Jordan's large
official holdings of foreign exchange reserves

eased the financial difficulties of the immediate
post-civil war period, when in addition to the suspension of Libyan and Kuwaiti aid, imports rose
greatly. [5]

After the Jordanian government began its
final military push against Palestinian commando
forces in Jordan in July 1971, Iraq and Syria
closed their borders and air space to Jordan. The
Iraqi closure, which lasted from mid-July to mid-
October of 1971, was not as serious as the Syrian
closure, which prevented the export of phosphates
to Europe and impeded the import of intermediate
goods needed for Jordanian industry. The Syrian
border closure was eased gradually throughout 1972
and completely terminated by the end of that year.

Some sectors, such as manufacturing and agriculture, began to recover in 1971, while other
sectors, particularly mining and construction, hit
bottom in 1971 and only began to recover in 1972.
By 1972 all sectors were expanding and the government had resumed systematic development efforts
after the essentially ad hoc approach of the 1967-
71 period. The government prepared a development
plan for 1973-75, initiated the rehabilitation of
the East Jordan Valley, and began a major irrigation project on the Zarqa River. The government's
efforts were assisted by an increase of over 30%
in its 1972 foreign aid receipts compared to 1971.

Severe frost and drought sharply reduced the
1973 harvest, but recovery continued in other
sectors during 1973. The Yom Kippur war of October
1973 had only a small and temporary adverse effect
on the Jordanian economy and its ultimate indirect
effects on the economy proved to be favorable in
several ways. As a result of the Jordanian com-
mitment of one armored brigade to the Syrian front,
the aid from Kuwait, agreed to at Khartoum in 1967
but suspended in 1970, was restored retroactive to
April 1973.

Throughout the 1950s and 1960s the rate of
inflation had remained relatively low. Beginning
in 1972 inflation, as measured by the change in
the Amman consumer price index, accelerated to
double-digit levels, with the most rapid price increases occurring in food. This was one of the
most important grievances that led to a brief army
mutiny in February 1974. In the aftermath of the
army unrest, pay of the armed forces was raised and
a new ministry, the Ministry of Supply, was created
to attempt to cope with inflation by such measures
as price regulation and subsidization of some food-

stuffs. Although the rate of inflation in food
prices declined from the 30% annual rate of 1972
and 1973, both the food price index and the overall
consumer price index subsequently continued to rise
at double-digit rates,[6] and the issue of inflation
continued to arouse widespread concern in Jordan.

In 1974 the economy benefitted from three
fortuitous events: an excellent crop year, a huge
increase in the world price of phosphates, and the
indirect impact of the oil-price revolution in the
Middle East. At the initiative of Morocco, the
world's largest exporter, world phosphate prices
were quintupled during 1974. In response, Jordan
raised 1974 phosphate production by more than 50%
over the 1973 level. The combined effect of higher
prices and increased volume produced an increase in
earnings from phosphate exports of almost 400% between 1973 and 1974.[7]

The economic boom in the oil-producing countries of the Arab Middle East brought about by the
oil-price revolution began to spill over into the
Jordanian economy in 1974, and by 1975-76 this
spill-over, in combination with other factors, had
produced boom conditions in the economy. Neighboring oil-producing countries flush with new oil
money increased their imports from Jordan. Even
more important, however, was the expansion of
opportunities for Jordanians to work in the oil
countries. The increased employment of Jordanians
abroad, their increased earnings, and the perception of greater security for funds invested in
Jordan since the defeat of the guerrillas all contributed to a huge increase in remittances from
Jordanians employed abroad.

The great increase in Arab governments' oil
wealth after 1973 contributed to the Jordanian
boom in another way, by facilitating a large increase in aid payments. The Arab summit conference
in Rabat in October of 1974 approved substantial
aid payments to Jordan in addition to those decided at Khartoum in 1967. Thus, according to
official statistics, transfer payments to the Jordan central government from Arab sources quadrupled
between 1973 and 1975 to a level of nearly $170 per
capita. The addition of recorded transfers from
other foreign donors raises the level of 1975 grant
aid per capita to around $220. This is nearly
2-1/2 times the corresponding figure for 1967-69,
which itself was remarkably high in comparison with
other LDCs. In addition, development loans during
1975 equalled about $30 per capita.[8] Further, it

is generally acknowledged that a substantial volume of foreign aid used to finance the import of military equipment was not recorded in the official statistics.

In 1975 several new factors were added to continued high receipts of foreign exchange from phosphate exports, foreign aid, and remittances from Jordanians abroad. The reopening of the Suez Canal restored Jordan's direct transport link with Europe through the port of Aqaba. The worsening civil war in Lebanon diverted to Jordan some economic activity, such as vacation travel by Arabs from the oil-producing countries of the Gulf. Although the majority of refugees from the fighting in Lebanon probably fled to Syria and Europe, some went to Jordan. Many international firms had maintained their Middle East headquarters in Beirut. As fighting there intensified, firms sought to set up Middle East offices elsewhere, especially Athens, but to some degree Amman as well as Cairo, Teheran, and cities in the Gulf States.

In combination, these developments by 1975-76 had brought about frenetic land speculation in Jordan--particularly in Amman, but not limited to it--and a boom in construction, both residential and nonresidential. The construction boom, in combination with the expansion of the armed forces, the restoration of agricultural activity in the East Jordan Valley, and the outflow of workers to take employment in the oil-producing states, produced an extremely tight labor market--one in which unemployment was virtually nonexistent and wages for unskilled workers in the Amman area had perhaps tripled over a two-year period.

It was in this setting of tight labor markets, inflation, rampant land speculation, and seemingly limitless availability of foreign aid that Jordan presented its Five Year Development Plan for 1976-80. Inevitably, the introduction of the plan was in a setting of uncertainty: To what degree were the unprecedented circumstances of the economy of 1976 evanescent phenomena destined to disappear within the lifetime of the plan and to what degree were they the harbingers of a permanent change in the economic environment? Indeed, not only was there doubt about where the economy was going, but it was by no means clear where the economy had been. It is the purpose of the remainder of this study to clarify at least partially these issues.

2. POPULATION

Different estimates of the number of persons who fled to the East Bank from the West Bank and Gaza after the 1967 war have been as low as 250,000 and as high as 400,000. Although there was no reliable count of these displaced persons as they entered Jordan nor has there been a complete census of the East Bank population since 1961, it is possible by indirect means to estimate the number entering the East Bank after the war.

According to the 1961 census, 47.2% of the population, or 805,450 persons, resided in the West Bank.[9] Between the 1952 and 1961 censuses the growth of the West Bank population--around 1% per year--had been much less than that of the East Bank population, due to migration from the West to the East Bank. There is evidence, although it is only partial, that the rate of migration was significantly lower between 1961 and 1967 than between 1952 and 1961 (see above, pp. 28-29). In light of this, I extrapolate the 1961 West Bank population to 1967 using an average annual growth rate of 2%, which gives a West Bank population of roughly 900,000 on the eve of the 1967 war. A census by Israel placed the September 1967 population of the West Bank, including East Jerusalem, at 665,000.[10] This implies that roughly 235,000 persons had fled the West Bank by September 1967. According to Israeli estimates, net migration from the West Bank, excluding East Jerusalem, was about 29,000 between September 1967 and the end of 1968, by which time the net outflow had slowed to a trickle.[11]

If there were no Arab emigrants from East Jerusalem between September 1967 and end-1968 and if all the West Bank emigrants went to the East Bank, then according to the calculations in the preceding paragraph the number of West Bankers who fled to the East Bank after the war would have been about 264,000. In addition, by mid-1968 about 47,000 persons from the Gaza Strip had arrived in the East Bank.[12] Allowing for the departure of a modest number of West Bank emigrants directly to other countries, it seems reasonable to place the number of postwar displaced persons entering the East Bank at roughly 300,000.[13]

By the end of 1968 the number of East Bankers exclusive of those who entered after the 1967 war would have been about 1,170,000.[14] Adding the

300,000 postwar immigrants gives a total East Bank population of very roughly 1,470,000 at the end of 1968. The calculations here are based upon a 1961-68 growth rate of the resident population of the East and West Banks, excluding the effect of the inflow from Gaza, of 3% per year—a conjectural figure. In view of the 2.8% rate that prevailed during 1952-61, the use of the 3% rate for 1961-68 would allow for a decline in emigration to foreign countries, due perhaps to improved employment opportunities in Jordan during 1961-66, or for a modest rise in the rate of natural increase. Unfortunately, we can only conjecture about the possibility of such trends.

The growth rate of the population equals the rate of natural increase (birth rate minus death rate) minus the net rate of emigration abroad. On neither of these are the available data satisfactory. The most recent reliable estimate of the rate of natural increase is for 1959-63 (see above, p. 27), and there has never been any reliable comprehensive estimate of the rate of emigration from Jordan.

Two considerations suggest that the rate of natural increase may have been increasing. The first is the expectation that mortality rates might decline as economic development raised the levels of nutrition and health care. The 1959-63 crude death rate in Jordan was similar to that of other LDCs at a comparable level of economic development. As economic development occurs, crude death rates typically decline. Even if a quite rapid improvement in life expectancy is assumed, the effect on the average annual rate of natural increase over the 1961-76 period as a whole would be modest: 0.2-0.3 of a percentage point.[15]

The second piece of evidence suggesting that the natural rate of population increase may have risen comes from a 1972 national fertility survey of a random sample of women between 15 and 49.[16] Age-specific cumulative fertility in 1972, as measured by this survey, was significantly higher than the levels recorded by the 1961 census. When these age-specific cumulative fertility rates are converted to a general fertility rate (births per 1000 women 15-49), that rate appears to have risen 18.6% since 1961.[17] Had the percentage of women 15-49 in the total population remained unchanged between 1961 and 1972, this would imply an increase in the crude birth rate of 18.6% between 1961 and 1972. A household sample survey for 1972 indicates

88

a decline in the percentage of women 15-49 in the total population, but the sample may not be a representative one.[18] If the decline shown in the household survey is correct, the net rise in the crude birth rate resulting from the combined effect of an increase in age-specific fertility rates and a decrease in the proportion of women 15-49 in the total population would be 11.4%, or from 47.1 per thousand in 1961 to 52.5 in 1972--an extremely large increase, which would make the 1972 crude birth rate in Jordan at or near the highest in the world.

If the findings of these sample surveys are accepted and if a significant increase in life expectancy between 1961 and 1972 is assumed, it is possible that the natural rate of population increase could have risen from 3.1% around 1961 to as high as 4.0% in 1972. It is difficult to reconcile such a remarkable increase with two pieces of evidence suggesting that the rate of natural increase may not have risen greatly since 1961. First, the rate appears to have been roughly constant over the period 1952-61 (see above, pp. 27-28). It is difficult to imagine why the rate of natural increase would remain steady for a decade and then suddenly shoot up in the succeeding decade. Second, birth and death rates in the occupied West Bank between 1968 and 1975 have been similar to those estimated for Jordan during 1959-63.[19]

The evidence suggesting a rise in the natural rate of increase is statistically weak. Since there are no reliable statistics on deaths,[20] the belief that the death rate may have fallen is based only on the evidence from other countries that death rates of LDCs normally decline as development occurs. Military and civil conflict between 1967 and 1971 must have contributed to increased mortality rates. The evidence of a rising birth rate comes from the 1972 fertility sample survey. This was the first such survey conducted by Jordan, and the interviewers used had no previous experience of this type. There is doubt about the reliability of this survey. In the 1961 population census, cumulative fertility of some women was inconsistent with their age and length of marriage, perhaps because they reported their husbands' children by previous marriage.[21] In the calculation of fertility rates for 1961 a correction was made for these inconsistencies. Although similar inconsistencies apparently appeared in the results of the 1972 fertility survey, no correction was made for them.

In conclusion, while some evidence points to a rise in the natural rate of population increase, the indicated rise is so great that evidence much better than what we now have is necessary before the conclusion can be accepted. Until that evidence is forthcoming, a more modest rise in the rate of natural increase seems more plausible. Nonetheless, there remains the possibility, to be confirmed or rejected by new evidence, that during the 1960s Jordan may have experienced a sharp increase in fertility.

The rate of growth of the resident population is affected not only by the possibility of a rise in the rate of natural increase but also by the likelihood of an increase in the rate of emigration abroad after 1967. Both push and pull forces may have been at work. The number of displaced persons that entered the East Bank after the 1967 war must have decreased employment prospects and prompted more Jordanians to seek employment abroad, a movement that would have been accelerated by the internal tensions culminating in the civil disturbances of 1970-71. After the oil-price revolution of 1973-74, pull factors must have become more important, as increased incomes in the oil countries expanded employment opportunities and salary levels there.

Only one study of emigration to foreign countries has been carried out and that study, while carefully conducted, was for a small and unrepresentative sample of the population: recent graduates of post-secondary vocational schools and teacher training centers. From a random sample of all such graduates between 1971 and end-1975, it was found that 31.3% were outside Jordan.[22] This strikingly high figure probably is unrepresentative of school-leavers in Jordan as a whole. School-leavers with post-secondary education, including university education, presumably were more likely to emigrate than others, since the greatest labor demand in the oil countries was for highly trained labor.

As a conjectural exercise, assume that 20% of all new entrants into the labor force since 1968 took employment abroad.[23] Suppose also that 4% of all workers in the labor force before 1968, who presumably were much less likely to emigrate than new entrants to the labor force, emigrated between 1968 and 1975. Together, these speculative assump-

90

tions imply an outflow of roughly 35,000 workers between 1968 and 1975 or about 5,000 per year. Although a significant number of emigrants must have been young single persons, and some other emigrants may have left their families in Jordan, many emigrants must have been accompanied by dependents not in the labor force. According to the 1961 census, 56% of Jordanians employed abroad were economically active.[24] This suggests that total outflow may have been about twice the number of workers emigrating, i.e., 10,000 persons per year or 70,000 in total between 1968 and 1975.

The preceding estimates have been extremely speculative, intended only to indicate broad orders of magnitude. They rely upon several numbers which are no more than plausible guesses. It is perhaps less misleading to suggest that the net outflow of population between 1968 and 1975 may have been around 50-100,000. Allowing for modest net emigration between 1961 and 1968, this suggests that the total number of Jordanians abroad may have risen from the 63,000 enumerated by the 1961 census to around 150-200,000 by 1975.

To project the population beyond 1968, I assume a natural rate of population increase of 3.5% per year, a substantial increase over the 3.1% rate that prevailed around 1961.[25] Applying this to my 1968 population estimate and allowing for emigration gives an estimated resident Jordanian population of about 1.75 million at the end of 1974. The official JDS estimate for the same time is 1.9 million, but the means by which this estimate was reached are patently erroneous.[26]

Another piece of evidence supports the belief that the official population figures are seriously overestimated. According to the multi-purpose household survey of 1974, 32.8% of the sample population was enrolled in school during 1974.[27] Because urban residents, who have higher enrollment rates, may be over-represented in the sample, the true proportion may be slightly less, but most likely no less than 30%.[28] According to the Jordan Ministry of Education, there were 501,468 students enrolled in schools of all types during 1973-74.[29] If these students represented 30% of the total resident population in early 1974, and allowing for population increase to end-1974, the resident population at the end of 1974 would be about 1.7 million--close to my previous estimate and much below the official estimate of 1.9 million. Subsequently, wherever estimates of the resident

Jordanian population are required, a figure of 1.75 million for end-1974, or extrapolations from it, will be used.

3. LABOR FORCE AND EMPLOYMENT

No comprehensive estimate of the postwar labor force exists, because no population census has been taken since 1961. However, two household sample surveys, while not fully representative of the population, indicate significant changes in labor force participation.[30] In these multi-purpose household surveys, conducted during the first four months of 1972 and 1974, respectively, certain population groups were omitted completely and others apparently were not represented in proportion to their size in the population. In particular, no households of armed forces members or wandering bedouins were included. Since household enumeration in cities was based on property tax records, most households living in squatter's dwellings must have been omitted. It appears also that Amman and urban areas in general probably were over-represented in the sample.[31] However, examination of the survey results indicates that labor force participation rates for Amman and urban areas in general were not greatly different from those for the entire sample. Hence, the possible over-representation of these groups in the sample should not distort the results severely. The omission of households of members of the armed forces probably is the most serious statistical defect of the multi-purpose household surveys.

In Table V.1 data derived from the 1972 and 1974 household surveys are compared with the 1961 census results. Because of the large population movement from the West Bank to the East Bank after 1961, it is not clear whether the East Bank in the 1970s is best compared with the East Bank or both banks in 1961. Therefore 1961 data for both Jordan and the East Bank are provided. As it turns out, the general conclusions are not greatly affected by the choice of comparison for 1961.

Row 1 of Table V.1 reveals a distinct decline in the overall labor force participation rate between 1961 and 1972-74. To analyze this change, it is sufficient to analyze the trends among males 15-64 years old, who comprised 85-90% of the labor force. As row 2 shows, other groups (women, child-

92

dren, and the elderly) in combination did not
account for any significant part of the change in
the overall labor force participation rate.[32]
Another reason for concentrating on males 15-64 is
the existence of serious statistical problems with
other groups in the labor force, particularly in
the agriculture sector. For example, different
studies of the labor force have produced vastly
different estimates of the proportion of women in
the total agricultural labor force: 2% in the 1961
census, 20% in the 1967 sample survey of the agriculture sector, 3% in the 1972 and 1974 multi-
purpose household surveys and 33% in the 1975 agriculture census.[33] It is obvious that these differences are caused by statistical inconsistencies,
not by changes over time.[34]

Virtually all the change shown in row 1 is
attributable to males 15-64 (row 3). Two developments account for the sharp decline shown in row 3:
First, males 15-64 were a smaller fraction of the
total population in 1972-74 than in 1961 (row 4).
Since males 15-64 have the highest labor force participation rate of any group in the population,
the fall in the relative size of this group reduced the overall participation rate. The decline
in the proportion of males 15-64 in the total population is best explained by emigration into employment abroad, heavily concentrated among working-
age males.[35]

The second source of the decline shown in row
3 is a fall in labor force participation rates
among males 15-64. Whereas 81-83% of males 15-64
were in the labor force in 1961, by 1974 only 75%
were (row 5).[36] This decline is more than explained by row 6. It is due to a large increase
in the proportion of working-age males enrolled in
school. Interestingly, the proportion of males
15-64 who were either in the labor force or in
school, which may be viewed as an expanded parti-
cipation-rate concept, increased significantly between 1961 and 1972-74 (row 7). This trend might
be explained by improvement in employment prospects
between 1961 and 1972-74. When unemployment rates
are high and employment prospects poor, some prospective workers are discouraged and stop seeking
work, thereby withdrawing from the labor force. When
employment prospects (domestic and foreign) improve, as they probably did in Jordan between 1961
and 1972-74, some "discouraged workers" become economically active. In Jordan they partly counter-

TABLE V.1.   THE LABOR FORCE PARTICIPATION RATE AND ITS DETERMINANTS, 1961, 1972, 1974 (percent)

	1961		East Bank	
	Jordan	East Bank	1972	1974
1. Labor Force Participation Rate	22.9	24.2	19.9	19.6
2. Labor Force Excluding Males 15-64 as % of Total Population	2.9	2.5	2.5	2.5
3. Males 15-64 in Labor Force as % of Total Population	20.0	21.7	17.4	17.1
4. Males 15-64 as % of Total Population	24.6	26.1	23.0	22.6
5. Males 15-64 in Labor Force as % of all Males 15-64	81.4	83.2	75.8	75.0
6. Males 15-24 in School as % of all Males 15-64	8.1	6.5	17.3	17.3
7. Males 15-24 in School plus Males 15-64 in Labor Force as % of all Males 15-64	89.5	89.7	93.1	93.0

SOURCES:

JDS, First Census, vol. I, pp. 29, 125-26, vol. II, pp. 3-4; JDS, Multi-Purpose Household Survey, January-April 1972, pp. 67-69, 113-20; JDS, Multi-Purpose Household Survey, January-April 1974, pp. 47, 99.

balanced a trend toward increased educational enrollment among working-age males.

It is possible that part of the decline in
labor force participation rates shown in Table V.1
is a statistical error, due to the omission of
households of members of the armed forces. Perhaps
a disproportionately large share of armed forces
members were young men, either single or with small
familes. If so, the labor force participation
rate of the households omitted in the 1972-74 surveys may have been above that of the population as
a whole, and the 1972-74 figures would be biased
downward. Even if this is so, this bias cannot
account for all the developments in labor force
participation behavior shown in Table V.1. In particular, while it may account for some of the decline shown in row 4, it does not explain the
trends in rows 5-7.

According to the multi-purpose household surveys, the unemployment rate was only 2.8% in 1972
and fell to 2.1% in 1974.[37] These estimates may
be seriously biased by the unrepresentativeness
of the sample, but it cannot even be determined
whether the direction of bias is upward or downward. On the one hand, the omission of squatter
households, among whom the unemployment rate
probably is high, may bias the unemployment rate
downward. On the other hand, the omission of
armed forces households, among whom the unemployment rate probably is low, may have the opposite
effect. Also, over-representation of urban households, who have higher unemployment rates than
rural households,[38] biases the unemployment rate
upward. In view of these drawbacks, little cre-
dence can be placed in the unemployment rates reported by the multi-purpose household surveys.
In particular, the 2.8% unemployment rate for 1972
seems implausibly low for a time when the economy
was still recovering from the dislocations of the
1970-71 civil strife.

The sampling biases in the multi-purpose
household surveys probably do not distort trends
in the unemployment rate nearly so much as the
level of the unemployment rate. Thus, the decline
in the unemployment rate between 1972 and 1974 is
more credible than the estimated unemployment rates
themselves. The decline certainly is consistent
with other evidence of a tightening labor market
at this time. While no systematic statistical
study of wage rates during this period has been

conducted, informal surveys leave little doubt that
during 1973-76 wages outside government employment
generally were rising much more rapidly than
prices.[39] By 1976 a modest number of foreign
workers had been imported temporarily to fill
specific labor gaps. By that time it was difficult to doubt that only a minimal amount of fric-
tional unemployment persisted.

4. THE GROWTH OF TOTAL OUTPUT

a. The Share of the East Bank in Total Output

     When the West Bank was occupied in June 1967,
no GDP estimates existed for either of the two
banks separately. Shortly after the war the JDS
unofficially estimated the breakdown of 1965 GDP
between the East and West Banks. Table V.2 presents this estimate of East Bank GDP and its sectoral composition. For comparison, it also presents corresponding estimates for the East Bank in
1967, made by the National Planning Council (NPC)
in 1975. In Table V.2 GDP and sectoral value added
for the East Bank are shown both in absolute terms
and in proportion to the total for the two banks
combined.
     Table V.2 reveals very large differences be-
tween the two estimates. While economic conditions
in the two years were quite different because of
the war and massive population shift that occurred
in mid-1967, this seems insufficient to explain
all the differences in Table V.2. If the figures
in Table V.2 were to be believed, it would mean
that East Bank GDP in current prices increased
at an average annual rate of 21-1/2% between 1965
and 1967. Even allowing for inflation, this cannot be believed. Nor is it probable that the
East Bank share in GDP rose from 62% or 64% to
80.6% in only two years, even allowing for the
likelihood that the postwar recession in the West
Bank was more severe than that in the East Bank.
     If there are errors in the statistical break-
down of GDP between the East and West Banks, the
agriculture sector is not a likely source. Table
V.2's agricultural sector estimates for 1965 and
1967, both relatively good crop years, are consistent with each other. Data on agricultural production has long been compiled according to geographical area, so that the division of agricultural

96

TABLE V.2.   TWO ESTIMATES OF EAST BANK GDP AND EAST BANK SHARE IN TOTAL GDP, BY SECTORS, 1965 and 1967

| | Value Added (J.D. million) | | Share in Total GDP (percent) | |
	1965 (1)	1967 (2)	1965 (3)	1967 (4)
Agriculture	21.5	25.2	63	65.0
Mining & Manufacturing	13.1	15.0	81	85.7
Construction	5.3	8.4	67	96.7
Electricity & Water Supply	1.2	1.3	69	73.0
Transport	6.7	13.9	53	93.7
Wholesale & Retail Trade	17.9	30.3	57	77.5
Banking & Finance	1.3	3.1	63	91.2
Ownership of Dwellings	6.3	8.2	59	68.9
Public Administration and Defense	17.6	25.6	82	98.4
Services	5.8	11.7	45	77.1
GDP at Factor Cost	93.6 (96.7)	142.7	62 (64)	80.6

NOTES: Column (1): Calculated by multiplying the percentages in column (3) times the corresponding 1965 value added estimates from JDS, The National Accounts, 1959-1967, p. 10. The alternative figure for 1965 East Bank GDP (shown in parentheses) is equal to the sum of the sectoral value added figures in column (1).

Column (2): From unpublished estimates of the National Planning Council.

Column (3): From N. I. Dajani, The Israeli Aggression: Economic Impact, Amman, 1967, p. 2. The alternative estimate of the East Bank share in total GDP (shown in parentheses) was derived by dividing J. D. 96.7 million from column (1) by 1965 GDP for the two banks combined, from JDS, The National Accounts, 1959-1967, p. 10.

Column (4): Derived by dividing the value added estimates of column (2) by the corresponding 1967 estimates for the East and West Banks combined, from JDS, The National Accounts, 1967-1973, Amman, [1975], p. 11.

97

value added between the East and West Banks is a
comparatively easy matter. Table V.2's mining and
manufacturing sector estimates for 1965 and 1967
are not inconsistent with each other, but they are
high in comparison with the 1967 industrial census,
which found 70% of 1967 mining and manufacturing
value added to have originated in the East Bank.[40]
According to the estimates for 1967, the East
Bank's share in total value added was over 90% in
construction, transport, banking and finance, and
public administration and defense. In none of
these sectors are such high East Bank shares very
credible, especially in comparison with the considerably lower estimates for 1965. While the
share of the East Bank may be overstated by the
1967 estimates, its share for some sectors probably
is understated by the 1965 estimates. In particular, it is difficult to believe that the share of
the East Bank in trade and transport value added
was less than its share in GDP as a whole, as implied by column (3) of Table V.2. In the East
Bank were located the longest and most important
transport routes, particularly the roads to Syria
and Aqaba which carried most imports and exports.
Wholesale and retail trade presumably was heavily
concentrated in the East Bank, where Amman served
as the country's major distribution center as well
as its largest market.

In view of these considerations, it appears
that the share of the East Bank in total GDP on
the eve of the 1967 war was somewhere between
Table V.2's estimates for 1965 and 1967 but closer
to the 1965 figure--probably about 70%, or a little
less. The estimate of 1967 East Bank GDP used
in Table V.2 is the first year in a time series
of postwar East Bank GDP estimated by the NPC and
JDS. If, as suggested here, 1967 East Bank GDP
in this time series were overstated, then it is
possible that the estimates for subsequent years
are also overstated. This possibility is one
reason why estimates of postwar East Bank GDP
and its growth cannot be accepted with complete
confidence. As we shall see in the next section,
there are other reasons.

b. Measuring the Growth of Output

Estimates of 1967-75 GDP for the East Bank
alone were made by the NPC, in cooperation with the
JDS. They are shown in Table V.3. Since these

98

TABLE V.3. GROSS NATIONAL PRODUCT, EAST BANK, 1967-75 (J.D. million in current prices)

	1967	1968	1969	1970	1971	1972	1973	1974	1975
Agriculture	25.2	16.2	22.5	15.6	23.86	26.56	17.57	30.30	26.00
Mining & Manufacturing	15.0	17.4	19.9	17.1	17.74	19.80	22.60	41.32	48.80
Construction	8.4	9.5	10.5	7.7	7.35	9.17	15.15	16.40	16.10
Electricity & Water Supply	1.3	1.9	1.7	1.9	2.18	2.48	2.77	2.85	3.10
Transportation	13.9	13.9	14.5	14.3	14.58	17.31	17.96	22.79	24.90
Wholesale & Retail Trade	30.3	24.9	31.5	30.4	31.20	34.00	36.50	36.90	43.90
Banking & Finance	3.1	2.7	3.9	3.9	3.07	3.08	3.01	3.39	4.30
Ownership of Dwellings	8.2	8.8	9.2	10.0	10.83	11.61	12.42	13.20	15.70
Public Administration & Defense	25.6	32.8	35.8	37.5	38.66	40.50	41.00	53.60	56.10
Services	11.7	12.8	14.1	16.4	16.45	18.26	19.96	23.57	30.60
GDP at Factor Cost	142.7	141.0	163.6	154.7	165.92	182.77	188.94	244.32	269.50
+ Indirect Taxes	17.0	17.8	20.8	19.7	20.24	24.40	29.40	33.06	37.00
GDP at Market Prices	159.7	158.8	184.4	174.4	186.16	207.17	218.34	277.38	306.50
+ Net Factor Income from Abroad	11.2	10.4	14.0	12.6	13.17	13.87	22.83	31.99	67.00
GNP	170.9	169.2	198.4	187.0	199.33	221.04	241.17	309.37	373.50

SOURCE: 1967-70 from Jordan National Planning Council.
1971-75 from CBJ, Monthly Statistical Bulletin, 13 (November 1977), Table 42.

99

NPC-JDS estimates for the East Bank alone were derived from JDS estimates for the East and West Banks combined, they will be affected by weaknesses in the all-Jordan figures and possibly by some additional ones. The numbers for 1967, 1970, and 1971 are especially weak because military conflict in those years hindered the collection of data necessary for the construction of GDP estimates. For a variety of other reasons, the all-Jordan estimates of GDP for all the postwar years are much less reliable than those for 1959-66.

The resources, both administrative and financial, allotted to the compilation of national accounts estimates were cut back during the postwar period. By the mid-1970s national accounts statistics were less thoroughly prepared than in the prewar period,[41] yet the time lag required for compilation and publication had lengthened to nearly two years. In the mid-1970s a number of estimates used to compute GDP still were based upon extrapolations from the results of sample surveys conducted in the early 1960s.[42] These results were obsolete not only because of the passage of time, but because they were representative of Jordan as a whole, not of the East Bank.

On top of these serious weaknesses in postwar GDP estimates came the most serious one of all: a sharp acceleration in the rate of inflation. The high rate of postwar inflation made it impossible to determine the growth rate of real output except with a great margin for error. Since 1967 the JDS has compiled consumer price indices for four cities in the East Bank.[43] For deflating GDP these indices have several failings: They do not represent all the population; they do not include prices of investment goods as would a true GDP deflator, and--as is the case in all countries, especially LDCs--the price data used are often erroneous due to faulty reporting, the prevalence of bargaining and sales in unorganized markets, and the problem of allowing for changes in quality of goods and services sold. Had the inflation rate been low, say under 5% annually, these sources of error would not be an insurmountable barrier to the deflation of current-price GDP estimates. But when the rate of inflation is 10-20%, an error of only 10% in the inflation rate statistics (and it could easily be greater) would produce an error of 1-2 percentage points in the annual growth rate of real GDP--a substantial change.[44]

Table V.4 presents GDP growth rates in current and constant prices for the postwar period, as

TABLE V.4. AVERAGE ANNUAL GROWTH RATE OF EAST BANK GDP, BY SECTORS (percent)

	1967/68-1974/75 at Current Prices (1)	1971/72-1975 at Constant Prices (2)
Agriculture	4.5	-2.7
Mining and Manufacturing	15.7 }13.6	8.9
Construction	8.9	
Wholesale and Retail Trade	5.6	4.5
Public Administration and Defense	9.4	2.7
Electricity and Water Supply	9.3	
Transportation	8.0	
Banking and Insurance	4.1 }9.1	6.2
Ownership of Dwellings	7.9	
Other Services	12.0	
GDP at Factor Cost	8.9	4.5
Indirect Taxes	10.5	7.0
GDP at Market Prices	9.0	4.8

NOTES: Column (1) calculated from data in Table V.3, column (2) from unpublished estimates of the National Planning Council. In column (2) constant prices are for 1971/72.

101

derived from NPC and JDS estimates.[45] Both current-
price and constant-price estimates are highly unreliable for the reasons mentioned in the preceding
paragraphs. In very broad terms these estimates
suggest that the growth of real GDP during the postwar period up to 1975 was negligible--probably no
more than 1% average annual growth. Inflation between 1967/68 and 1974/75 roughly equalled the
growth of current-price GDP, implying negligible
real growth.[46] The annual real growth of nearly 5%
for 1971/72-75 shown in column (2) of Table V.4 may
be attributed to recovery from the 1970-71 recession, which had been brought on by Jordan's civil
war.

If it were true that constant-price GDP in the
East Bank did not increase over the postwar period
as a whole, then average GDP per person or per worker would have decreased by over one-third, since
the population and labor force in the East Bank
both increased by more than a third between early
1967 and 1975. Unsystematic evidence on the tightness of labor markets and the rise in wage rates
(especially in 1969 and again after the civil war
in 1975-76) makes it difficult to believe in so
marked a decline in productivity and living standards.[47] In part (a) of this section it was suggested that the estimates of 1967 East Bank GDP
overstated the share of the East Bank in Jordan's
GDP. If East Bank GDP were overstated for 1967,
but not (or not so greatly) for subsequent years,
the true growth of GDP might be somewhat greater
than that suggested by the estimates of the NPC and
the JDS.

In conclusion, the best available evidence--
and it is not very good--suggests that the growth
of real GDP during the postwar period was modest--
certainly modest considering the growth in the
labor force. It probably did little more than keep
up with the large increase in the East Bank population, and it well may not have done even that. Given
the quality of available national accounts data and
the problems of deflating them, it would be misleading to suggest anything more precise.

Like the overall GDP growth rate, the sectoral
growth rates shown in Table V.4 can be accepted
only in very broad terms, but their general pattern
is reasonably credible. Agricultural production at
best stagnated during the period; the Israeli shelling of the East Jordan Valley was an important reason. The most important cause of the rapid growth
of value added in mining and manufacturing was the

quintupling of world phosphate prices during 1974 and the associated increase in Jordan's phosphate exports--apparently only a transitory phenomenon since by 1976 world phosphate prices had declined sharply below their recent previous peak.

NOTES

1. Net official loans contributed an additional $6 per capita per year. The grant and loan figures used are not authorizations, but are the actual figures recorded in the balance of payments estimates of the Jordan Central Bank.

2. The Institute for Strategic Studies, The Military Balance, 1967-1968, London, 1967, p. 45; and idem, The Military Balance, 1969-1970, London, 1969, p. 35.

3. Assuming 300,000 refugees by 1968, of whom about 20-25% were in the labor force, and assuming both the total number of refugees and the number of refugees in the labor force increased at 3% per year due to the natural increase of population.

4. One estimate of the damages was J.D. 16 million or about $45 million. Hanna S. Odeh, Economic Development of Jordan, 1954-1971, Amman: Ministry of Culture and Information, 1972, p. 42. For comparison, gross domestic investment for all Jordan in 1966 was about $80 million.

5. Jordan's total foreign reserves fell from J.D. 94 million at the end of September 1970 to J.D. 83 million at the end of June 1971. Central Bank of Jordan (CBJ), Monthly Statistical Bulletin, 7 (June 1971), Table 3.

6. JDS, Consumer Price Index for Amman, Zarqa, Irbid, Aqaba and Civil Servants, various issues.

7. CBJ, Monthly Statistical Bulletin, 11 (May 1975), Tables 23 and 36.

8. Per capita grants and loans calculated from data in ibid., 12 (May 1976), Tables 23 and 36.

9. JDS, First Census, vol. I, p. 29. The population excludes Jordanians resident abroad and includes foreigners resident in Jordan.

10. Israel Central Bureau of Statistics, Statistical Abstract of Israel, 1967, Jerusalem, p. 581.

11. Calculated from idem, Statistical Abstract of Israel, 1973, Jerusalem, p. 693.

12. This is the number that was registered for rations, either with UNRWA or the Jordan government. United Nations, Report of the Commissioner-General, pp. 4-5.

13. Apparently, the new arrivals in the East Bank were not representative of the population of the area departed, but were heavily weighted with former residents of refugee camps. See D. R. Campbell, "Jordan: The Economics of Survival," International Journal, 23 (Winter 1967-68), 121-22. In parti-

103

cular, the large West Bank camps near Jericho in the Jordan Valley were virtually completely depopulated after the war. Presumably, many camp residents felt they had little to lose by leaving. Also, many camp residents received remittances from relatives abroad or on the East Bank and may have feared the loss of these remittances if they remained under Israeli occupation.

14. Calculated by extrapolation from the 1961 census using average annual growth rates of 4% between late 1961 and mid-1967 and 3% between mid-1967 and end-1968. The 4% growth rate for the earlier period includes the effect of West-Bank-to-East-Bank migration during that period.

15. Calculated from projections in JDS, Analysis of the Population Statistics, Fourth Report, pp. 5, 8. A steady increase in life expectancy from 52 years in 1961 to 62 years in 1981 is assumed.

16. Hanna Rizk, Summary of Findings and Conclusions of the National Fertility Sample Survey, Amman: Jordan Department of Statistics, 1972.

17. General fertility rate for 1961 from JDS, Analysis of the Population Statistics, First Report, pp. 8-9. General fertility rate for 1972 calculated according to the same methods from data in Rizk, p. 9, Table IV.

18. Figure for 1972 calculated from JDS, Multi-Purpose Household Survey, January-April 1972, Amman, 1974 (Arabic text, tables in English), p. 67. For the weaknesses of the sample taken for this survey, see p. 92. Figure for 1961 calculated from JDS, Analysis of the Population Statistics, Fourth Report, p. 5.

19. Arie Bregman, Economic Growth in the Administered Areas, 1968-1973, Jerusalem: Bank of Israel Research Department, English edition, 1975, pp. 27-30; and Israel Central Bureau of Statistics, Quarterly Statistics of the Administered Territories, 6 (May 1976), Table A/1. The population of East Jerusalem is not included in either of these sources.

20. Deaths consistently have been grossly under-reported in Jordan.

21. JDS, Analysis of the Population Statistics, p. 8.

22. From preliminary results of a study by Salem O. Ghawi, chief of the Manpower Planning Section of the National Planning Council. I am grateful to Mr. Ghawi for making these data available to me. For males, who comprised over 70% of the graduates, the percentage abroad was 38.3%, while for females it was only 13.3%.

23. Since about one-third of new entrants into the labor force had some post-secondary education, the 20% figure used here would be consistent with a 30% emigration rate among new entrants with some post-secondary education and a 15% emigration rate for those with less education.

24. JDS, First Census, vol. I, p. 329.

25. But not as large an increase as would be indicated

by the results of the somewhat suspect 1972 fertility sample survey.

26. In the JDS estimates, the East Bank population in- creases each year by 3-4% until 1968. Between 1968 and 1969 the population increases by 474,000, or 42%. Presumably, this increase is meant to reflect the inflow of displaced persons to the East Bank after the 1967 war, but besides the obviously incorrect timing, the number (474,000 compared to my estimate of 300,000) is much too large to be credible. In addition, the JDS estimate makes no allowance for emigration from Jor- dan. See JDS, Statistical Yearbook, 1974, pp. xii-xiv, 2-3.

27. JDS, Multi-Purpose Household Survey, January-April 1974, Amman, 1976, p. 104. This study is similar to that for 1972 and covers most of the same households.

28. The enrollment rate was 27.4% for rural residents, 35.1% for urban residents (ibid., p. 104). The enrollment rate is consistent with that for earlier years from other sources: 16.4% in 1961, 21.2% in 1966 and 31.1% in 1972. The last figure, from the 1972 multi-purpose household survey, in which urban households are also probably over-represented, is probably an overestimate; in comparison with the 1974 figure it indicates the continuing upward trend in the enrollment rate.

29. Jordan Ministry of Education, Statistical Yearbook of Education, 1973-74, Amman, n.d., pp. 84-85. This includes all students in Jordan, not solely those in Ministry of Educa- tion schools.

30. JDS, Multi-Purpose Household Survey, 1972 and 1974 editions.

31. For details of the sampling procedure see pp. 15-19 (in Arabic) of the 1972 survey. I am grateful to Mohammad Hassan Ismail of the JDS Economic Section for helpful comments on the methods of the multi-purpose household surveys. The same dwellings were visited in the 1972 and 1974 surveys, with one important exception: The 1974 survey added households from 25 East Ghor villages, so that this irrigated agricultural area probably was over-represented in the 1974 sample.

32. There was a substantial percentage increase in the labor force participation rate of women, but this originated from a very small base and was largely offset by trends for children and the aged.

33. JDS, First Census, vol. 2, p. 10; JDS, Population and Labor Force in the Agriculture Sector, 1967, Table 4; JDS, Multi-Purpose Household Survey, 1972, p. 168; JDS, Multi- Purpose Household Survey, 1974, p. 202; unpublished prelimi- nary results of the JDS 1975 agricultural census.

34. Probably the most important inconsistencies are caused by differences in the seasons during which the censuses and surveys were taken (women, children, and the aged entering the labor force during peak seasons and withdrawing during slack seasons) and differences in the criteria by which per-

105

sons were judged to be in the labor force.

35. Over 54% of those abroad in 1961 were economically active males and another 12% were males attending school or university (JDS, First Census, vol. I, p. 329).

36. Of the fall in the proportion of males 15-64 in the labor force to the total population shown in row 3, roughly 60% was due to the decline in the proportion of all males 13-64 to the total population (row 4) and the other 40% to the reduction in the proportion of males 15-64 participating in the labor force (row 5).

37. JDS, Multi-Purpose Household Survey, 1972, p. 177, and JDS, Multi-Purpose Household Survey, 1974, p. 55.

38. Ibid., 1972, p. 92, and 1974, pp. 71-72.

39. Informal inquiry among large private contractors in Amman by economists from the U.S. Department of Labor indicated increases of 100-200% in the wages of ordinary construction workers between 1974 and 1976 and comparable increases for most skilled construction labor. Other, less systematic, inquiries generally confirm the finding of large wage increases outside government employment.

40. JDS, Manufacturing Industrial Census, 1967, Amman, 1968, pp. 18, 63.

41. For example, after 1972 the JDS no longer carried out systematic analysis of the sources and uses of commodity flows, a procedure which, among other things, facilitates the distinguishing of intermediate from final products, the estimation of different forms of expenditure, and the determination of value added in the trade and transport sectors.

42. For examples, see JDS, The National Accounts, 1967-1973, pp. 26-48.

43. Published in JDS, Consumer Price Index for Amman, Zarqa, Irbid, Aqaba and Civil Servants, Amman, monthly.

44. Suppose the annual growth rate of GDP in current prices is 20%, while the measured rate of annual inflation is 14%. Then the measured growth rate of GDP in constant prices is 5% per year--about average for an LDC. But if the true rate of inflation were 12%, rather than 14%, the true growth rate of constant-price GDP would be 7% per year--an outstanding growth performance.

45. The choice of years for column (2) was dictated by availability; the NPC did not make constant-price estimates for years prior to 1971/72. The estimates in column (2) are considered rather crude ones; the methodology of the estimation has not been published.

46. Between 1967/68 and 1974/75 the average annual inflation rate in consumer prices was 8.9% for Amman and 7.9% for Zarqa (calculated from CBJ, Monthly Statistical Bulletin, various issues).

47. Admittedly, labor markets may tighten due to factors not entering the growth of GDP, such as recruitment of Palestinian commandoes in 1968-69. Note also that the tight-

ening in 1975-76 occurred particularly in the latter year, when there was a large increase in total product--31% in current-price GDP and 46% in current-price GNP between 1975 and 1976 according to preliminary estimates. CBJ, _Monthly Statistical Bulletin_, 13 (November 1977), Table 42.

6
The Anatomy of Postwar Development

1. SECTORAL ALLOCATION OF EMPLOYMENT AND PRODUCTION

The 1961 population census provided the only comprehensive statistics on the distribution of employment among sectors. In 1974-75 the JDS carried out three censuses (of agriculture, industry, and manpower), which together provided estimates of employment in all sectors, except the armed forces. However, because these censuses seriously underrecorded employment in many sectors and probably counted some other employment twice, the census estimates require substantial revision--unfortunately based largely on guesswork--before even a rough outline of the sectoral pattern of employment may be drawn.

Column (1) of Table VI.1 presents the sectoral distribution of employment as estimated by the three censuses. Results from the industrial census (lines 2.a and 3.a) refer to 1974, the remainder to early 1975.[1] Alternative estimates, based partly on conjecture, are shown in column (2) of Table VI.1. The biggest adjustment occurs in public administration and defense, to correct for the failure of the censuses to include employment in the armed forces, about 80-90,000 in 1974-75.[2]

The estimates of agricultural employment raise two problems: workers recorded as employed only a small fraction of available time and farm operators whose main occupation was not agriculture. Many "casual workers" (defined as those employed in agriculture on a single holding for less than a third of available time)[3] should not be included in normal agricultural employment; many were students, and others were employed mainly in nonagricultural activities. However, probably some casual workers were employed on several farm holdings, and if all their employment were taken together would have

TABLE VI.1. EMPLOYMENT BY SECTORS, 1974-75

	Census Results (thousands) (1)	Adjusted Estimates (thousands) (2)
1. Agriculture	125.1	75
a. Permanent Workers	73.3	55
b. Temporary Workers	15.4	15
c. Casual Workers	36.4	5
2. Mining		5
a. Industrial Census	2.4	
b. Manpower Census	2.7	
3. Manufacturing		27
a. Industrial Census	24.5	
b. Manpower Census	19.6	
4. Construction	8.4	33
5. Electricity and Water Supply	2.1	2
6. Transport	13.9	18
7. Wholesale and Retail Trade	20.8	28
8. Banking and Finance	2.6	3
9. Public Administration and Defense	12.3	100
10. Services	45.2	55
11. Not Clearly Specified	.6	
Total Employment	c. 253-258	346
Unemployment		7
Labor Force		353

NOTES   Column (1): Rows 1, 1.a, 1.b, and 1.c from preliminary results of 1975 agricultural census. Rows 2.a and 3.a from preliminary results of 1974 industrial census. Rows 2.b, 3.b, and 4-11 from preliminary results of 1975 manpower census.

Column (2): Agriculture and public administration and defense sectors adjusted as described in the text. Adjustments in other sectors are very rough approximations based on subjective assessment of the likely degree of under-recording of each sector's employment by the censuses.

been mainly occupied in agricultural labor. To allow for this last group, a small number of casual
workers are recorded as employed in column (2) of
Table VI.1. Column (2) counts all agricultural
"temporary workers" (defined as those employed one-
third to two-thirds of available time on one agricultural holding) as employed in agriculture. The
agricultural census defined as permanent workers
those employed more than two-thirds of available
time in agriculture and all those who operated a
holding, no matter how much time they devoted to
agriculture. In fact, a significant number of farm
"operators" were mainly employed outside agriculture.[4] These persons are omitted from the number
of permanent agricultural workers in column (2).

The 1975 manpower census was intended to enum-
erate employment in all activities except agriculture and the armed forces. It was based upon information derived from establishments. While an attempt was made to gather information on employment
outside establishments or in unlicensed establishments, it was evident that much employment was not
recorded. For some sectors the probable degree of
underenumeration is great; for others, small. It is
possible only to make plausible guesses at the magnitudes. In mining, employment in stone crushing
and quarrying is under-recorded; in manufacturing,
employment in handicrafts and other household activities; in commerce, petty trading; and in services,
casual labor and domestic services. Much employment in the transport sector is believed to have
been missed. Probably the greatest degree of underenumeration was in the construction sector, mainly
an industry of small operators, who keep no employment records, and of casual labor which often
changes employers and construction sites. The fact
that East Bank construction employment recorded by
the 1975 manpower census is far below that recorded
for 1961 by the population census corroborates this
belief.[5]

To arrive at the adjusted estimates for mining,
manufacturing, construction, transport, trade, and
services in column (2), the estimates of the manpower census were revised upward in rough proportion
to the probable degree of underenumeration in each
sector. These are little more than plausible guesses, intended only to suggest broad orders of magnitude. Adding a rough estimate for unemployment
gives an estimated total labor force that is consistent with the labor force participation rate and my
estimate of Jordan's population.[6]

110

The estimates in column (2) of Table VI.1 were used to arrive at columns (2) and (4) of Table VI.2. Unpaid family workers, who were included in the estimates of Table VI.1, were excluded from those of Table VI.2.[7] To permit analysis of changes over time, Table VI.2 also presents both absolute and relative sectoral employment for the East Bank in 1961, as recorded by the 1961 population census.

A striking shift in the pattern of East Bank employment between 1961 and 1974-75 is indicated by Table VI.2. Despite a large increase in total population and employment, there appears to have been no increase in the number employed in agriculture. The proportion of the labor force employed in agriculture declined sharply from a 1961 level already low compared to other LDCs. Failings in the agricultural employment statistics cannot plausibly account for this trend. Coverage of the 1975 agricultural census is believed to have been over 95% complete. Also, 1961 agricultural employment may be understated because employment was recorded in a month of low farm labor demand.

Corresponding to the decline in the employment share of agriculture between 1961 and 1974-75 was a sharp increase in the share of services employment, mainly in the armed forces. By 1975 about a quarter of total employment was in the armed forces, including public security forces. Between 1961 and 1975 military employment nearly tripled, while civilian employment increased by about two-thirds. Although the number in the armed forces is not officially released by the Jordan government, but must be estimated, there is little likelihood that errors in estimation could account for much of this disproportionate growth in armed forces employment.

Table VI.2 compares the sectoral distribution of employment in the East Bank for 1961 and 1974-75. If the comparison were between both banks in 1961 (see Table IV.1, p. 64, above) and the East Bank in 1974-75, the fall in the share of agriculture and the rise in the share of services would be even greater. In addition, Table VI.2 was calculated on the assumption that all the 1961 armed forces employment was on the East Bank; if some were on the West Bank, the rise in the share of services in total East Bank employment between 1961 and 1974-75 would be even greater. In Table VI.2, other than in "agriculture" and "other services," no significance should be attached to sectoral trends, which could easily be due to errors in the highly

111

TABLE VI.2. SECTORAL DISTRIBUTION OF EMPLOYMENT, EAST BANK, 1961 AND 1974-75, AND TYPICAL COUNTRY

	Number (000s) East Bank		Share in Total Employment (percent)		
			East Bank		Typical Country
	1961	1974-75	1961	1974-75	
	(1)	(2)	(3)	(4)	(5)
I. Primary Production	65	64	35	20	50.7
A. Agriculture	60	59	32	18	49.7
B. Mining	5	5	3	2	1.0
II. Industry	39	60	21	18	20.8
A. Manufacturing	17	27	9	8	15.5
B. Construction	22	33	12	10	5.4
III. Services	85	204	45	62	28.5
A. Transport	8	18	4	5	4.1
B. Trade, Banking, and Insurance	17	29	9	9	8.2
C. Other Services	60	157	32	48	16.2
Total Employment	189	328	100	100	100

NOTES

"Electricity and water supply" is included as part of "other services."

Column (1) is from JDS, First Census, vol. 2, pp. 11-15. Family workers, unemployed workers, and those of unclassified economic status are not included. To limit the compounding of rounding error, column (3) was calculated from the original data, rather than the rounded-off figures in column (1).

Column (2) was derived from column (2) of Table VI.1 Employment recorded here is reduced by the number of family workers recorded in the JDS censuses: 16,000 in agriculture and 2,000 in trade, banking, and insurance. Column (4) was derived from column (2) of Table VI.2.

In Column (5) items I.A, III.B, and III.C are for group V in Kuznets, "Quantitative Aspects II," pp. 23-27. Unpaid family workers are excluded from the definition of the labor force. Items I.B, II.A, and III.A are for the shares in 1960 labor force of a country at $300 GDP per capita for 1958, from Kuznets, Economic Growth of Nations, p. 203.

conjectural estimates for these other sectors.

Column (5) of Table VI.2 presents the sectoral shares in total employment of a typical country at Jordan's 1974-75 level of GDP per capita. The major trends in sectoral employment already identified--an increasing share of public administration and defense (under "other services" in Table VI.2) and a decreasing share of agriculture--have magnified disparities between Jordan and the typical LDC which were already significant in 1961.

To a degree, the developments which have altered the sectoral distribution of employment have also affected the sectoral distribution of production. Column (3) of Table VI.3 presents the shares of sectoral value added in East Bank GDP for the combined years 1973/74. These ratios were derived from the NPC estimates of East Bank GDP; the serious weaknesses of those estimates should be kept in mind when interpreting Table VI.3. Column (4) presents comparable ratios characteristic of the average country at the East Bank's 1973/74 levels of GNP per capita and, usually, population. For comparison, columns (1) and (2) present ratios for all Jordan in 1961/62 and the average LDC of comparable income per head and population; these ratios correspond to those in columns (3) and (4), respectively, for the East Bank in 1973/74. Because available data only permit comparison of all Jordan before the 1967 war with the postwar East Bank, it is hazardous to identify trends in sectoral shares from the data in Table VI.3. Some of the differences between columns (1) and (3) are simply because the shares of some sectors in GDP are different for the East Bank compared to Jordan as a whole. For example, this could account for column (3)'s higher share for construction, an activity that had been disproportionately concentrated in the East Bank since long before the 1967 war.

As Table VI.3 indicates, the small (relative to the average LDC of comparable income and population) share of agriculture in Jordan's GDP continued into the mid-1970s. Agriculture's share in GDP declined significantly after 1961/62, but an important part of this decline was the normal fall in agriculture's share associated with Jordan's increase in GNP per capita.[8] The share of manufacturing rose from far below average in 1961/62 to nearly the level typical of the average comparable LDC in 1973/74.[9] In part, this increase is spurious, the result of comparing the more industrialized East Bank in 1973/74 with all Jordan in 1961/62. But the increase in the

114

TABLE VI.3. SECTORAL DISTRIBUTION OF GDP: JORDAN OR EAST BANK AND TYPICAL COUNTRY, 1961/62 AND 1973/74 (percent)

	1961/62		1973/74	
	Jordan (1)	Typical Country (2)	East Bank (3)	Typical Country (4)
I. Primary Production	22.2	36.6	14.4	31.4
A. Agriculture	21.0	35.2	11.0	26.4
B. Mining	1.1	1.4	3.4	2.4
II. Industry	11.4	17.2	18.9	20.0
A. Manufacturing	6.6	12.4	11.6	12.5
B. Construction	4.9	4.8	7.3	5.1
III. Services	66.4	42.3	66.9	43.6
A. Transport	11.5	5.8	9.4	6.6
B. Trade, Banking, and Insurance	23.1	17.3	18.4	17.5
C. Public Administration and Defense	15.4	6.4	21.8	7.7
D. Other Services	16.5	15.7	17.3	15.4

NOTES

Columns (1) and (2) are reproduced from Table IV.1 above. Column (3) is calculated from Table V.3 above and from unpublished NPC data on value added in mining. As in column (2), items I, II, and III for column (4) were calculated from the B equations for small countries given in Chenery and Taylor, p. 396, and items I.A, I.B, II.B, and III.A from equations in Chenery, p. 634. For both equations GNP per capita of $300 (in 1960 prices) and population of 1.7 million were used. The ratios for III.B, III.C, and III.D in column (4) are for the benchmark value of $300 GDP per capita in Kuznets, Economic Growth of Nations, p. 111.

115

share of manufacturing also reflects a rapid expansion of the manufacturing sector in the early 1960s to make up for a "structural disequilibrium" in manufacturing.

Jordan's atypically large concentration in services, which was identified and explained for the prewar period in Chapter 4, also prevailed for the postwar East Bank, and for some of the same reasons. While Jordan's comparative advantage in tourism and the historical underdevelopment of its manufacturing sector accounted for some of its prewar concentration in services, these factors probably did not contribute significantly to services concentration in the postwar East Bank. However, the two most important causes of prewar services concentration—Jordan's import surplus and its large defense burden—also must have been the primary causes of postwar services concentration in the East Bank. Since postwar national accounts statistics are much poorer than those for the prewar period, the quantitative effects of these different factors on the share of services in GDP cannot be measured adequately, as they were in Chapter 4 above. The great expansion of manpower in the armed forces after 1961 leaves little doubt that the defense burden accounted for an important part of the East Bank's postwar concentration in services—probably significantly more than in prewar Jordan.[10] In comparison with prewar Jordan, the import surplus of the postwar East Bank was about equally large in proportion to GDP.[11] Therefore, the import surplus, as it did in prewar Jordan, must have accounted for very roughly half, or a little more, of the difference between the services share of the postwar East Bank and of the typical LDC with comparable income per head and population.

2. INTERNATIONAL TRANSACTIONS

Jordanian international trade and balance of payments statistics do not include transactions occurring between the East Bank and the Arab territories occupied by Israel as a result of the 1967 war. The trade in services, remittances, and capital flows may be prohibitively difficult to measure accurately. However, Israel publishes statistics on merchandise trade between the Occupied Territories (including the Gaza Strip, but excluding East Jerusalem) and the East Bank, which have been used to compile Table VI.4. From Table VI.4 it is evident that merchandise trade with the Occupied

TABLE VI.4. MERCHANDISE TRADE OF EAST BANK WITH OCCUPIED TERRITORIES (EXCLUDING JERUSALEM),
1971/72 AND 1974/75

	Average 1971/72	Average 1974/75	Average Annual Growth Rate 1971/72-1974/75
MERCHANDISE EXPORTS			
1. In Current J.D. Million			
a. Agricultural Products	.392	.223	-17.1%
b. Industrial Products	1.027	1.244	6.6
c. Total	1.419	1.466	1.1
2. Total Merchandise Exports to Occupied Territories as % of Merchandise Exports to All Destinations	4.8%	2.9%	
MERCHANDISE IMPORTS			
1. In Current J.D. Million			
a. Agricultural Products	3.933	6.365	17.4
b. Industrial Products	4.899	5.819	5.9
c. Total	8.832	12.184	11.3
2. Total Merchandise Imports from Occupied Territories as % of Merchandise Imports from All Sources	4.9%	5.9%	

NOTES

Merchandise trade with the Occupied Territories is from Israel Central Bureau of Statistics, Quarterly Statistics of the Administered Territories, Jerusalem, vol. 3, no. 3, 1973, pp. 8-9, and vol. 6, no. 1, 1976, pp. 6-7. The data are converted from Israel pounds to Jordan dinars using the free market rate of exchange for each year, supplied by Arie Bregman of the Research Department of the Bank of Israel. Total merchandise exports (including re-exports) and imports for Jordan are from CBJ, Monthly Statistical Bulletin, various issues.

117

Territories was a relatively minor part of the East
Bank's total merchandise trade. Over the period
covered in Table VI.4--the period of recovery and
expansion after the 1970-71 civil war--there was
some growth in the East Bank's merchandise imports
at current prices from the Occupied Territories,
but at constant prices the imports must have declined. The East Bank's miniscule exports to the
Occupied Territories did not grow significantly in
current prices and must have declined substantially
in constant prices. In its balance of merchandise
trade with the Occupied Territories, the East
Bank ran a proportionately large deficit, imports
being six (in 1971/72) to eight (in 1974/75) times
exports.

The small and diminishing importance of the
East Bank's trade, especially its exports, with
the Occupied Territories was due to the trade-
diverting effects of economic measures applied by
Israel to the Occupied Territories. Trade barriers
between Israel and the Occupied Territories were
eliminated while Israel's high protective tariff
rates were applied to imports of the Occupied
Territories from the rest of the world, including
the East Bank.[12] Both measures diverted the trade
of the Occupied Territories away from the East
Bank toward Israel. By 1975 91% of the imports of
the Occupied Territories were from Israel, 1.5%
from Jordan, and 7.5% from other countries; for
exports the corresponding shares were 65%, 27%, and
8%, respectively.[13] About half of the exports from
the Occupied Territories to the East Bank were agricultural products, primarily citrus fruits, and
half were industrial products, mainly processed
agricultural products, such as olive oil, vegetable
shortening, and soap. A significant fraction of
these exports to Jordan may have been re-exported
to other countries.

No estimate of nonmerchandise transactions between the East Bank and the Occupied Territories
has ever been published, but they may be much more
important than merchandise transactions. In particular, there probably were important flows of
tourism and other travel services in both directions. Like all transactions between the East Bank
and the Occupied Territories, these flows were not
recorded in the official balance of payments statistics for Jordan. Remittances from abroad to the
Occupied Territories which passed through the banking system of the East Bank have been recorded as
remittances to Jordan; no accounting was made of

their subsequent outflow to the Occupied Territories. An interesting, if quantitatively minor,
transaction is the continued payment of salaries
by the central government in Amman to some of its
civil servants remaining in the West Bank.[14]

Table VI.5 shows the relative importance of
major components of Jordan's balance of payments
during 1965/66, 1969, and 1974. The two postwar
years were ones of comparative normality, both relatively good crop years and both years of cyclical-
ly high employment. Table VI.5 refers to all Jordan for 1965/66 and to the East Bank alone for 1969
and 1974, but the latter data do not include trade
between the East Bank and the Occupied Territories.[15]

Statistical data on Jordan's balance of payments prior to the 1967 war suffered from some
serious deficiencies, but postwar balance of payments data were even less reliable.[16] Because of
internal disturbances, the data gathered for 1969-71
were particularly weak. Also, some imports of military supplies, and the foreign aid which financed
them, went unrecorded in Jordan's balance of payments estimates.[17] Estimates of expenditures by
foreigners on travel in Jordan became progressively
less reliable, as the survey data used to estimate
average expenditure per visitor became more and more
outdated.[18]

One vital area where the data are particularly
weak is the receipt of remittances from Jordanians
abroad. In this respect Table VI.5 does not give
an adequate picture of the striking growth in remittances occurring in the postwar period. Extremely rapid growth occurred after 1974, the last year
shown in Table VI.5. Remittances, as officially
recorded, increased more than five-fold between 1974
and 1976. Between 1971 (when remittances hit a low
point due to the 1970-71 civil strife in Jordan) and
1976, they increased at an average annual rate of
94% per year. Remittances during 1976 averaged over
$220 per East Bank resident, or roughly one-fourth
of GNP per capita in the East Bank.[19] If we assume
100,000 Jordanians employed abroad, this amount of
1976 remittances would average about $4,000 per
Jordanian worker abroad.

What makes these remittance figures even more
remarkable is that they are probably understated,
possibly very greatly. Official statistics record
only remittances passing through the banking system, but a large fraction, perhaps the greater part,
of remittances passes through private money chang-
ers. Several factors work in the opposite direction,

119

TABLE VI.5. BALANCE OF PAYMENTS: MAJOR COMPONENTS AS PROPORTION OF TOTAL CURRENT FOREIGN
EXPENDITURES, 1965/66, 1969, 1974 (percent)

	As Proportion of Total Current Foreign Expenditures (percent)			Average Annual Growth Rate (percent per year)
	1965/66	1969	1974	1969-74
I. Exports of Goods and Services	35.5	29.4	45.8	21.5
A. Goods Exports and Re-Exports	14.5	13.5	26.6	27.5
1. Re-Exports	2.7	2.6	5.5	29.5
2. Domestic Exports	11.8	10.9	21.1	27.0
a. Fruits and Nuts	1.4	1.3	2.3	24.1
b. Vegetables	3.6	3.3	2.6	6.5
c. Cigarettes	.5	.5	.4	4.9
d. Phosphates	4.0	3.3	10.5	40.5
e. Olive Oil	.1	.3	.2	6.2
f. Cement	---	.4	2.2	53.4
g. Batteries	.2	.2	.3	18.9
h. Miscellaneous	2.0	1.6	2.7	23.5
B. Travel	15.0	4.1	9.3	30.7
C. Other Services	6.0	11.8	9.9	7.3
II. Total Factor Income	20.7	13.5	18.3	18.1
A. Remittances	14.1	6.3	12.9	28.4
B. Interest and Dividends	4.4	6.3	4.7	5.2
C. Pipeline Transit Fees	2.2	1.0	.6	1.6
III. Current Transfers to Households	13.9	3.7	2.4	2.5
TOTAL CURRENT RECEIPTS	70.1	46.7	66.5	19.4
TOTAL CURRENT EXPENDITURE	100.0	100.0	100.0	11.3
CURRENT ACCOUNT DEFICIT	29.9	53.3	33.5	1.4

IV. Foreign Transfers to Government	31.5	35.9	38.5	12.8
V. Net Foreign Loans	5.6	3.6	4.8	18.2
VI. Errors and Omissions	3.5	3.9	3.8	10.5
VII. Net Change in Foreign Assets	10.8	-10.0	13.6	---

NOTES

Sources: CBJ, Fourth Annual Report, 1967; CBJ, Monthly Statistical Bulletin, various issues; JDS, External Trade Statistics, 1965 and 1966 issues; JDS, The National Accounts, 1959-1967; JDS, The National Accounts, 1967-1973, and unpublished materials of the CBJ and JDS.

tending to cause remittances to be overstated by
the official statistics, but the effect of these upward biases is probably less than the downward bias
caused by the failure to record remittances passing
outside the banking system. Some of the remittances
passing through the East Bank banking system and
recorded in balance of payments statistics may ultimately pass to the West Bank, where the Jordan
dinar is legal currency as well as the Israel pound.
Also, some of the payments recorded as remittances
in 1975 and 1976 may actually have been capital
flight from Lebanon in the wake of the civil strife
there.

A primary cause of the rapid growth in remittances was the increase in employment and earnings
of Jordanian workers in the oil-producing countries
of the Arab Middle East after the oil-price revolution of 1973. But the increase in remittances began around 1971-72--well before the oil-price revolution. The upsurge in remittances then probably
was chiefly due to the restoration of stability
after the civil war and the preceding years of tension and uncertainty. The restoration of a secure
investment climate in Jordan drew in remittances to
be invested in bank deposits, industrial shares,
and housing. Demand from Jordanians working abroad
or their families must have played a major role in
the frenetic bidding-up of land prices in Jordan,
which was under way well before the civil war in
Lebanon added to the demand for housing in Jordan.

This remarkable growth in remittances means
that when we talk about the growth of total product,
it makes a considerable difference whether we mean
Gross Domestic Product or Gross National Product.
For example, between 1967 and 1975 the average
annual growth rate in current prices of GNP was 1.8
percentage points higher than that of GDP at market
prices, and for the subperiod of maximum remittance
growth, 1971-75, the difference was 3.7 percentage
points.[20] Therefore, it is possible, for example,
that GDP per capita might have stagnated over the
1967-75 period while there could have been a modest,
but not negligible, growth in GNP per capita.

As Table VI.5 indicates, by 1974 current receipts from abroad financed about two-thirds of total current foreign expenditure--a considerable increase over 1969, but still slightly less than in
1965/66, when it was 70%. The most important single
cause of the rapid rise in current recepits between
1969 and 1974 was a very rapid growth in receipts
from domestic merchandise exports, which nearly

122

doubled as a proportion of current receipts. However, while receipts from domestic merchandise exports grew at an average rate of 27% per year between 1969 and 1974, the quantum index of exports increased at an average annual rate of only 9%.[21] The remainder of the increase in merchandise exports receipts was due to inflation in export prices, part of which reflects temporary circumstances of exceptional foreign demand. In particular, the huge rise in receipts from phosphate exports, which accounted for more than half of the 1969-74 increase in receipts from domestic merchandise exports, is at least partly transitory, due to temporarily high prices and world demand for phosphates during 1974-75.[22] To a degree, the high level of receipts from cement exports also seems to have been transitory, due to temporary excess capacity in Jordan and a construction boom in nearby oil-producing states; the 1975 value of cement exports was less than half that of 1974.[23] However, in the longer run cement may become a more important export product, for Jordan has planned to establish a cement plant in the south of the country, much of whose output would be exported, mainly to Saudi Arabia.[24]

When allowance is made for rapid inflation in export prices and for the probably transitory nature of some 1974 export receipts, there does not appear to have been much change in the overall pattern of Jordan's merchandise exports since the immediate prewar period. A few new export products have emerged--pharmaceutical products, worsted textiles, paper products--but they remain quantitatively of minor importance, and in some cases the domestic value added is a comparatively small fraction of the value of the export. In the case of services exports there has been a significant change in the pattern since the prewar period--hardly a surprising one. Although earnings from travel grew rapidly between 1969 and 1974, by 1974 they financed only 9% of current expenditures, compared to 15% in 1965/66. The obvious reason is the loss of the West Bank tourist attractions in 1967.

The great increase in aid received after 1973 was noted in Chapter 5. To some degree, the increase can be seen in the 1974 figures in Table VI.5 and the 1975 figures show a large further increase. The financial transfer in 1974 and again in 1975 was significantly greater than the real transfer of resources (the excess of imports over exports) because Jordan was accumulating large amounts of foreign reserves in those years, in part perhaps

123

because the sudden increase in foreign exchange receipts from aid, remittances, and phosphate export was too unexpected to lead quickly to government expenditure and other measures sufficient to absorb the new inflow of foreign exchange. Jordan's external public debt grew rapidly in the postwar period, tripling between the end of 1969 and mid-1976.[25] Nonetheless, principal and interest payments on the external public debt for 1975 were less than 5% of the value of exports that year and less than 2% of receipts from exports, factor income, and public and private transfer payments from abroad.[26] Thus, debt servicing continued to be not a serious problem.

3. PUBLIC FINANCE

The major trends in the government budget are shown in Tables VI.6 and VI.7. The tables are derived from central government budget data, which exclude revenues and expenditures of municipalities and autonomous governmental or semigovernmental agencies.[27] It is generally acknowledged that a significant amount of foreign aid in the form of military equipment is not included in the budget accounts. The budget items for 1975 are preliminary. Even for earlier years, the budget is not fully reliable.[28]

The trends in government revenue shown in Table VI.6 must be interpreted cautiously because of weaknesses in the data, the impact of partition in 1967, and exceptional circumstances (primarily the phosphate boom) in 1974/75. The effect of the loss of the West Bank may be clearly seen in the comparison between 1964/65 and 1968/69, when tax revenue fell sharply in relation to total government revenue even though it rose in relation to the GNP of a truncated Jordan. The consequences of the phosphate boom are visible in the rising shares between 1968/69 and 1974/75 of three revenue sources: income taxes (from corporate income taxes on the phosphate company), interest and profits (the government's profits from the phosphate company, in which it holds most of the shares), and oil transit and phosphates (phosphate royalty payments).

Perhaps the most striking development shown in Table VI.6 is the great increase after the 1967 war in the importance of foreign grants and loans. According to budget estimates, the share of foreign resources in total central government revenues declined during 1968/69-74/75. Clearly, this was due

TABLE VI.6. RELATIVE IMPORTANCE OF MAJOR COMPONENTS OF CENTRAL GOVERNMENT REVENUE (percent)

	Share in Total Central Government Revenue			Share in GNP		
	1964/65	1968/69	1974/75	1964/65	1968/69	1974/75
I. Domestic Revenue	55.7	39.9	45.0	14.6	16.0	22.0
A. Taxes	40.1	28.5	30.7	10.5	11.4	15.0
1. Indirect Taxes	35.1	25.8	25.8	9.2	10.3	12.6
a. Customs	23.2 {	13.2	11.0	6.1 {	5.3	5.4
b. Excise		7.9	5.8		3.2	2.8
c. Others	12.0	4.7	9.0	3.1	1.9	4.4
2. Direct Taxes	5.0	2.8	4.8	1.3	1.1	2.4
a. Income	3.4	2.7	4.5	.9	1.1	2.2
b. Other	1.6	.1	.4	.4	.02	.2
B. Nontax Revenue	15.6	11.3	14.3	4.1	4.5	7.0
1. Interest and Profits	5.9	5.1	5.8	1.5	2.0	2.8
2. Oil Transit and Phosphates	9.7 {	1.7	2.3	2.5 {	.7	1.1
3. Others		4.6	6.2		1.8	3.0
II. Foreign Resources	44.3	60.1	55.0	11.6	24.1	26.8
A. Grants	33.8	53.2	44.3	8.8	21.4	21.6
B. Loans	10.5	6.9	10.7	2.8	2.8	5.2
TOTAL REVENUE	100.0	100.0	100.0	26.1	40.1	48.8

NOTES

CBJ, Monthly Statistical Bulletin, various issues, and Table V.3 above.

The year 1964/65 represents the average for the two fiscal years from April 1964 to March 1966. In computing the share in GNP, which is estimated on a calendar-year basis, an appropriately weighted average of 1964-66 GNP was used. In 1966 the fiscal year was changed to coincide with the calendar year, so that all figures for 1968/69 and 1974/75 are on a calendar-year basis.

mainly to the rapid rise in domestic revenue, for
the share of foreign resources in GNP continued to
rise during the period. However, there is a very
great difference between foreign grants and loans
to the central government as recorded by the government budget and by the balance of payments. While
the balance of payments records aid when received,
the budget does not record it until committed to be
spent. Foreign grants and loans to the central
government were much greater in the balance of payments estimates. If the balance of payments figures
are used, foreign grants and loans to the central
government rose as a percentage of GNP from 18% in
1964/65 to 29% in 1968/69 and 39% in 1974/75. As a
percentage of total central government revenues they
rose from 59% in 1964/65 to 65% in 1968/69 and continued at 65% in 1974/75.[29]

Although Table VI.6 shows a not insubstantial
rise in the share of taxes in GNP, this increase
should not be taken as evidence of any great change
in Jordan's fiscal system. As it was before the
1967 war, in the postwar period the share of GNP
raised in tax revenue by Jordan continued to be below average for a country of Jordan's per capita income and degree of openness.[30] Since Jordan's economy was considerably more open in 1974/75 than
1964/65, a rise in the share of taxes in GNP was to
have been expected; the expected rise in the ratio
of taxes to GNP due to increased openness could
account for about half of the increase in the ratio
occurring between 1964/65 and 1974/75.[31] The share
of income taxes in GNP rose, but the effect was
small.

While some attempt was made to improve income
tax enforcement, most of the prewar problems of tax
administration remained.[32] Despite repeated proposals for taxation of capital gains and inheri-
tances,[33] there was no significant broadening of
the direct tax base. The share of nontax revenue
in GNP rose significantly, but this was partly due
to the exceptional, and temporary, circumstances of
the phosphate boom, which increased government
royalties and profits on its phosphate company
shares, and interest on Jordan's much increased
foreign reserves.[34] In conclusion, there is no
evidence of a significant structural change in the
raising of domestic government revenues in the postwar period.

The major specific proposal for changing the
tax system in the 1976-80 plan was for a tax on
capital gains from the sale of real estate, a

narrower version of the tax on capital gains proposed in the 1973-75 plan. Other major proposals--
for improvement of tax administration and of tariff
legislation--were in general terms only.[35]

The summary of government expenditure and
budget trends in Table VI.7 reveals a very marked
change in the growth of defense expenditure over
the postwar period. Between the prewar and the
early postwar years the relative defense burden increased remarkably, from 12.6% of GNP in 1964/65 to
23.0% in 1968/69, due to the decline in real GNP
caused by the loss of the West Bank and to a large
absolute increase in the size of the armed forces.
In the later years of the postwar period defense
expenditures decelerated and fell sharply as a percentage of GNP;[36] even so, by 1974/75 the relative
defense burden was still significantly higher than
in the immediate prewar years. The increase in defense expenditure during the early postwar period
did not prevent an almost equally rapid growth of
nondefense government expenditure at the same time.
The sharp increase in foreign aid permitted both.
In the later postwar years the growth of nondefense
expenditure accelerated.

In the postwar years the share of government
spending in GNP reached remarkably high levels. By
the mid-1970s total government spending (including
current expenditure, capital expenditure, and transfer payments) equalled roughly half of East Bank
GNP. In the average LDC the comparable ratio is
well under a quarter.[37] Hence, despite a fundamentally free-enterprise philosophy of economic policy,
postwar Jordan, through its uncommon access to
foreign assistance, had arrived at an economy in
which government expenditure predominated to an
extraordinary degree.

Not all government expenditure represented com-
mand over goods and services, for some of it was in
the form of subsidies and other transfer payments
to the private sector. Subsidies, both explicit
and implicit, became more important around 1974-75.
The most important explicit subsidies were to wheat
and sugar, and followed sharp rises in world prices
of those products. A largely implicit subsidy was
represented by the domestic sale of petroleum products at less than world prices, not recorded in
the government budget because of the special circumstances surrounding the dispute with Tapline over
the price of imported oil.

It is tempting to interpret the increased resort to subsidies, which coincided with a steep in-

TABLE VI.7. RELATIVE IMPORTANCE OF MAJOR COMPONENTS OF CENTRAL GOVERNMENT BUDGET (percent)

	Share in Total Central Government Expenditure			Share in GNP		
	1964/65	1968/69	1974/75	1964/65	1968/69	1974/75
EXPENDITURE						
Defense	48.4	50.1	28.0	12.6	23.0	14.6
Recurring	48.2	50.0	28.0	12.6	23.0	14.6
Development	.1	.1	--	--	.1	--
Nondefense	51.6	49.9	71.9	13.5	22.9	37.5
Recurring	29.3	22.5	39.3	7.6	10.3	20.5
Development	22.3	27.4	32.6	5.8	12.6	17.0
Total	100.0	100.0	100.0	26.1	46.0	52.0
Recurring	77.5	72.5	67.3	20.2	33.3	35.1
Development	22.5	27.5	32.6	5.9	12.7	17.0
REVENUE	100.2	87.3	93.5	26.1	40.1	48.8
DOMESTIC BORROWING	--	5.4	5.6	--	2.5	2.9
RESIDUAL	.2	-7.3	-6.4	0.1	-3.4	-3.4

Sources: CBJ, Monthly Statistical Bulletin, various issues, and Table V.3 above. The treatment of calendar and fiscal years is the same as in Table VI.6.

crease in aid receipts, as a measure to channel
some of the increase in foreign resources to the
private sector, perhaps because of a limit to ab-
sorptive capacity in the government sector or because of a philosophical desire to hold down the
scope of the government sector. However, when the
history of these subsidies is examined, this interpretation appears incorrect. All the subsidies
were for politically sensitive goods whose world
price had risen precipitously. As time passed, all
three subsidies were reduced significantly--partly
through a fall in the world price (sugar, wheat),
partly through government measures to increase the
domestic price (wheat, petroleum products). In retrospect, these subsidies may be seen as largely
emergency measures and probably politically astute
ones with--in the cases of sugar and wheat--great-
est benefits for low-income groups. They were not
devices to funnel foreign aid to the private sector,
although their adoption was undoubtedly facilitated
by the plentiful availability of foreign assistance.

Probably not too much significance should be
attached to trends in the relative importance of
recurring and development expenditure in Table VI.7.
The distinction is not a precise one. Many recurring expenditures contribute to development. Over
time some budget items have been shifted from the
development classification to the recurring. For
what it is worth, there was a steady rise in the
relative importance of development expenditure, but
not for the same reason throughout the postwar
period. In the early years the proportion of nondefense outlays devoted to development expenditures
rose, but in the later years it did not. In the
later years the relative share of total development
expenditures rose simply because of the declining
importance of defense expenditure, virtually all of
which was recurring expenditure.

4. SAVING AND INVESTMENT

Gross fixed investment averaged 27.6% of GDP
at market prices in the East Bank during 1973-75,[38]
compared to 17-18% for all Jordan during 1959-66.
The 1959-66 ratio was about average for LDCs at a
comparable level of income, that for 1973-75 well
above average.[39] Estimates of investment and GDP
are less accurate for the postwar than the prewar
period, but it seems extremely unlikely that statistical errors could be great enough to account for
most of the recorded increase in the investment

ratio. At least in part, the difference may be due
to the difference in geographical areas covered by
the two estimates; in prewar Jordan investment
probably was a significantly larger share of GDP in
the East Bank than in the West Bank. Aside from this,
the investment ratio may have increased over time, perhaps mainly due to the increase in foreign aid supplied.
      The NPC has calculated the gross ICOR for the
East Bank during 1973-75 at about 5.[40] Such a figure, if correct, would be considerably greater than
the prewar ICOR (about 2-1/2 for 1959-66) and the
ICOR for an average LDC (about 3). For two major
reasons, no confidence can be placed in the estimated ICOR for 1973-75. First, the time period is
too short to eliminate the influence of transitory
elements. Second, and more important, accurate estimation of the ICOR requires an accurate estimate of
the growth rate of constant-price GDP. Because the
statistical reliability of estimates of postwar current-price GDP is low and because it is impossible
to deflate these estimates with sufficient accuracy,
no estimate of postwar real growth can be relied upon.
      The distribution of East Bank gross fixed in-
vestment among using sectors is shown in Table VI.8.

TABLE VI.8. SHARE OF USING SECTORS IN GROSS FIXED CAPITAL FOR-
         MATION, 1973-75 (percent)

	Private	Government	Total
Agriculture	2.2%	7.9%	10.0%
Industry & Electricity	14.4	5.2	19.7
Tourism	2.2	0.4	2.6
Transport	11.8	13.1	24.9
Communications	--	3.1	3.1
Housing	20.5	1.3	21.8
Other	4.4	13.6	17.9
Total	55.5	44.5	100.0

Source: NPC, Five Year Plan, p. 35.

For some sectors, particularly "industry and electricity" and "other," there is considerable doubt
about the completeness of coverage and the reliability of the estimates. But three sectors--agri-
culture, transport, and dwellings--are likely to be
almost as reliable as the corresponding estimates
for 1959-66 in Table III.1, p. 38, above and may
safely be compared with them. The shares of agriculture and transport in total gross fixed investment are very similar for the two periods. But investment in dwellings, which comprised about 30% of

fixed investment in 1959-66, was only a little more
than 20% during 1973-75. The share of housing in
total fixed investment was for 1959-66 well above
average for an LDC, but for 1973-75 only about average. If 1976, a year of stepped-up housing construction, were included, the picture might be different.

The contribution of different sources to the
financing of investment is shown in Table VI.9.

TABLE VI.9. SOURCES OF FINANCING GROSS DOMESTIC INVESTMENT,
1973-75

	Share in Gross Domestic Investment (percent)
1. Deficit on Foreign Current Account	98.4
2. Gross Domestic Saving	1.6
3. Gross Government Saving	-57.0
4. Gross Private Saving	58.6

NOTES

Sources: NPC, Five Year Plan, pp. 31, 39, 40, 111; JDS,
unpublished materials; Israel Central Bureau of Statistics,
Quarterly Statistics of the Administered Territories, 6 (May
1976), pp. 6-7.

The deficit on foreign current account includes the deficit on merchandise trade, but not services, with the Occupied Territories. The exchange rates used to convert from
Israel pounds to Jordan dinars were 14.0 pounds/dinar for
1973, 16.0 for 1974, and 23.7 for 1975.

The figures there must be considered extremely speculative and subject to a great margin of error.
The estimates of the deficit on foreign current account in row 1 and of gross government saving in
row 3 are handicapped by weaknesses in the statistics of international transactions and the government budget, respectively. Since gross private
saving in row 4 is derived as a residual from estimates of gross investment, the deficit on foreign
current account, and gross government saving, it
will be affected by errors in any of these items
and is therefore especially dubious. Given the wide
margin of error which must be allowed, comparison of
the postwar period with the prewar period (shown in
Table III.7, p. 53, above) does not indicate any
statistically significant change in the relative
importance of different sources of investment

131

finance between the two periods.

5. MONEY AND INFLATION

In the prewar and early postwar periods price increases were relatively gradual, notwithstanding some sharp year-to-year changes due to harvest fluctuations. In 1972 inflation accelerated sharply to double-digit levels and remained in the 10-20% range for every year from 1972 to 1975. The postwar trend in prices is indicated by column (1) of Table VI.10. Although the index is subject to significant error due to incompleteness of coverage and difficulties of accurately gathering price statistics, it surely must represent the general trend adequately, if not the precise magnitude of changes.

Columns (2)-(4) of Table VI.10 show the postwar changes in East Bank GNP in current prices, the money supply, and the relationship between them. They show velocity declining as the money supply growth exceeds that of GNP. However, the decline in velocity shown may be exaggerated, as 1967 GNP probably was overstated.[41] In addition, the relationship between the money supply and East Bank GNP is complicated by the fact that the Jordan dinar is one of two legal currencies in the Occupied Territories.[42]

Until about 1969 the monetary base (currency plus bank reserves) in Jordan was essentially determined by the state of the balance of payments; the Central Bank of Jordan (CBJ) had virtually no discretionary control over it.[43] The monetary base tended to expand when balance of payments surpluses increased the foreign exchange holdings of the CBJ, and to contract as a consequence of deficits. After the government introduced the first treasury bills in 1969 and longer-term development bonds soon thereafter, the close link between the CBJ's foreign reserves and the monetary base was greatly attenuated.[44] This is evident in the growing importance after 1968 of dinar assets in the total assets of the CBJ, shown in column (1) of Table VI.11. Nonetheless, even after 1969 the balance of payments sometimes had an important influence on the monetary base.[45]

The growth of the total money supply was determined not only by the growth of the monetary base, but by the reserve-holding behavior of the commercial banks and the currency-holding behavior of the public, both of which changed significantly in the postwar period. Although legal reserve requirements

132

TABLE VI.10. INDEXES OF PRICES, GNP, AND MONEY SUPPLY, AND LEVEL OF VELOCITY, 1967-75

	Consumer Prices (1)	Indexes (1967 = 100) East Bank GNP in Current Prices (2)	Money Supply (3)	Velocity (4)
1967	100.0	100.0	100.0	2.3
1968	99.9	99.0	116.9	1.9
1969	106.7	116.1	127.9	2.1
1970	114.1	109.4	140.2	1.8
1971	119.5	116.6	143.5	1.8
1972	128.4	129.3	152.9	1.9
1973	141.7	141.1	185.1	1.7
1974	168.9	181.0	226.2	1.8
1975	188.4	218.5	290.4	1.7

NOTES

The consumer price index is a weighted average of the price indexes for Amman and Zarqa, from CBJ, Monthly Statistical Bulletin, various issues. The indices are weighted according to the relative population sizes of the two cities in 1967, from JDS, Population Census and Internal Migration, p. 9.

East Bank GNP in current prices is from Table V.3 above. The money supply is defined as currency outside banks plus demand deposits, from CBJ, Monthly Statistical Bulletin, various issues. Velocity equals East Bank GNP in current prices divided by the money supply at the end of the period.

TABLE VI.11. SOME MAJOR MONETARY RATIOS, 1967-75 (percent)

	CBJ Dinar Assets as % of Total Assets (1)	Commercial Bank Reserves as % of Demand Deposits (2)	Currency as % of Monetary Base (3)	Currency as % of Money Supply (4)
1967	5.9	34.5	73.6	68.5
1968	4.6	32.2	78.5	72.2
1969	7.3	25.5	83.2	74.1
1970	14.7	26.7	84.7	78.2
1971	20.7	27.6	83.5	76.9
1972	12.4	26.3	80.9	70.8
1973	24.5	22.0	83.8	70.0
1974	28.4	21.8	82.5	67.8
1975	18.8	22.7	79.5	63.6

NOTES

Source: CBJ, Monthly Statistical Bulletin, various issues.
The monetary base is defined as commercial bank reserves plus currency in the hands of the public.

were first imposed in 1969, raised in 1971, and
raised again in 1974, the actual ratio of reserves
to demand deposits declined greatly over the 1967-75
period [column (2) of Table VI.11]. The reason
seems evident: The availability of government securities beginning in 1969 caused banks to switch
precautionary balances from the low-yielding form of
excess reserves to the higher-yielding form of
government securities.[46] Thus, the behavior of commercial banks had a significant expansionary effect
on the money supply in the postwar years. This is
evident in columns (3) and (4) of Table VI.12.

The currency-holding behavior of the public
exerted a contractionary effect on the money supply
in the early part of the postwar period and an expansionary effect in the later years [columns (3)
and (4) of Table VI.11]. Until 1970 internal tensions and the threat of civil war induced the public
to hold a larger fraction of its money balances in
the form of currency, rather than bank deposits.
After the civil clashes of September 1970, which
effectively settled the issue, this trend reversed
itself and bank deposits became a steadily larger
fraction of the money supply--the usual trend as
countries develop and one which had prevailed in the
prewar period.

By 1972 all three major influences on the money
supply--the monetary base, the reserve-holding behavior of commercial banks, and the currency-holding
behavior of the public--were acting in the same
direction: toward rapid expansion of the money supply. It was at this time that sustained, rapid inflation made its first appearance in the state of
Jordan. After 1972 a number of selective measures
were adopted in an attempt to alleviate the inflationary impact on certain groups or sectors. These
included subsidies to some staples, mainly wheat and
sugar. In 1973 the CBJ resorted to moral suasion in
an effort to channel credit of the commercial banks
to "productive" (noncommercial) activities and to
trade in nonluxury goods.[47] This was a departure
from previous policy, which had largely limited itself to measures to change credit conditions in
general. As such, the effect on the overall rate
of monetary growth and inflation probably was minimal. Beginning in 1974, the CBJ adopted measures
which combined direct limitation on credit expansion
by commercial banks with exemptions intended to
channel credit to favored sectors or activities.[48]
Although the CBJ claimed some success in reducing
credit expansion by these direct measures,[49] the

TABLE VI.12. INDEX NUMBERS OF PRINCIPAL MONETARY AGGREGATES, 1967-75 (1967 = 100)

	Total CBJ Assets (1)	Monetary Base (2)	Commercial Bank Reserves (3)	Commercial Bank Demand Deposits (4)	Currency Outside Banks (5)
1967	100.0	100.0	100.0	100.0	100.0
1968	115.0	115.8	94.6	101.5	123.3
1969	109.2	122.5	78.3	107.5	138.4
1970	115.5	139.0	80.5	104.1	160.0
1971	121.5	142.2	89.2	111.7	161.1
1972	119.4	143.9	104.0	136.5	158.1
1973	143.7	166.2	102.1	160.6	189.2
1974	166.2	200.0	132.6	209.7	224.2
1975	215.9	249.9	194.1	296.0	269.9

Source: CBJ, Monthly Statistical Bulletin, various issues.

record of monetary growth and inflation suggests
that they could have played only a marginal role in
combatting inflation. Their major significance is
as an indication of a new, more interventionist,
CBJ approach to control of commercial banking and
credit.[50]

While the monetary developments reviewed here
may have been the proximate cause of the 1972 acceleration in inflation, their ultimate source must
be sought in developments abroad. During 1974-75
exports plus imports equalled 90% of GNP. A country so exposed to the world economy must be expected
to import inflation from abroad unless it is offset
by exchange rate appreciation. If the dollar prices
of Jordan's purchases rise, the dinar prices must
rise as well, unless the exchange rate is appreciated or special measures (such as tariff reductions
or subsidies) are adopted. When the U.S. dollar
was devalued at the end of 1971, the old exchange
rate of the dinar vis-à-vis the dollar was retained,
so that the dinar was effectively devalued relative
to other currencies as a whole. This must have been
one of the causes of the acceleration of Jordanian
inflation in 1972. After 1972 the dinar remained
fairly stable in relation to other currencies as a
whole.[51] As a result the acceleration in worldwide
inflation which began in 1973 was transmitted to
Jordanian prices.

The foreign inflation which was transmitted to
Jordan after 1972 was not simply that of the world
as a whole, but was disproportionately that of the
neighboring region. For some goods and services,
most importantly perishable agricultural products,
the market is essentially regional, not worldwide.
It is no surprise that the most rapid inflation was
in fruits and vegetables, whose prices were pulled
up by skyrocketing demand in neighboring countries
benefiting from the oil boom. The rapid inflation
in neighboring Saudi Arabia (24% per year between
1972 and 1975), combined with depreciation of the
Jordan dinar relative to the Saudi Arabian riyal
(over 8% between 1972 and 1975), must have transmitted especially strong inflationary pressures to
Jordan.[52] Although the dinar appreciated slightly
relative to the Syrian pound, it was not great
enough relative to Syrian inflation during 1972-75
to prevent strong inflationary pressures from that
direction as well.[53]

The one measure capable of reducing Jordanian
inflation significantly during this period was appreciation of the dinar. Since this was a period

of large aid inflows and balance-of-payments surpluses, such a measure could not be ruled out on balance of payments grounds. In the minds of Jordanian policy-makers the primary obstacle to exchange rate appreciation as an anti-inflation measure appears to have been its effect on Jordan's competitive position, both current and prospective, in international markets. Against this it may be argued that the inflation which ensues from failure to revalue the dinar itself worsens Jordan's competitive position in international markets. But there is more to the question than this, and the issue of the appropriate exchange rate is a fundamental and difficult one.

Were it not for the large inflow of aid Jordan has been receiving for over two decades, the exchange value of the dinar would have been much lower. For years Jordanian policy-makers have proclaimed the goal of reducing dependence on foreign aid which, if achieved, would be likely to require an ultimate decline in the external value of the dinar. Thus, there is a possible conflict between the short-run and long-run functions of the foreign exchange rate, on which a rough balance must be struck. In the short run a high external value of the dinar serves the functions of dampening inflationary pressures and facilitating the net transfer of real resources (in the form of an import surplus) that is required for the financial transfer of aid funds to contribute to development. However, the current exchange rate also performs the longer-run role of guiding investment decisions. Too high an external value of the dinar will discourage investment in activities producing for export or for import-substitution in favor of investment in the production of nontradeable goods and services.[54] If the CBJ anticipates a future equilibrium exchange rate for the dinar much below the present one it may be justified in maintaining a current exchange rate below its short-run equilibrium level.

NOTES

1. The difference between the manpower census and the industrial census in the estimate of manufacturing employment probably is due to greater coverage by the industrial census. The larger estimate of mining employment by the manpower census may be because the industrial census refers to 1974 employment and the manpower census to employment in 1975, at a time when the mining sector was expanding.

2. See International Institute for Strategic Studies, The Military Balance, 1974-75 and 1975-76 editions.

3. The 1975 agricultural census enumeration was conducted during April-June, a time of high seasonal demand for agricultural labor. All workers employed on a holding during the week preceding the enumeration of that holding were recorded as employed in agriculture. In determining the amount of time worked on that holding in order to distinguish between casual, temporary, and permanent workers, the reference period was the preceding year.

4. According to the preliminary results of the 1975 agricultural census, about 19,000 holdings were operated by individuals whose main occupation was not farming. In rainfed cereal cultivation especially, it is often possible for a person to cultivate a holding with very little expenditure of his own time, by hiring custom tractor operators, custom sowers, and casual labor for the harvest. On such farms the technical level of cultivation practiced usually is low.

5. Excluding family workers, those seeking work, and those of unclassified economic status, there were 22,000 workers in construction in the East Bank during 1961. (JDS, First Census, vol. 2, pp. 11-15.) The 1975 manpower census enumerated less than 9,000 workers in construction (Table VI.1, line 4).

6. The labor force participation rate implied by the labor force estimate in Table VI.1 and my estimate of early 1975 population is 20.2%--slightly above the 19.6% estimate of the 1974 multi-purpose household survey. The difference is to allow for apparently greater coverage of female farm employment in the 1975 agricultural census than in the multi-purpose household survey.

7. Only the agriculture and trade sectors were adjusted for unpaid family workers. According to the preliminary results of the 1975 agriculture and manpower censuses these were the only sectors in which unpaid family labor was of quantitative significance. The reason for removing unpaid family workers is to eliminate the bias caused by inconsistent coverage of such workers in different surveys and censuses.

8. In absolute terms, the decline in the Jordan/East Bank agricultural share (10.0 percentage points) only modestly exceeded that for the typical country (8.8 percentage points). However, in relative terms, the Jordan/East Bank share declined from 60% of the average comparable country's share to 42%. In view of this, some, but not all, of the decline in the Jordan/East Bank agricultural share may be attributed to the rise in income per head.

9. Little significance should be attached to the sharp rise in the share of mining between columns (1) and (3), which is largely due to two factors: the concentration of phosphate mining in the East Bank and the extremely favorable world market for phosphates in 1974, the latter evidently only a

transitory phenomenon.

10. Note the increased share of public administration and defense in column (3) compared to column (1).

11. For 1959-61 Jordan's import surplus was 37% of GDP at factor cost--a percentage which was gradually declining in the prewar period. For 1973/74 the East Bank import surplus was 35% of its GDP at factor cost. The import surplus was calculated from balance of payments estimates in Central Bank of Jordan, Monthly Statistical Bulletin, 12 (August 1976), Table 23, and adjusted for the East Bank import surplus in goods, but not services, in trade with Israeli-occupied territories. Without the adjustment for the East Bank's trade with the Occupied Territories, the East Bank import surplus was 33% of its GDP at factor cost.

12. See Abba Lerner and Haim Ben-Shahar, The Economics of Efficiency and Growth: Lessons from Israel and the West Bank, Cambridge, Mass.: Ballinger Publishing Company, 1975, pp. 170-73.

13. Israel Central Bureau of Statistics, Quarterly Statistics of the Administered Territories, vol. 6, no. 1, 1976, pp. 6-7. In 1968 the East Bank's share in the trade of the Occupied Territories had been 80% in imports and 46% in exports (Israel Central Bureau of Statistics, Monthly Statistics of the Administered Territories, vol. 1, no. 1, Jerusalem, 1971, pp. 6-7).

14. These payments were halted after the suspension of the Khartoum subsidies from Kuwait and Libya in 1971 but were resumed in 1974 after the restoration of the subsidy from Kuwait.

15. While it would be possible to adjust it to include merchandise trade between the East Bank and the Occupied Territories, much more important transactions--particularly travel and remittances--must be omitted for lack of data. Since it might be misleading to include a few minor transactions with the Occupied Territories while omitting much more important transactions, no transactions at all were included.

16. In the treatment of oil imports the 1974 balance of payments estimates in Table VI.5 may be unrepresentative. After the 1973 rise in world oil prices Jordan continued to receive Saudi Arabian oil from Tapline, but the price was in dispute. Oil imports during 1974 were recorded in the balance of payments statistics at the price prevailing before the oil-price revolution. Subsequently, Jordan agreed to pay world oil prices retroactively. Therefore, the 1974 value of imports (included in "total current expenditure") may be understated significantly in Table VI.5. Subsequent increases in aid from Saudi Arabia may have been intended at least partially as compensation to Jordan for accepting this agreement.

17. This was also true, but in lesser degree, for the prewar data. Whenever there was an omission, both the import

and the aid financing it were excluded from the accounts. Therefore, the omission had no effect on the net balance in the balance of payments.

18. Postwar estimates of average expenditure per visitor were based on a prewar survey supplemented by a very limited survey of tourist expenditure in the postwar period and adjusted annually by means of a price index.

19. CBJ, Monthly Statistical Bulletin, 9 (December 1973), Table 15; and 13 (June 1977), Table 23. The number of East Bank residents in 1976 is assumed to be 1.85 million. The exchange rate used is $1 = J.D. 0.333.

20. Calculated from Table V.3 above, p. 98.

21. JDS, Statistical Yearbook, 1974, p. 243. The usual criticism of such indices--that they do not adequately account for the changing composition of different import categories-- is not a serious criticism of the index for Jordan's exports, which were mainly homogeneous products like phosphates, cement, and agricultural products.

22. Between 1969 and 1974 the quantity of phosphates exported rose 58% while the average price per ton rose 246% (calculated from data on quantity and value of domestic phosphate exports in JDS, Statistical Yearbook, 1969 and 1974 editions). Revenues from phosphate exports in 1975 were about equal to those for 1974, but in 1975 world phosphate prices began a sharp decline which continued into 1976. The high prices and world demand in 1974-75 seem to have been largely transitory, caused by the ability of Morocco, the world's biggest phosphate exporter, to exploit some short-run monopoly power.

23. CBJ, Twelfth Annual Report, 1975, p. 55. However, there may have been some smuggled exports of cement; the Jordan government controlled the domestic price of cement and restricted its export.

24. National Planning Council (NPC), Five Year Plan for Economic and Social Development 1976-1980, [Amman, 1976], mimeographed version, pp. 347-48.

25. CBJ, Monthly Statistical Bulletin, 6 (February 1970), Table 28; and 12 (September 1976), Table 39. The proportion of the loans undisbursed rose from 32% in 1969 to 42% in 1976.

26. CBJ, Monthly Statistical Bulletin, Table 32 of May, September, December, 1975, and January, 1976 issues.

27. E.g., the University of Jordan (partially financed by an earmarked tax not included in the government budget accounts), the Aqaba Port Authority, and the Agricultural Credit Corporation.

28. Reportedly, it was dissatisfaction with the quality of budget accounts that led to the proposal in the 1976-80 plan for the establishment of a consolidated Treasury Account at the CBJ (NPC, Five Year Plan, p. 96). It was hoped that such a measure, scheduled to begin in 1976, would provide alternative data (on a cash basis) in addition to the estimates

of the Budget Department of the Ministry of Finance.

29. The balance of payments estimates are from CBJ, Monthly Statistical Bulletin, various issues.

30. Typical "tax effort" of LDCs is from Hinrichs, p. 40; and Lotz and Morss.

31. The degree of openness (exports plus imports as a proportion of GNP) rose from 51% in 1964/65 to 90% in 1974/75. The expected effect of this on "tax effort" is calculated using equation (2) for low-income countries from ibid., p. 497.

32. See above, p. 57.

33. E.g., NPC, Three Year Development Plan 1973-1975, n.p., n.d., p. 40.

34. The interest is received by the CBJ, but CBJ profits are transferred to the government treasury.

35. NPC, Five Year Plan, pp. 93-97.

36. This should be qualified by recalling the under-recording of imports of military equipment, which may have been relatively greater in the later years.

37. For 37 developing countries in the 1960s the average was 21.5% (calculated from Lotz, p. 125).

38. NPC, Five Year Plan, pp. 30-31. A high margin of error should be attached to this estimate.

39. Chenery and Syrquin, p. 201.

40. NPC, Five Year Plan, p. 31.

41. See above, pp. 95-97.

42. It is not clear how this would affect the velocity estimate in column (4) of Table VI.10. On the one hand, the holding of Jordanian dinars by residents of the Occupied Territories may be increasing more rapidly than that by East Bank citizens because of the faster growth of incomes in the Occupied Territories. On the other hand, the progressive integration of the Occupied Territories into the economy of Israel may be reducing the desire to hold dinars there.

43. See Michel Isa Marto, A Money Supply Model: Jordan, Amman: Central Bank of Jordan, 1974, originally a Ph.D. dissertation in economics at the University of Southern California, 1970. An updated version was published as idem, An Econometric Money Supply Model for Jordan, Amman: Royal Scientific Society, 1974. See also Umayya Salah Tukan, An Analysis of Central Banking in Jordan, Amman: Central Bank of Jordan, 1974; and J. E. Hazelton and G. E. Khoury, Monetary Analysis of Balance of Payments Surpluses and Deficits: A Review, Amman: Royal Scientific Society, 1974.

44. For example, 82% of the growth in the total assets of the CBJ between end-1968 and end-1974 was due to the growth in dinar assets. CBJ, Monthly Statistical Bulletin, 9 (September 1973), Table 5; and 12 (September 1976), Table 6.

45. In 1975 the CBJ holdings of gold and foreign exchange reserves rose by 47%, more than offsetting a 14% decline in CBJ dinar assets, as total CBJ assets rose by 30%.

Ibid., 12 (September 1976), Table 6.

46. The ratio of commercial bank reserves plus holdings of government securities to demand deposits actually rose modestly from 34.5% in 1967 to 38.1% in 1975. Ibid., 7 (September 1971), Table 6; and 12 (September 1976), Table 7.

47. CBJ, Tenth Annual Report, 1972, pp. 110-11.

48. CBJ, Eleventh Annual Report, 1974, pp. 33-36.

49. Between end-1972 and end-1973 incremental commercial bank loans and bills discounted were 87% of incremental deposits in commercial banks. The ratio declined to 81% for 1974-75 and 76% for end-1975 to September 1976. CBJ, Monthly Statistical Bulletin, 12 (September 1976), Tables 7, 10.

50. In early 1976 the CBJ for the first time imposed minimum interest rates on bank deposits and commercial leading by banks.

51. On exchange rate experience see Andreas S. Gerakis, "Pegging to the SDR," Finance and Development, 13 (March 1976), 35-38; CBJ, Tenth Annual Report, 1973, pp. 103-4; and CBJ, Eleventh Annual Report, 1974, pp. 69-73.

52. International Monetary Fund, International Financial Statistics, Washington, D.C., September 1976, pp. 224-25 and 324-25.

53. Between 1972 and 1975 Syrian consumer prices rose at an average 17% per year between 1972 and 1975. Over the same period the Jordan dinar appreciated about 5% relative to the Syrian pound (ibid., pp. 224-25 and 360-61).

54. It may be argued that potential investors will foresee future depreciation of the dinar as a result of the future reduction in aid inflows and will be guided in their investments by this anticipated future exchange rate, rather than by the current one. It seems highly unlikely that many investors would act thus on the basis of such uncertain information.

143

Part 3
Development Policies
and Prospects

7
Agriculture

1. THE SETTING

For over a decade preceding the 1967 war the growth of agricultural value added at constant prices averaged around 6% per year--a high rate in comparison with most LDCs. In the postwar period to 1975 there has been no perceptible growth in agriculture.

The data on agricultural development are best for the period 1959-66. During this period the average annual growth of agricultural value added in constant prices was nearly 6%. The sources of agricultural growth in this period can be broken down roughly as follows:[1]

2%	East Ghor Canal project
1/2%	fruit and vegetable increases from other sources
1%	poultry
2-1/4%	livestock
5-3/4%	increase in agricultural value added

During this period the growth of grain output was nil. On the other hand, the growth of fruit and vegetable production accounted for over 40% of the increase in the total value of agricultural production. The greater part of this increase in fruit and vegetable production may be attributed to the East Ghor Canal project.[2] This project diverted water by gravity flow from the Yarmouk River into a 70-kilometer (43.5-mile) canal in the Jordan Valley running parallel to the Jordan River on its east bank. The system also received water from seven small perennial streams that flow westward to the Jordan River. Construction of the main canal was begun in 1959 and completed by 1963. By

1966 all the lateral canals and primary drains had
been completed and the full 30,000 acres of the
project area brought into irrigated cultivation.

Over half of agricultural growth during 1959-
66 came from the livestock and poultry sector.
The growth in poultry was due partly to the adoption of modern commercial methods in broiler production.[3] Adoption of the new technology began in
the late 1950s in Jordan and was stimulated by its
earlier success in nearby Lebanon and by government
restrictions on the import of live broilers. The
new technology, a comparatively simple one without
great capital requirements, has contributed to the
growth of the poultry industry widely in the less
developed world. An increase in egg production
also contributed significantly to the growth of
poultry output, but this appears to have been more
the expansion of existing methods than the adoption of greatly improved techniques.

Somewhat surprising is the rapid growth (9-1/2%
per year between 1959 and 1966) of non-poultry
livestock production, which accounted for almost
two-fifths of the growth in total agricultural production during this period. For the earlier
period, 1954-59, the growth rate of non-poultry
livestock production was almost as great. This
high level of sustained growth is surprising because there is little evidence of significant advance in methods in the non-poultry livestock sector.[4] By 1966, after more than a decade of rapid
growth, most production in the sector came from
traditional breeds of sheep and goats grazed on
grasslands, desert, and stubble by nomads and, to
a lesser degree, settled villagers. Errors in
statistics might account for a part of the reported
high growth rate,[5] but surely not for most of it.

Most of the growth in non-poultry livestock
production must have been expansion of traditional
activities from a very small base. As a result of
the expansion of its livestock herds, Jordan on the
eve of the 1967 war suffered from destructive overgrazing.[6] Perhaps partly because of the excessive
livestock numbers, average weight of the animals at
slaughter was quite low.[7] By 1966 there appeared
to be little possibility for non-poultry livestock
output to grow in the way that it had for more than
a decade previously. If much further growth were
to occur, it would require the adoption of new
methods, perhaps including improved breeds.

Although the rate of growth of total agricultural value added during 1954-59 was similar to

that for 1959-66, the pattern of growth was dis-
tinctly different. Poultry and fruit production,
which made important contributions to agricultural
growth during 1959-66, had a negligible impact on
agricultural growth during the earlier period. The
growth of grain production was negligible during
1954-59 as it was during 1959-66. Over 90% of the
growth of agricultural production during 1954-59
was due to growth in the production of vegetables
(especially tomatoes, watermelons, and cucumbers)
and non-poultry livestock. No single irrigation
project comparable to the East Ghor Canal project
contributed to growth during 1954-59. However,
the expansion and intensification of production
in the Jordan Valley, much of it under irrigation,[8]
probably was the major source of the increase in
vegetable production during this period. Many
Palestinian refugees settled in the Jordan Valley
during the early 1950s, bringing with them new
techniques from the more advanced agriculture of
Palestine. As a result of the new methods and the
larger labor force in the Jordan Valley, irrigation
was expanded, the cultivated area was enlarged,
land was cropped more frequently (by reduced fallow-
ing of rainfed land and double-cropping of irrigated land), and the cropping pattern was shifted
somewhat away from cereal cultivation toward more
labor-intensive fruits and vegetables.[9]

Over the period 1967 to 1975 there was no perceptible trend in total East Bank agricultural output aside from large year-to-year fluctuations due
to the weather.[10] The failure of rainfed cereal
production to increase was merely the continuation
of the prewar pattern. The failure of livestock
production to grow in the postwar period perhaps
is not surprising since by 1966 Jordan appeared to
have exhausted most of the potential for livestock
growth without the adoption of new techniques.
Production in Jordan's major irrigated area, the
Jordan Valley, was interrupted by hostilities until
1970. By 1975 production there had been restored
to somewhere near 1966 levels and future increases
seemed assured, both from fuller exploitation of
irrigation projects already completed and from new
projects under way.

Because of rainfall variations, year-to-year
changes in agricultural output have been very great.
Wheat production in a good year may be four or five
times that in a bad year. As production of poultry
and irrigated crops (neither affected by rainfall
variations) became relatively more important in the

years before the 1967 war, the relative size of the
fluctuations in total agricultural production declined somewhat, but remained large. Surprisingly,
these large fluctuations in the agricultural sector
do not appear to have generated significant fluctuations in other sectors. For the period 1954-66,
for which the data are best, there was no significant correlation between year-to-year value added
changes in agriculture and those in nonagriculture
or its major components.[11]
    There are several reasons why fluctuations in
agriculture had little effect on the rest of the
economy. Since agriculture provided a small share
of GDP compared to other LDCs, its fluctuations
naturally would not have so great an impact on the
rest of the economy. The ready availability of
food aid from abroad kept domestic supplies relatively stable. Since much of the food aid was dis-
tributed through normal commercial channels, the
commerce and transport sectors were not so greatly
affected by fluctuations in domestic production of
food grains. More generally, in some LDCs fluctuations in production of primary products may be
transmitted to the rest of the economy through the
resulting balance of payments problem and the measures adopted by the government to deal with it.[12]
Because abundant foreign aid permitted large holdings of foreign reserves, Jordan did not have to
undergo this. During bad crop years, rather than
undertaking measures to restrain imports, Jordan
increased its import surplus by drawing down its
stock of foreign reserves. Finally, agricultural
fluctuations did not have great repercussions on
the rest of the economy because agriculture was not
very important either as purchaser of intermediate
inputs from the rest of the economy or as supplier
of intermediate inputs to manufacturing.[13]
    It was shown above (pp.111-13) that there has
been virtually no change in the size of the agricultural labor force between 1961 and 1975. Given
the high natural rate of growth of the rural population, this implies substantial emigration from
rural areas. Probably the rate of emigration was
greater after 1967, when agricultural income stagnated, than during the 1961-67 period. The rate of
rural-to-urban migration in the East Bank after
1967 may have been almost as high as the relatively
high level prevailing in Jordan before 1961.[14]
    By 1975 Jordanian agriculture was largely com-
mercialized. However, 48% of the total number of
land holdings (but representing only 25% of the

land area in all holdings) were producing "mainly" for home consumption. Even most of these must have had important connections with the market. Not surprisingly, the average holding producing mainly for sale was almost 3 times the size of the average holding producing mainly for home consumption.[15]

2. LAND TENURE

a. Distribution of Ownership and Holdings

The distribution of agricultural land may be measured in two ways, each related to a different issue of policy. Studies of land tenure in Jordan commonly have blurred the distinction between these two different concepts. First is the distribution of ownership, which is connected to the issue of equity. In an LDC agricultural land may be the most important form in which wealth is held, so that a highly unequal distribution of agricultural land ownership could by itself generate an unequal distribution of total wealth. The second concept is the distribution of holdings, or units of operation, which raises issues primarily of efficiency in production, rather than distributional equity.[16]

The size distribution of land ownership is shown in Table VII.1 and that of land holdings in Table VII.2. Not too much importance should be attached to such highly aggregated figures. Where the quality of land in different areas varies greatly (as it does in Jordan between the irrigated land of the Jordan Valley, the rainfed wheat lands of the northern plateau, and semi-desert lands cultivated only in years of unusually good rainfall), measuring the distribution of land by area alone without allowing for differences in land quality may produce misleading results.[17]

The degree of inequality in land ownership shown in Table VII.1 is considerably less than that in most of Latin America, or pre-revolutionary Iraq and Egypt, and perhaps comparable to that of India during the 1950s.[18] If the figures in Table VII.1 are correct, the degree of inequality in land ownership is substantial in Jordan, but not comparable to that in those LDCs with the greatest inequality. The effect of inequality in ownership of agricultural land on the overall inequality of wealth and income is attenuated by the fact that agriculture generates a comparatively small part of total national income in Jordan. In the East Bank crop production accounted for only about 10% of national

149

TABLE VII.1. SIZE DISTRIBUTION OF AGRICULTURAL LAND OWNERSHIP, EAST BANK (percent)

| Size Class (dunums) | As Percentage of Total | | | |
| | East Bank excluding the Ghors, 1971 | | Ghor Areas of East Bank, 1974 | |
	Number	Area	Number	Area
Less than 10	30.0	3.6	18.6	1.5
10-29	34.8	15.4	23.1	8.9
30-49	13.6	13.8	36.9	25.1
50-99	12.3	22.8	12.0	15.6
100-199	5.7	22.5	5.4	13.7
200-499	2.9	20.6	3.2	17.8
500-999	.6	9.5	.6	8.2
1,000 and over	.2	9.8	.3	9.3

NOTES

1 dunum = 1/10 hectare = c. 1/4 acre

The Ghor areas are the cultivable areas of the Jordan Valley and include all of the East Ghor Canal project area.

Sources: JDS, Agricultural Statistical Yearbook and Agricultural Sample Survey, 1974, Amman, 1975, p. xvii; JDS, The Agricultural Sample Survey in the Ghors, 1974, Amman, 1975, pp. 1-2.

150

income. Of this 10%, certainly no more than half represents returns to ownership of land, the remainder being returns to labor and capital. In Jordan returns to privately owned land probably account for a very small fraction of income from animal production, much of which comes from grazing livestock on unowned land or from raising poultry, which requires little land.

Four studies have been carried out on the distribution of land ownership in limited areas of the postwar East Bank and all show somewhat less inequality than that in Table VII.1. Three of them covered regions of rainfed cereal cultivation and all indicated that the 10% of landowners with the largest ownership had about 35-45% of the land area while the 75% of landowners with the smallest ownership had about 30-40% of the land area.[19] A fourth study, of the area irrigated by the East Ghor Canal, showed a distribution of ownership more equal than in the rainfed farming areas studied; the 6% of landowners with the largest holdings had only 14% of the total land area.[20] One reason is the land reform measures which have been applied to the East Ghor Canal project area.[21]

The difference in the inequality of land ownership between the aggregate figures of Table VII.1 and the studies of particular areas may have several explanations. Of course, the area surveyed may be unrepresentative of the East Bank as a whole. If large landowners own land both within and outside the limited area surveyed, the extent of their holdings and the degree of the inequality will be understated by the studies of restricted areas. If land quality and ownership size are inversely correlated, statistics for limited areas, within which land quality is relatively homogeneous, will show greater equality of distribution.[22] Finally, there is the possibility that the ownership data from which Table VII.1 was compiled may be inaccurate.

Some doubt is cast on the reliability of data on the distribution of land ownership shown in Table VII.1 by inconsistencies between them and the results of the 1975 agricultural census, which recorded the distribution of land holdings, rather than ownership. The 1975 census probably should be considered the more reliable of the two data sources,[23] so that discrepancies between them are more likely to be due to errors in the ownership data. If so, the most likely error is that the ownership distribution data used to derive Table VII.1 includes many plots with the same owner.[24]

151

TABLE VII.2. SIZE DISTRIBUTION OF AGRICULTURAL LAND HOLDINGS, EAST BANK, 1975 (percent)

Size Class (dunums)	Number of Holdings As % of Total	Area of Holdings As % of Total
Less than 10	24.4	1.1
10-29	24.2	5.6
30-49	15.1	7.3
50-99	17.0	14.9
100-199	10.7	18.3
200-499	6.6	24.2
500-999	1.4	11.4
1,000 and over	.7	17.0

Source: JDS, 1975 agricultural census, preliminary results, unpublished.

NOTES

The table excludes a small number of holdings held by squatters, on a tribal basis, or in miscellaneous tenure forms. Together the area of the excluded items is less than half of one percent of the total area. "Holdings" without land (mainly landless owners of livestock) are not included in the table.

Such an error would cause the average size of land ownership to be understated. It is not clear whether it would have a significant effect on the percentage distribution of land ownership shown in Table VII.1. If there were an effect, it seems more likely that larger landowners might have a larger number of dispersed parcels and hence that the degree of inequality might be understated somewhat by Table VII.1.[25]

Most studies of land tenure in Jordan have been based on statistics of holdings, as shown in Table VII.2. The issue of the efficiency of different holding sizes is difficult to determine since economists are not agreed on the effect of holding size on efficiency in agriculture. There is well-documented evidence from many LDCs that the larger is farm size the lower is average output per acre. Whether this constitutes an argument for breaking up large farms depends on the cause of the inverse relationship observed and on that there is disagreement. Explanations for the inverse relationship have included diseconomies of scale,[26] better land on small holdings,[27] and a variety of institutional or market failures.[28] The variety of explanations and the experience of land reforms do not yet permit any ready generalization about the effect of breaking up larger holdings on the efficiency of agricultural production.

The preceding paragraph discussed the possible inefficiencies of large holdings. Sometimes it is possible inefficiencies of small holdings which are stressed. If there were increasing returns to scale in LDC agriculture, the existence of small holdings might reduce agricultural output. Economies of scale often are imputed to LDC agriculture by a false analogy with agriculture in the developed countries. In much of U.S. agriculture the scarcity of labor relative to capital and land makes it efficient to spread labor over large farm units by the use of labor-saving, but indivisible, farm equipment; large farm units may be necessary to fully utilize farm equipment. In the LDCs labor-saving farm machinery generally is not efficient because labor is abundant.[29] Most studies of LDC agriculture do not find significant scale economies.[30]

In some crops at least, Jordan may be an exception to the generalization that scale economies are unimportant in LDC farming. Increasing demands for labor in Jordan's urban areas and in neighboring countries drew off potential farm labor and increased the incentive to use labor-saving equipment, primarily tractors and combines, in the cultivation of rainfed grain crops. To the degree that these had indivisibilities and could not be used to cultivate more than one holding, the existence of small holdings in Jordan's grain-producing areas might have been an obstacle to efficiency. However, in the dryland grain areas of Jordan a well-developed network of custom operators provided tractor and combine services for hire.[31] In some areas agricultural cooperative societies provided comparable services. Since these services were widely available and widely utilized, the existence of some comparatively small holdings does not appear to have been a serious obstacle to the utilization of such indivisible capital goods.

b. Fragmentation of Holdings

In some respects it is the size of fragments, rather than holdings, which may affect agricultural efficiency. An operator may have a single holding composed of several scattered fragments, often long strips running from top to bottom of a hill. This may reduce efficiency by the waste of time in travel between strips, greater costs of fencing, or boundary disputes, but it is not clear that such costs are significant.[32] Probably much more significantly, fragmentation may be an obstacle to contour plowing and terracing, which could alleviate Jordan's severe problem of soil erosion in the rainfed areas.

Fragmentation of holdings was significant in Jordan, and it was greater in the dryland areas, where its consequences may be more serious. For the East Bank as a whole in 1975, 49% of the total number of holdings were in a single parcel; the other 51% of holdings averaged 3-1/2 fragments per holding. For the two groups combined the overall average was about 2.3 fragments per holding.[33] There is little disagreement that the cause of the fragmentation is the partition of land upon inheritance.

In the East Ghor Canal project area land tenure legislation produced more consolidated holdings and restricted further fragmentation. As a result, in 1971 the average there was only 1.2 fragments per ownership. However, de _facto_ fragmentation exceeded this, because--contrary to the intent of the law--in ownerships which were jointly held by more than one owner the land frequently was worked by

individual owners in fragments smaller than the
legal minimum.[34]

The problem of land fragmentation as an obstacle to contouring may be attacked in two ways:
(1) reducing land fragmentation by such measures
as compulsory land consolidation or changing inheritance laws; (2) cooperation in cultivation among
farmers with adjacent strips. The evasion of minimum size requirements in the land tenure legislation for the East Ghor Canal area suggests that the
first option may not succeed, at least in the short
run. One survey of farmer attitudes in two villages
in the rainfed grain-producing areas found strong
opposition among farmers to both inheritance law
reform and land consolidation measures.[35] It appears that reducing land fragmentation is at best
an objective for the longer run, only after fundamental changes in attitudes have occurred.

In the near term the best prospect for reducing soil erosion through adoption of contouring appears to be by measures to promote cooperation in
cultivation among holders of adjacent strips. A
survey of 200 farmers in Jordan's major wheat-
growing area found that four-fifths would be willing to participate in collective tillage arrangements.[36] Since ignorance, as well as land fragmentation, is an obstacle to the adoption of contour
plowing, measures to promote cooperation in cultivation probably are best introduced as part of a
package of innovations. This strategy has been
adopted for several dryland farming assistance projects, applied to limited areas only, which have
been carried out by UN agencies and Jordan government bodies.

c. Forms of Land Tenure

According to the 1975 agricultural census, almost three-fourths of the agricultural holdings in
the East Bank were entirely owned by the operator.
Of the remaining holdings, some were entirely rented, others were partly owned and partly rented. In
total, roughly 15-20% of the agricultural land was
rented. Very little of this land was rented for a
fixed amount; much the greater part of it was sharecropped.[37]

The preponderance of sharecropping among farm
rental contracts has concerned some economists in
Jordan because of its alleged inefficiency. However the presumed inefficiency of sharecropping,
long taken for granted by economists, has been

155

strongly challenged in recent years.[38] The long-accepted argument was that sharecropping caused the tenant to apply insufficient variable inputs because he would receive only a fraction of their incremental output. The new "sharecropping is efficient" school asked why landlord and tenant would voluntarily adopt an inefficient contractual arrangement and observed empirical evidence that sharecropped farms were equally efficient as comparable farms under alternative tenure arrangements.

The new school of thought does not argue that sharecropping is invariably the most efficient form, but that tenurial contracts generally are made by economically rational persons, and in circumstances where sharecropping contracts are chosen they generally are the most efficient form of contract available. A variety of factors may affect the attractiveness of sharecropping. Sometimes the landlord and tenant provide certain inputs in the same proportion that they share in output. Sometimes the agreement may specify the level of certain inputs to be applied by the parties. In contrast to a fixed-rent tenancy, sharecropping permits the tenant to reduce his risk from crop failure by sharing the risk with the landlord.[39] Sometimes it is efficient for tenant and landlord each to specialize in different managerial functions; the provision of a share in output to each party gives each an incentive to improve performance. Reid argues that sharecropping may permit better adjustment to unforeseen changes during the year than would fixed-rent tenancy.[40]

The "sharecropping is efficient" view is not universally held.[41] Nonetheless, there is sufficient force to the argument that it cannot be presumed that sharecropping in Jordan is inefficient without empirical evidence. The evidence available from Jordan lends little support to the view that sharecropping is an inefficient form of tenure. Frequently, both landlord and tenant shared in the costs of many inputs, often in proportion to their respective shares in output.[42] Landlords usually visited sharecroppers frequently and production decisions often were made by mutual agreement.[43]

Two studies have computed net returns per dunum in two areas of irrigated farming in Jordan for several crops under owner-operation, sharecropping, and fixed-rent tenancy. In one study the highest returns by far were on the sharecropped farms.[44] In the other study the results were mixed with no evident difference between any of the three

156

tenure forms.[45] These studies might have been carried out more elaborately[46] and no comparable evidence exists for rainfed farming areas. Nonetheless, the burden of proof would appear to be on the advocates of legislation to restrict sharecropping agreements or to alter their terms. At present there is almost no evidence that such legislation would make a significant positive contribution to agricultural production in Jordan.

One form of tenancy legislation that might contribute to agricultural efficiency and growth would require upon termination of a tenancy that compensation be paid by landlords to tenants for unexhausted and unremovable improvements to the holding made by the tenant. Such a provision could be applied equally well to sharecropped and fixed-rent tenancy and might promote innovation and investment by the tenant. Such legislation should not be adopted without study of its feasibility and likely payoff in the Jordanian environment. Verifying tenant contributions in the courts, or other adjudicative bodies, may be practically difficult. And it is possible that the contribution to growth would be minimal, if the legislation simply causes the tenant to make the investments the landlord otherwise would have made. Nonetheless, such a measure at least seems preferable to commonly made proposals for legislation to require longer-term tenancy contracts, as opposed to the one-year (but frequently renewed) oral contacts currently widespread in Jordan. Requiring long-term tenancy contracts may reduce output by delaying the removal of an inefficient tenant and may cause landlords to switch from renting to self-cultivation using hired labor.

3. DRYLAND AGRICULTURE

a. Stagnation of Dryland Crop Production

Rainfed crop production in Jordan comprises a variety of crops, but wheat cultivation is much the most important. In the more arid areas, barley often is grown instead of wheat. Two- or three-year crop rotations are widespread and commonly involve wheat, lentils, and a summer crop, such as watermelons. Especially in the more arid areas, the cultivation of cereals may be combined with livestock production. In the hills, where rainfall is high and the land is steep, stony, and eroded, fruit and olive trees have been replacing crops. This section will concentrate on wheat, which constitutes about three-fifths of the total value of dryland crop production and which has been the primary object of the government's development efforts in the dryland areas. At the end of the section, we shall briefly discuss livestock production, primarily a dryland area activity.

Table VII.3 presents annual indices of area, production, and yield (output per dunum) of the three major dryland field crops.[47] The large size of year-to-year fluctuations in production and yield is striking. While these fluctuations may obscure underlying trends, it appears from the table that there is no discernible upward trend in area, production, or yield of any of the three major dryland field crops in the postwar period. Regression analysis indicates that when rainfall variation is allowed for, there was an upward trend in the production of all three crops during 1967-75, but in no case was the trend statistically significant.[48]

The stagnation in dryland field crop production in the postwar period is nothing new. Growth in grains and legumes was negligible for more than a decade preceding the 1967 war. The postwar stagnation especially invites inquiry because the efforts of the government and assistance agencies to promote dryland agriculture were intensified in the mid-1960s. Why, despite the professed intentions of policy-makers, has there been so little progress in dryland agriculture in the postwar period?

It is now well established that rapid advance in LDC agriculture cannot come solely from increased investment in existing methods or a reorganization of existing techniques, but requires the adoption of new technologies.[49] New crops, improved seed varieties, increased water supplies, new inputs--such as chemical fertilizers, herbicides, and pesticides--and other innovations have greatly accelerated agricultural growth in some parts of the less developed world. For the most part this has not happened in Jordan's dryland agriculture. In the past decade the most important innovations in Jordan's dryland crop production have been the adoption of mechanical equipment--primarily tractors and combine harvesters--to replace human and animal power. While these may increase output,[50] the lack of growth in dryland crop output suggests that their main effect may have been to somewhat reduce labor inputs in dryland agriculture.

There are many possible reasons why the adoption of new technology has been so limited

TABLE VII.3. INDICES OF AREA, PRODUCTION, AND YIELD OF
PRINCIPAL GRAINS AND LEGUMES, EAST BANK,
1967-75

(1967 = 100)

	Area	Production	Yield
Wheat			
1967	100	100	100
1968	97	48	50
1969	73	81	112
1970	99	28	28
1971	108	86	79
1972	99	108	109
1973	108	26	21
1974	109	125	114
1975	52	25	49
Barley			
1967	100	100	100
1968	122	31	25
1969	98	67	69
1970	70	9	12
1971	90	41	46
1972	104	54	52
1973	91	9	10
1974	111	63	57
1975	91	19	21
Lentils			
1967	100	100	100
1968	99	45	45
1969	101	81	80
1970	90	27	30
1971	90	86	95
1972	125	93	74
1973	106	20	19
1974	95	122	129
1975	65	21	33

Source: JDS, Statistical Yearbook, various years.

159

in Jordan's dryland crop production:

1. Appropriate new technologies do not exist because

   (a) new technologies have not been developed;
   (b) they have not been adapted to Jordanian
       conditions;
   (b) even if adapted, they could not be produc-
       tive enough in Jordan to justify their
       cost.

2. Efficient new technologies appropriate to Jordan exist, but are not sufficiently adopted
   because of

   (a) institutional obstacles, such as land
       tenure;
   (b) personal characteristics (e.g., illiter-
       acy) of Jordan's dryland farmers;
   (c) distorted prices, which make efficient
       technologies privately unprofitable;
   (d) inadequacies in the system of delivering
       new technology to the farmer (farm input
       suppliers, agricultural extension, agri-
       cultural cooperatives).

Most, if not all, of these factors have contributed to the absence of growth in dryland crop
output in Jordan. In the following paragraphs
these factors are examined. While it is impossible
to numerically measure the effects of each factor,
we may arrive at a rough idea of which are likely
to be more important and what they arise from.

Availability of New Technologies. The best-
known of recent innovations in LDC agriculture, the
so-called Green Revolution plant varieties, are not
applicable to Jordan's rainfed crop production because they require too great a water supply. Discoveries to date in dryland crop technology do not
promise such extraordinary grains, although gains
possible from some improved varieties in rainfed
production are hardly inconsequential.[51] Given
this and the extremely arid character of much of
Jordan's rainfed crop land, it would be unrealistic
to expect sudden and remarkable advances. Nonetheless, Jordan's dryland wheat yields are among the
lowest in the world, and some new inputs and
methods used elsewhere appear appropriate to the
conditions of Jordan's rainfed agricultural areas.
In part, the level of dryland crop cultivation may

160

be raised by achieving greater use of inputs currently extant, but under-utilized, in Jordan.
Chemical fertilizer is used by a small minority of
Jordan's dryland wheat farmers, even those in the
best rainfall areas,[52] and, where used, it is not
very intensive. Herbicides, almost unknown in the
grain-producing areas in the early 1970s, began to
be adopted on a significant scale in the middle of
the decade. Other innovations adopted elsewhere,
such as improved tillage practices, seed drills,
and rod weeders may be appropriate for Jordan.
    Wheat seeds used in Jordan are either impure
local varieties or breeds that have been well established for several decades. The use of cleaned
seeds treated with fungicide is an innovation that
has been widely adopted in the wheat-growing areas
of moderate rainfall and above. Government plans
have aimed to promote increased supplies of certified seeds of traditional varieties. But new
higher-yielding varieties are virtually unknown in
the wheat-growing areas. Although a program of
wheat breeding and testing has existed for years,
it has not made superior varieties available to the
farmer. Reasons for this failure to deliver improved varieties include lack of adequate research
personnel and field support, lack of coordination
and communication among researchers and with extension personnel and farmers, and failure to recognize
the increased need for improved varities as farmers
adopt other modern cultural practices to which improved varieties would respond better than the traditional breeds.[53] Both financial and managerial
resources have been deficient. Although it requires time, an adequate effort to develop new vari-
eties--building upon and adapting discoveries in
plant breeding outside Jordan--may have a substantial payoff and more so as farmers further adopt
other improved cultural practices in the future.
    It is not only seed varieties that need adap-
tation to Jordanian conditions. For other innovations, such as chemical fertilizer application and
moisture-conserving tillage methods, very little is
known about the practices appropriate to the different soils and moisture levels in different areas of
Jordan. Between 1967 and 1975 over 500 dryland
wheat demonstrations were conducted in Jordan, but
with minor variations all were based on only two
packages of new practices, one of which (clean summer fallow) appears economically unsuitable for Jordan. Practices demonstrated and recommended to

161

Jordanian dryland wheat farmers were based upon
those appropriate to eastern Oregon and Washington,
presumed to be climatically and topographically
similar to the major wheat-growing areas of Jordan's
East Bank. Since the individual components of the
package (including improved tillage, seed drill,
chemical fertilizers, herbicides) were not varied
between demonstrations, their separate contributions to increases in yield could not be determined, nor could their optimum input levels and how
they might vary with soil quality and moisture
availability. In particular, there is little knowledge for different soil and rainfall zones of the
optimal input levels of the various soil nutrients
or of the appropriate tillage practices and crop
rotations.[54]

Because of the high variability of rainfall,
it will require years of experimentation to determine the levels of application of new practices appropriate to the different parts of Jordan's dryland wheat-growing areas. Years also are needed to
adapt and develop high-yielding grain varieties
appropriate to Jordan. Because of both financial
and administrative shortfalls, adaptive research,
which typically has a high payoff in LDCs, in the
past has been one of the weakest links in Jordan's
agricultural development system.[55]

Although experimental evidence is limited,
there is enough information to suggest that some
recommended new practices should not be adopted in
Jordan because their returns do not justify their
costs. This is particularly true for the practice
of clean summer fallow, a moisture-conserving technique that has been recommended for rainfed crop
areas with very low rainfall.[56] Likely returns
from this practice evidently fall short of the high
costs of the numerous tillage operations required
and the loss of livestock forage on weedy fallow.[57]
Still unclear is the economic feasibility of the
seed drill, whose capital costs are high. It may
be desirable only in the best of Jordan's rainfed
wheat lands.[58] Conceivably, a simple, inexpensive
grain drill suitable for Jordanian circumstances
might be developed. In general, innovations which
are highly cost-effective in areas of good rainfall
may be economically irrational in the more arid
wheat-growing areas, where normal yields are so low
that even if an innovation doubled them the increased yield might not justify the cost of the innovation. In areas of very low rainfall the adoption of most new practices, including chemical fer-

162

tilizer and herbicides, has been nil.[59] In most
cases, the new practices probably are not efficient
in these areas. Moisture-conserving practices,
such as herbicides, are a possible exception.

Despite the unsatisfactory nature of the evi¬
dence, it seems evident that there do exist some
innovations that would be efficient in Jordan's
most important wheat areas and yet, as of 1976, had
been only slowly adopted and often insufficiently
applied. Chemical fertilizers and herbicides clearly appear to be efficient in areas of at least moderate rainfall and improved tillage practices may
be.[60] Why then were these innovations not more
widely adopted and more intensively applied?

Obstacles to Adoption of New Technologies. Institutional obstacles may hinder the adoption of
some improved practices, but they cannot account
for most of the shortfall in adopting new techniques. The small size, irregular shape,and fragmentation of many landholdings (see section 2 of
this chapter) may obstruct the adoption of improved
tillage practices by necessitating cooperative tillage arrangements among a number of farmers. Small
landholdings may hinder the use of indivisible
machinery with scale economies, such as tractors,
combines, and seed drills, but the prevalence of
custom machinery services substantially attenuates
this problem. Weaknesses in land tenure cannot
have been a serious obstacle to the adoption of
such highly divisible inputs as fertilizer and
herbicides. And since fertilizer and herbicides
are divisible inputs requiring only seasonal credit,
defects in agricultural credit institutions are unlikely to have seriously obstructed their adoption.
The widespread use of tractors and combines suggests that even for indivisible inputs requiring
long-term credit, deficiencies in agricultural
credit cannot have been a great hindrance to innovation.

Inadequate education and illiteracy may have
been an obstacle to the adoption of new practices
by Jordan's dryland farmers. Compared to other
LDCs at a similar level of economic development,
Jordan appears to have been about average in literacy and primary school enrollment rates. In 1960
in the East Jordan Valley, an area where new practices were adopted subsequently, age- and sex-
specific literacy rates actually were less than for
the 1961 non-nomadic rural population of Jordan as
a whole.[61] Several studies in limited areas of

163

dryland farming have shown high rates of illiteracy
(60% and up) among farm operators. However, many
of these farm operators were elderly and had liter-
ate grown sons participating in the cultivation of
the holding.[62] In conclusion, while the level of
education of dryland crop producers is less than
ideal, as it is in all LDCs, there is no evidence
that this impediment to development is more serious
than in other LDCs or more serious in Jordan's dryland crop areas than in its irrigated areas. Therefore, it cannot be considered a principal cause of
the poor development performance of Jordan's dryland crop production compared to other LDCs or to
Jordan's irrigated crop production.

Gotsch has pointed out that beginning in 1973
the Jordanian government's wheat price policy, by
distorting the relationship between prices for outputs and inputs, curtailed the incentive of wheat
farmers to adopt improved technology.[63] When world
grain prices skyrocketed in 1973 and 1974, the
government held down domestic wheat prices by subsidized wheat imports, supplemented by export controls, in order to hold down the domestic price of
bread. These measures were remarkably successful
in restraining bread prices,[64] but at the expense
of restraining the price for wheat received by
farmers.[65] While the domestic price of wheat was
held well below rising world prices, domestic input
prices remained in line with world prices, which
were also rising sharply. Consequently, the ratio
of wheat output to input prices declined. Using
fertilizer as an illustration, Gotsch showed that
at the prices prevailing for the 1973-74 and 1974-75
crop years the use of fertilizer was not very profitable for farmers even under optimistic assumptions about the impact of fertilizer on yields.[66]

Beginning in 1975 the wheat-fertilizer price
ratio became more favorable as world prices of fertilizer fell and domestic prices of wheat received
by farmers were increased. In retrospect, the
1973-75 episode appears to have been the temporary
response to remarkable and transitory circumstances
in world markets. The maintenance of steady retail
bread prices in urban markets may have been a politically astute measure and eased the burden of the
world commodities boom on the urban poor in Jordan.
Nonetheless, the episode brought about at least a
temporary setback to the efforts of government and
foreign agencies to promote the development of dryland crop production. Just when many farmers had
become exposed to improved practices through demon-

stration projects, government price policy sharply, albeit temporarily, reduced the profitability of adopting new technologies. As an alternative policy, part of the government's subsidies to bread consumers might instead have been used to further subsidize modern inputs to wheat production (there was in fact a very limited amount of input subsidization). A modest rise in the dinar price of bread could have been allowed; as it was, a constant dinar price for bread when wages and prices in dinars were soaring constituted a marked decline in the real cost of bread. In any event, the diminution since 1975 in the price disincentive against wheat inputs such as fertilizer promises some acceleration in the adoption of improved technologies over the near term.

The system for delivering new technologies and inputs to the farmer has both private and public components. In the private sector are suppliers of custom services and sellers of agricultural inputs. While several agricultural specialists have examined these sectors, it has been only in a very impressionistic fashion. In general, they conclude that suppliers of custom services (such as plowing, herbicide spraying, and combine harvesting) are competitive, but not fully informed of the best methods of using the new technologies.[67] Since custom operators often are farmers themselves, or at least rural residents, their need for more knowledge should be considered just a part of the general need in the rural areas for greater knowledge of new technologies. From this viewpoint extension and demonstration work should be directed at both farmers and custom operators. The impressions of specialist observers also suggest that private merchants of modern inputs (such as farm implements, fertilizers, and herbicides) are reasonably competitive. While they do not supply much technical assistance to farmers, as farm input suppliers in the U.S. often do, they probably are not a serious obstacle to adoption of new technologies in rural areas.[68]

The government's role in delivering new technologies to dryland crop producers has been handicapped by flaws in conception and execution. Demonstration efforts have been based upon the "package of practices" approach now widely advocated for the agricultural development of LDCs.[69] With the package approach a number of new practices are presented to the farmer to be adopted virtually simultaneously. The approach is predicated on the belief

165

that positive interactions among the separate components of the package are so great that innovations not very productive when adopted singly generate very large output increases (greater than the
sum of the parts) when adopted as a package.   In
Jordan as a consequence of this approach, demonstration wheat experiments in the dryland areas
each embodied five or more improved practices.

The drawback to the package approach is that
it is much more difficult to induce a small farmer
to adopt five or six innovations and apply them to
the optimal degree than to adopt them selectively,
singly, and gradually.   His reluctance typically is
well founded on high risk, high capital costs, and
the difficulty of learning enough to apply all the
innovations properly.   Where the interaction effects are strong enough, the package approach is
capable of overcoming these obstacles.   In the case
of Jordan's dryland crop production, it appears
that the new practices being promulgated in the
early and mid-1970s did not have sufficiently high
interaction effects to warrant a package approach.
Where irrigation and new crops or seed varieties
are to be adopted, the interaction effects are likely to be high, but neither was among the new practices being made available in the rainfed areas in
the early and mid-1970s.   Judging by the differences in rates of adoption of different components
in the wheat technology package,[70] it is evident
that they were being adopted singly and not as
parts of a package.

It appears that the adoption of the package
approach for new wheat technologies was inappropriate.[71]   The approach seems to have been based on a
false analogy with the agricultural development of
the East Jordan Valley, where the package approach
was considered to have been a success.   But the
situation was different there, where the irrigation
of new land necessitated new cropping patterns and
a variety of other innovations.   In the drylands
the presentation of new technologies in demonstrations as an inseparable package, although in truth
they were not inseparable, made it more likely that
the farmer would adopt none of the innovations, for
it was impossible for him to observe from the demonstrations the effects of any of the innovations
in isolation.   Another, and related, adverse consequence of the package approach was that its complex-
ity caused wheat project staff to concentrate on
the technical and management requirements of the
demonstrations to the neglect of communicating the

new package of practices to extension workers, let alone most farmers.[72]

For years the agricultural extension service has fallen short of expectations. Every one of Jordan's four development plans since 1962 has found the extension service wanting and called for its upgrading. Agricultural specialists have blamed its shortcomings on a variety of factors: an inadequate number of agents, low pay, insufficient training, lack of transport and materials, low status of agents' positions, and poor management.[73] Direct evidence of an inadequate system is seen in high turnover rates of extension agents and lack of contact between extension agents and most farmers.[74]

While the shortcomings of the extension service are undeniable, it would be a mistake to place on it much of the blame for the failure of dryland crop production to grow. Virtually all the shortcomings of Jordan's agricultural extension service are common complaints in other LDCs as well. It appears that the transplantation of agricultural extension, which has been so successful in the United States, to the very different environment of today's LDCs is by no means an easy task.[75] For the East Bank as a whole, Jordan's ratio of extension workers per farm (about 1:700) is greater than the average for LDCs (about 1:1600).[76] It is doubtful that expansion and improvement of the extension service should have been a high priority development objective (as in fact it was not). Evidence from India indicates that investments in agricultural research have had a much higher rate of return than investments in agricultural extension.[77]

In many LDCs failure of farmers to adopt new technologies has been blamed on the extension service, but in fact has been due to low profitability of the technologies the extension agent has to deliver. To an important degree, this has been the situation in Jordan's dryland crop-producing areas.[78] Some new practices were known, but knowledge of their best use in different areas of Jordan was lacking, they were made temporarily unprofitable by the government's wheat price policy, and--in cases such as fertilizer and herbicides--other channels of transmitting new practices to the farmer could substitute for extension. Agricultural extension has not been a critical bottleneck in the past and it is unlikely to become one in the future, at least until adaptive research begins to provide new technologies which are both profitable and demanding of agricultural extension for successful delivery to the farmer. Efforts to improve the extension service should continue in anticipation of the time when it may be a critical factor, but there is time and it cannot be considered a top priority project for the near term.

Agricultural cooperative societies can be an instrument for the delivery of new technologies to farmers, but in Jordan they played a minor role at least until the mid-1970s. In the dryland areas only about 10% of the wheat farmers were members of cooperatives in 1975. In the mid-1970s some agricultural cooperatives, encompassing a small minority of dryland wheat farmers, appeared to have made significant advances in promoting integrated technological change and increased production. On the basis of these limited successes and the presumed success of an integrated approach in the East Jordan Valley, the 1976-80 Five Year Plan made integrated development administered through agricultural cooperative societies the keystone of its program for agriculture. The agricultural cooperative society was to be "the basic unit from which the work of the agricultural extension agent begins."[79] The cooperatives were to be expanded to include as many farmers as possible and inputs, including credit, were to be channeled through them. Thus, however minor may have been the past role of the cooperatives, if the government perseveres in its professed intention to use them as the basic channel for disseminating new inputs and practices, their future significance will be great indeed.

The Jordanian cooperative movement, which has included both agricultural and nonagricultural societies, was essentially begun in 1952. For the next two decades most of the agricultural societies were limited to the function of saving and credit; i.e., they were merely rural credit unions. Generally, they were small and very limited in financial resources.[80] After the 1967 war several major and interrelated changes occurred in the cooperative movement and its role in agriculture. Beginning in 1968 centralized management and services for the cooperative system, previously dispersed among four functional bodies, were consolidated in a single agency, the Jordan Cooperative Organization (JCO). Second, although no great change in the number or membership of agricultural cooperatives occurred, there was a shift toward multi-purpose societies (see Table VII.4), which are more suited to the de-

168

TABLE VII.4. AGRICULTURAL COOPERATIVE SOCIETIES IN THE EAST BANK, 1968-75

	Multi-Purpose Agricultural		Agricultural Credit & Thrift		Other Agricultural		Total	
	Societies	Members	Societies	Members	Societies	Members	Societies	Members
Number								
1968	7	510	120	4,617	24	830	151	5,957
1969	19	610	107	3,959	17	602	143	5,171
1970	23	819	106	4,382	17	637	146	5,838
1971	15	1,068	104	3,352	19	683	138	5,103
1972	31	1,589	99	2,753	15	552	145	4,894
1973	23	1,749	84	2,222	17	525	124	4,754
1974	32	2,293	77	1,925	15	536	124	4,754
1975	66	4,654	28	717	9	365	103	5,736
% of Total								
1968	4.6	8.6	79.5	77.5	15.9	13.9	100.0	100.0
1969	13.3	11.8	74.8	76.6	11.9	11.6	100.0	100.0
1970	15.8	14.0	72.6	75.1	11.6	10.9	100.0	100.0
1971	10.9	20.9	75.4	65.7	13.8	13.4	100.0	100.0
1972	21.4	32.5	68.3	56.3	10.3	11.3	100.0	100.0
1973	18.5	38.9	67.7	49.4	13.7	11.7	100.0	100.0
1974	25.8	48.2	62.1	40.5	12.1	11.3	100.0	100.0
1975	64.1	81.1	27.2	12.5	8.7	6.4	100.0	100.0

Source: Jordan Cooperative Organization, unpublished.

169

livery of new practices.[81] Third, in 1975 the JCO began its first serious efforts to supply agricultural inputs (including fertilizer, seeds and seedlings, pesticides, herbicides, and equipment--often at subsidized prices) to member societies. Also in 1975 the JCO, in cooperation with the Ministry of Agriculture and the UNDP/FAO, began a project for integrated agricultural development of rainfed areas in the Irbid district, Jordan's major wheat-growing area. The project included cooperative cultivation of fragmented units, supply of new inputs, improved tillage and soil conservation practices, planting of fruit trees, and development of livestock production.

Since 1975 the cooperative system has provided a variety of inputs and services (often on subsidized terms) to members of agricultural cooperatives. Inputs sold to farmers at below-market prices included fertilizers, seeds and seedlings, packing materials, herbicides and pesticides.[82] Often cooperatives purchased equipment and rented it to members. In some cases (tractors, combine harvesters) the cooperatives were in competition with private custom operators; in other cases (seed drills) comparable custom services were not available. Although the cooperative system sees itself as cooperating with extension agents rather than performing the extension function itself, in fact the multi-purpose cooperatives--generally provided with both a manager and an agronimist by the JCO-- evidently carried out some technical assistance themselves as well. Cooperative societies provided low-interest loans to members; since the interest rates were below market rates the maximum borrowing permitted to members generally was limited to modest amounts.[83] Marketing of output has not been an important function of agricultural cooperatives in the dryland areas.

While economies of bulk buying account in part for the below-market prices of some services and inputs provided by the agricultural cooperatives, there also was a substantial subsidy element financed by grants and low-interest loans to the JCO from the government, the Agricultural Credit Corporation, the CBJ, and foreign donors. In addition, the government on occasion has provided inputs (such as fertilizers, herbicides, and cleaned and treated seeds) for distribution through the cooperative system, often at subsidized prices. The JCO in turn pays the salaries of the manager and agronomist of each multi-purpose agricultural cooperative and provides low-interest loans to the local cooperative societies.

The number of East Bank dryland farmers belonging to multi-purpose agricultural cooperative societies grew steadily in the years after the 1967 war and accelerated sharply after 1974. Although only about 10% of dryland wheat farmers were members in 1975, if the 1974-75 rate of membership growth were maintained, half would be members by 1980.[84] The acceleration in membership coincided with a large increase in the provision of subsidized inputs by cooperatives. It is unclear to what degree new memberships were attracted by the subsidies. The lowest rates of membership are in the marginal rainfall areas, where cooperatives are generally unavailable and where most new practices would not be cost-effective in any case. In higher rainfall areas lacking local cooperatives, some farmers would join cooperatives, if available.[85] There also is evidence that many cooperatives have failed to reach all prospective members and to explain themselves adequately.[86] Thus, there may be possibilities for further expansion of cooperative membership by establishing additional societies and by improving communications with prospective members.

Potentially, cooperative societies can enhance the effectiveness of other parts of the technology delivery system, particularly the extension service. In LDCs, where the ratio of farmers to extension agents typically is very high, the services of agents can be extended more widely by directing them through groups, rather than to individuals, as is the practice in the U.S. Extension services in some LDCs have been moving away from the focus on individuals to one on groups.[87] The government's promotion of the cooperative system as a focus for introducing new practices into dryland farming may be a means of supporting the research and extension service of the Ministry of Agriculture (MOA) by multiplying its effectiveness. This certainly is the professed intention of the new emphasis on cooperatives. However, the new reliance on cooperatives to promote dryland farming was partly motivated by dissatisfaction with the performance of agencies, primarily the MOA, that had previously been responsible for the development of dryland agriculture. The relationship between the cooperative system and the MOA, while intended to be complementary, is partly rivalrous as well.

If the strategy of channeling the promotion of

171

dryland farming through cooperatives is to be maintained, the challenge to the Jordanian government
will be to establish an effective working relationship between the two agencies. Alternatively, dryland development efforts may evolve so as to confer
the dominant role on a largely autonomous cooperative system, much as the semiautonomous Jordan Valley Commission has been delegated a dominant role
in the development of that area. The creation of
autonomous agencies, often able to attract away
the best of the civil service, frequently is com-
pellingly attractive as a means of sidestepping the
accumulated weaknesses of existing institutions.
However, the proliferation of autonomous agencies
has its own drawbacks, including overlapping responsibilities and lack of coordination of efforts.[88] In some circumstances, perhaps where the
task assigned to the autonomous agency is complex
and not highly interconnected with activities outside its domain, it may be worth the price; the
Jordan Valley Commission may be an example. But excessive reliance upon autonomous agencies runs the
risk of undermining established institutions with
a broader mandate, such as the MOA. Since a crucial missing link in Jordan's dryland crop development has been the adaptation of improved seed varieties and inputs to Jordanian conditions, a function which the cooperative system would be ill-
equipped to perform, it is likely to be crucial to
develop an effective relationship between the cooperative system and the MOA, which could provide
new practices to be adopted. In the long run measures to improve the performance of agencies like
the MOA are likely to be more effective than progressively delegating its functions to an increasing number of autonomous agencies.

Properly combined with the efforts of other
agricultural development agencies, the agricultural
cooperative societies may play a valuable role in
the development of dryland crop production. In a
society that is group-oriented compared to the more
individualistic farmers of, say, the United States,
new agricultural practices may be more readily
adopted if they are communicated to groups rather
than individuals. Cooperative societies may then
play a quite strategic communication role.[89] They
may be particularly valuable in securing cooperative tillage practices to offset the adverse consequences of land fragmentation. As previously noted,
they may multiply the effectiveness of the limited
resources available for agricultural research and

extension. In remote areas their role as supplier of inputs not otherwise available may be critical.[90]

While cooperatives have the potential to make a significant contribution to the development of dryland crop production, the very heavy reliance on cooperatives by the 1976-80 Five Year Plan raises a number of unresolved questions. Already noted is the question whether the cooperative system, the MOA, and other agencies promoting dryland development can establish an effective working arrangement. Given the limited resources to be provided to dryland cooperatives, the Five Year Plan's goals may be overambitious. If input subsidies to cooperative members are to be temporary, as has been planned, will their withdrawal retard--or even reverse--the growth of agricultural cooperative membership in the dryland areas? Might the recruitment of new members of agricultural cooperative societies run into diminishing returns? There may be an early phase when the farmers best suited to benefit from cooperative membership join the movement, after which additional members become progressively more difficult to recruit. Finally, is the potential of the JCO for promoting dryland agricultural development diluted by its responsibility for supervising nonagricultural cooperatives, such as consumer, housing, and crafts cooperatives?[91]

Conclusion. Why has Jordan's dryland field crop production grown so little and what are the implications for the future? Although Jordanian development planners and policy-makers have been preoccupied with the delivery system--especially the inadequacies of the extension service and the prospects for success of agricultural cooperatives--the principal obstacles to growth have been elsewhere. In the prewar period government efforts to promote dryland crop production were minimal. In the postwar period serious efforts were made to promote dryland agriculture. The failure of grain farmers to adopt new practices in the first half of the 1970s appears to be due primarily to two factors: inadequate adaptive research and price policies discouraging the use of modern inputs. Adaptive research failed to provide improved seed varieties suitable for Jordanian research and it failed to determine the appropriate level of use of new inputs and practices (such as fertilizers and new tillage practices and crop rotations) for different parts of Jordan's dryland area. And where modern inputs or practices might have been adopted, they were discouraged by a price policy which held down wheat prices while allowing input prices to rise. Since the disincentive effect of Jordan's price policy has been steadily reduced, there is some cause for optimism for the near-term future.

It is undeniable that the technology delivery system, especially the extension service, has serious limitations in Jordan, as it does in most LDCs. However, the new technology made available to the delivery system was limited and not fully adapted to Jordanian circumstances. And in any case, farmers were not well disposed to adopt the new technology because of the disincentives exerted by price policy. For the future, the government may continue to promote the development of the delivery system, but the danger is that it will concentrate its attention on this task to the near exclusion of an equally or more important function: adaptive research to develop new practices appropriate in different dryland areas of Jordan.

In the near term farmers may continue to adopt such readily understood practices as chemical fertilization and herbicide application. But the next breakthroughs are likely to take years. Time is needed to perform experiments to determine the appropriate use of new practices, including fertilization, in different rainfall and soil areas; where rainfall is as variable as it is in Jordan, an extra long period of experimentation may be required. New seed varieties will require time to be adapted to Jordanian conditions and produced in adequate quantities. Among the next generation of new practices (after mechanization, fertilizers, and herbicides) are likely to be new tillage practices. Not only will these require time for experimentation to adapt them to Jordanian conditions, but they make greater management demands upon the farmer and hence will be only gradually adopted. Here the delivery system may play a more important role.

Development policy-makers probably are wise to promote the development of the cooperative system in the dryland areas. The cooperative system is one of the more dynamic development agencies in the country and its early successes, though limited in area, provide some basis for optimism. The danger is one of overoptimism and overreliance upon the cooperative system. Early success in promoting the adoption of new practices often comes from adoption by the most progressive farmers in areas for which the new practices are best suited. Subsequent adoptions must come from more marginal farmers and

174

come with greater difficulty. Expectations based
upon linear extrapolations of striking early successes are almost certain to be disappointed. Even
if the cooperative system is very successful, it
can be only one of the instruments for promoting
dryland agriculture. Equally important, and here-
tofore neglected, is the system of adaptive research. The shelf of available new technology
adapted for Jordan's dryland agriculture is comparatively bare. Only when adaptive research has
made substantial additions to the technology available can the instruments for delivery of new technology, including the extension service and the cooperative system, be expected to play their full
role.

b. Livestock

Output from non-poultry livestock (mainly
sheep, cattle, and goats) has not increased significantly in the postwar period. Recorded growth
before 1967 was substantial, although there is some
question about the reliability of the statistics.
The prewar growth in output did not represent great
progress, as there was only limited change in techniques and the expansion merely added to livestock
numbers on rangeland that already was overgrazed.
Current practices in the raising of sheep,
cattle, and goats in Jordan fall far short of the
levels achieved in developed countries such as the
United States. It is common to represent this gap
between current and optimum practices as a potential for future growth. The real question, however,
is not the room for improvement, which is vast, but
the effort and time likely to be required to close
the gap. In the case of Jordan's dryland non-
poultry livestock sector, it may require decades
and something approaching a "cultural revolution"[92]
before practices currently recommended are generally
adopted.
Significant progress in non-poultry livestock
production in the dryland areas appears to require
the adoption of a particularly demanding package of
practices, including not only breed improvement and
better disease control but also a combination of
measures that together would constitute a revolution
in land-use practices.[93] Perhaps the easiest such
change in land use to bring about--and none too
easy at that--would be the incorporation of fodder
crops into crop rotations. More demanding yet is
the complex set of changes required for proper use

175

of pasture areas, of which the primary and indis-
pensible requirement is controlled access to range
land. As long as grazing areas are the common
property of all, overgrazing will continue because
individual livestock owners cannot benefit from
their own forebearance in the use of pasture land.
While the problem has been recognized in Jordan, no
effective measures have been implemented and it
seems unlikely that they can be, except over a very
extended period. The control of access to grazing,
which involves a significant alteration in long-
established bedouin grazing rights and practices,
probably will require major changes elsewhere before it can be established. The settlement of bedouin tribes--a gradual and costly process currently underway--would facilitate the adoption of controlled grazing, as would increased supplies of
animal feed from other sources, such as the irrigated areas or changed crop rotations in the dryland areas. Even when controlled access is
achieved, further innovations in range management
practices will be required. In particular, livestock operators will need to be taught to limit
their annual offtake of forage from range land,
leaving part of it ungrazed each year--a new technique which is likely to be adopted only gradually.[94]

In the past range lands in Jordan have been
diminished by the encroachment of cereal crops into
arid areas, which were ill-suited to them. The reversal of this process, with some of the arid lands
being planted to perennial grasses, could increase
the fodder supply and reduce soil erosion, but difficulties of administration and enforcement are
likely to make this a gradual process. Imports
are another potential source of fodder supply, but
except for poultry feed, this appears to be uneconomical.[95] The introduction of fodder crops,
such as vetches, clover, or sorghum, into the dryland crop rotation could increase fodder supplies.
The best near-term prospects for increased fodder
production probably lie in the irrigated areas,
where fodder acreage, particularly in alfalfa, has
expanded in response to attractive prices. The
Five Year Plan for 1976-80 projected a major increase in fodder supplies from this source.

Aside from measures to increase fodder production, the Five Year Plan's efforts to promote livestock production are limited principally to dairy
cattle and eggs. The emphasis may be misdirected.
Egg production, and in fact poultry production
generally, has been developing well on a private

basis. There is no evidence of any strong need for a semi-public company to (among other things) establish farms for egg production, as proposed by the Five Year Plan. Past and proposed efforts to develop the cattle industry have concentrated on increasing the numbers of Holstein-Friesian cattle for dairy production and, secondarily, for meat. There is general agreement that neither attempts to improve traditional cattle breeds nor beef production (except as a by-product of dairy farming) would be cost-effective in Jordan.[96] For raising dairy cattle, whose suitability to Jordan is questionable, it is doubtful that significant new government investment, as projected by the Five Year Plan, is warranted.[97]

The raising of sheep and goats received little attention in the Five Year Plan. Yet they contribute more to agricultural income than cattle or poultry, appear to have substantial prospects for development, and probably could benefit greatly from the proper sort of government assistance. Sheep and goats are more efficient meat producers than cattle in Jordanian conditions. Sheep herds may be improved by selective breeding improvement of the indigenous variety, while the goat population may be upgraded by increasing the numbers of improved breeds, particularly the Shami breed from Syria.[98] Both sheep and goat production may be expanded by the adoption of better fattening programs; partly due to ignorance traditional livestock producers typically underfeed their animals in order to maintain excessive numbers. Veterinary services also have much room for expansion and improvement. These needs provide ample opportunity for government-supported technical assistance.

In summary, the ultimate development of dryland livestock production will require revolutionary changes, which can only be implemented gradually over a period of decades. Development policy should promote measures, such as bedouin settlement, with this long-range objective in view. Measures with a shorter-term impact also are called for, but the Five Year Plan's emphasis on cattle and poultry should be at least partially redirected toward sheep and goat production.

4. IRRIGATED AGRICULTURE

The story of the development of irrigated agriculture in Jordan, which is largely the story of irrigation in the Jordan Valley, is in three chap-

177

ters: (1) a major development, the East Ghor Canal project, in the years preceding the 1967 war; (2) almost a decade of potential progress lost to internal and external conflict; (3) a resumption of Jordan Valley irrigation development with ambitious plans to increase irrigated acreage and output there several-fold in the future. Thus, the most important part of the story lies in the future, and the recent history of the irrigated area cannot be much of a guide.

Agriculture in the Jordan Valley on the eve of the 1967 Middle East war has been studied in detail by three sample surveys.[99] Compared to rainfed agriculture in the uplands, Jordan Valley agriculture--predominantly under irrigation--involved greater use of modern methods, including chemical fertilizers, pesticides, and fungicides, imported certified vegetable seeds, and more intensive land preparation. Very few farm operators in the Jordan Valley were engaged in off-farm employment, and employment of hired labor on farms was nearly universal. Vegetables, particularly tomatoes, predominated in the crop mix, but 30% of the cultivated area was devoted to wheat, primarily for home consumption. Because of their high water requirements, citrus fruit and bananas were limited to only about 10% of the cultivated area, but provided almost 30% of net income from crops in the immediate prewar years. Animal husbandry was of negligible importance.[100]

Irrigated yields in the Jordan Valley were comparable to those in other LDCs, but well short of maximum achievable yields.[101] In part, this was because the East Ghor Canal project had not been fully realized by the time of the 1967 war; in particular, many citrus trees, which normally require 10-15 years to reach maximum bearing potential, were only recently planted. Aside from this prospect, there was in the immediately prewar period also considerable scope for improved practices, such as better water management and the use of herbicides.

The original East Ghor Canal project was intended to be only the first part of an ambitious project to produce electricity and increase the land irrigated in the Jordan Valley: the Yarmouk project. The other important components of the Yarmouk project were the following: (1) construction of two dams on the Yarmouk River and two power plants, providing water for irrigation and hydroelectric power; (2) raising the sides of the exist-

178

ing East Ghor Canal to accommodate a larger flow
and construction of an extension running 40 kilo-
meters southward to the Dead Sea; (3) construction
of a 47-kilometer West Ghor Canal running parallel
to the Jordan River on its west bank southward to
the Dead Sea together with a siphon across the
Jordan River to connect the West Ghor Canal with a
60-kilometer canal to be constructed on the east
bank parallel to the existing East Ghor Canal; (4)
construction of seven dams to regulate the seasonal
flow of seven perennial streams (side wadis) flowing into the Jordan Valley from the east; (5) construction of nine pumping stations to provide water
to irrigable lands above the level of the two main
canals; (6) land improvement and construction of
lateral canals and flood protection and drainage
facilities in the area to be irrigated by the foregoing projects.

In the original 1955 plan for the Yarmouk project, the East Ghor Canal accounted for only about
one-fourth of the total area to be irrigated and
one-tenth of the total project cost.[102] The 1967
Middle East war interrupted the progress of the
Yarmouk project. In addition to the East Ghor
Canal project itself, only the construction of
three side wadi dams and the raising of the sides
of the East Ghor Canal had been completed by
1968. Construction of the Khalid Ibn El-Walid Dam,
one of the two proposed Yarmouk River dams, was begun in early 1967, but was halted by the Israeli
occupation of Syrian land on the opposite bank of
the Yarmouk River.

After the 1967 war the East Jordan Valley
(EJV) was increasingly used by the growing Palestinian commando movement. Israeli reprisal at-
tacks and shellings seriously damaged the East Ghor
Canal and destroyed buildings and fruit trees.
Agricultural activity in the EJV was greatly
diminished as most of the population sought refuge
in the highlands of the East Bank. In 1970 and
1971 the area was the scene of battles between Jordanian troops and Palestinian commandos. Not until
mid-1971 was peace restored to the EJV and its rehabilitation begun. Members of the EJV population
who had fled the fighting there gradually returned
after 1971. In 1973 the population of the EJV
reached 64,000--probably still a little below its
level on the eve of the 1967 Middle East war.[103]

In 1972 the government prepared the 1974-75
three-year plan for the rehabilitation and development of the EJV. In the following year it created

the Jordan Valley Commission (JVC) as an autonomous
agency with overall responsibility for the development of the Jordan Valley--responsibility which
previously had been divided among a number of
government agencies, including the Jordan River and
Tributaries Regional Corporation, Natural Resources
Authority, and the Ministry of Agriculture. The
1973-75 plan for the Jordan Valley was to have begun development of the area on an integrated basis.
As it happened, very little of the plan, which was
conceived hastily after peace was restored to the
Jordan Valley, could be implemented within the plan
period. For most of the plan's projects, construction did not even begin during the plan period. For
the most part, the JVC's activities during the
1973-75 period were confined to planning, design,
and award of contracts. Among the causes cited for
the failure to implement the plan on schedule were
the JVC's lack of experience, problems of coordi-
nating the JVC with other cooperating agencies, and
the unexpected acceleration of worldwide inflation.[104] Perhaps also the plan was simply unrealis-
tically ambitious.

In 1975 the JVC issued a Jordan Valley Development Plan for 1975-82, which was intended to triple
the irrigated area in the EJV.[105] The 1975-82 plan
contained uncompleted projects of the 1972-75 plan,
including the King Talal Dam on the Jordan River--
much the most important of the side wadi dam projects. The area expected to be irrigated by water
from the King Talal Dam equals roughly a sixth of
the total of 36,000 hectares expected to be irrigated in the EJV by 1982; it is about half the size
of the area irrigated by the original East Ghor irrigation project. All the projects carried over
from the 1972-75 plan were due to be completed no
later than 1977.

The major new project in the 1975-82 plan and
the single biggest project in the history of Jordan
Valley development is the Maqarin Dam on the Yarmouk River. It is expected to irrigate almost
15,000 hectares, or about 42% of the 1982 total
anticipated irrigated area in the East Jordan Valley. The dam will store Yarmouk River water during
the winter months of high water flow for use during
the summer. The project includes a hydroelectric
power plant. The construction of the other dam
originally planned for the Yarmouk River was halted
in 1967 by the Israeli occupation of the opposite
bank of the Yarmouk River and there are no current
plans for its resumption.

The 1975-82 plan calls for the adoption of sprinkler irrigation in virtually the entire irrigated area of the EJV. Since almost all irrigation was by surface methods in 1975, this requires the conversion of existing areas to sprinklers as well as their adoption in newly irrigated areas. The use of sprinkler methods is expected to reduce the loss of water in conveyance and field application from an average of 45% to an average of 20%. The use of sprinklers would also make arable some lands previously considered too uneven or sloping for cultivation, but the plan makes no provision for their irrigation during 1975-82. Aside from these areas, which may be as much as a quarter of irrigable land in the EJV, most of the potentially arable areas in the EJV are planned to be irrigated by 1982. The plan anticipates that an increase in multiple cropping will increase the cropping intensity from 106% to 132% of the cultivated area by 1982.

Although the irrigation projects proposed by the plan are scheduled for completion by 1982, they would not have their full effect on output until about 1987. The plan anticipates the value of EJV crop output in constant prices will rise by 300% between 1975 and 1982--most of the increase due to the new projects to be completed during that time. If the post-1982 impact of the projects in the 1975-82 plan is included, the total increase would be 346%. The increase in EJV GDP per capita, including the post-1982 impact of plan projects would be 123%--a much smaller increase because the success of the plan requires a doubling of EJV population between 1975 and 1982.

For the combined irrigation projects in the plan the JVC estimates an internal rate of return of 12.4%. If accurate, this rate of return would justify the investments, as the opportunity cost of foreign capital--currently abundantly available to Jordan for such projects--is doubtless well below that figure. The rate of return is probably slightly overstated, however. The JVC's estimate did not include projects that did not contribute directly to output, but may do so indirectly, such as road improvements, housing subsidies, schools, and health centers.[106] Of the total plan outlays about 65% were to be for irrigation projects. The other 35% were to be for transportation, utilities, social services, and housing--over 60% of which was for grants and loans to farmers for housing construction.

Since the 1950s, Jordanian agricultural policy has concentrated heavily on the Jordan Valley as the area of greatest development potential. In this it has surely been correct. The low-lying Jordan Valley is like a natural greenhouse with a winter climate much milder than neighboring upland areas; crops can be harvested there early in the year when there is little competition from other areas in Jordan or abroad. The potential payoff to irrigation projects in the Jordan Valley is greater and more certain than to most investments in dryland agriculture or livestock production. Past advances in agricultural research in both developed and less developed countries can provide new irrigated farming methods for adaptive borrowing.[107] In dryland farming the shelf of available new technology is not nearly so well supplied.

While the decision to concentrate heavily on the agricultural development of the EJV during 1975-82 is justified and the major irrigation projects chosen seem unexceptionable, some questions still need resolution. One obvious potential problem is the likelihood of delay in the completion of the projects in the 1975-82 EJV plan. This seems highly likely since most of the 1972-75 EJV plan projects fell far behind schedule, since the scheduling of projects in the 1975-82 plan is quite tight, and since the continuing boom in construction and shortages of labor in Jordan and nearby countries tends to delay the completion of projects. However, since the possibility of delays could be foreseen by almost everybody from the beginning of the plan, the plan's optimism in scheduling is unlikely itself to affect significantly the effectiveness of project implementation. Of course, a stretching out of the plan's timetable by, say, three years would imply significantly lower average annual growth rates for irrigated acreage and output than given by the plan.

Perhaps the most serious challenge to the success of the plan is posed by its need for a doubling of the EJV population between 1975 and 1982. Only about a quarter of the projected increase could come from natural growth of the EJV population; the remainder must come from in-migration. The plan projects a steady in-migration of 8,000 persons per year for five years from 1977 on, but this would still leave the 1982 population short of the target by almost 20,000. Furthermore, the assumption of steady annual in-migration between

1977 and 1982 seems quite optimistic, since most of the newly irrigated land will not be irrigated until 1982, and then only in the unlikely event that the plan is completed on schedule. The plan assumes that prospective high incomes in the EJV (planned to be higher in 1982 than for the country as a whole) and the improvement of housing and social services in the EJV will attract settlers from elsewhere in Jordan. Much may depend on the state of the labor market in Jordan's cities and elsewhere in the Arab Middle East; if the strong demand for labor continues into the 1980s, it may be very difficult to achieve the necessary migration to the EJV. If so, development of the EJV may need to be on a less labor-intensive basis with somewhat larger farm sizes. The JVC needs to prepare for such a contingency. Even if the required migration does take place, it is likely to come somewhat later than the JVC projects and will be further delayed to the extent that completion of the plan projects is delayed.

The plan for the EJV projects a major change in the cropping pattern between 1975 and 1982. Of the total cropped area, a quarter would be in fodder crops (alfalfa, berseem, fodder maize) by 1982. The increase in the share of fodder crops from a negligible level in 1975 to a quarter in 1982 would be roughly matched by a decline in the share of vegetables and citrus fruit. The increase in the share of fodder crops is predicated upon rapid expansion of livestock, and especially dairying, as planned by the government. However, the economic merit of the planned expansion in beef and dairy production has not been established.[108] The JVC needs to re-examine the optimal level of fodder production for the contingency that the government's planned expansion of beef and dairy production may be curtailed.

In 1974 the Jordan government established the Jordan Valley Farmers' Association as a primary instrument for the development of the irrigated areas in the Jordan Valley. Membership is compulsory for all farm operators in the irrigated areas of the EJV. Members of local councils and two-thirds of the Association's board of directors are elected by the members. The responsibilities of the Farmers' Association include supplying agricultural equipment, fertilizers, seeds, and pesticides; providing services such as pest control, harvesting, transportation, and marketing, and making seasonal loans to farmers. It is to cooperate with the Ministry

183

of Agriculture to determine cropping patterns and rotations.

In most respects, the Farmers' Association, as planned, resembles the cooperative system and it may evolve to be essentially the same.[109] Currently, when the Farmers' Association is at an early stage in its evolution, the planners' intention seems to be for the Farmers' Association to be somewhat more comprehensive, both in the range of tasks assumed and in the percentage of farmers covered, and to rely more on direct controls and compulsion.[110] There are justifications for adopting a more comprehensive and coercive approach to the development of a newly irrigated area: The new techniques are more complex and a greater departure from existing methods; farmers from outside the EJV and unfamiliar with agricultural practices there must be adapted to the new system; irrigation systems increase the interdependence--and hence need for control--between farms in the system. However, there are also limits to the extent of control that will be effective. Most importantly, the low level of development of Jordan's research and extension system limits the potential effectiveness of any comprehensive control system. When erroneous advice is more likely, it becomes less attractive to apply that advice comprehensively and on a compulsory basis. The JVC and the Farmers' Association may need to circumscribe more narrowly the spheres in which they claim competence to direct the development of the EJV. In its potential influence upon the course of agricultural development in the Jordan Valley, this choice of fields of operation may be one of the most consequential decisions to be made.

5. AGRICULTURAL MARKETING AND CREDIT

Until relatively recently, it was common to consider private agricultural marketing systems in LDCs as economically inefficient and monopolistic. The accumulation of research results from a variety of LDCs now suggests that this picture is more the exception than the rule.[111] These studies indicate that private agricultural marketing systems are generally economically efficient within the limitations set by a low general level of economic development, such as high transport costs and limited information networks. Monopoly power frequently is restrained by the fact that entry into the business of agricultural marketing is fairly

easy in most cases. Research on LDC farm marketing
systems is handicapped by many limitations in the
data available and there is no reason to think that
the new picture of private marketing systems applies everywhere without exception. Nonetheless,
these research results suggest that in the evaluation of particular cases the burden of proof probably should be on those who propose corrective
measures for a private marketing system they diag-
nose to be inefficient and monopolistic.

The information available on agricultural marketing in Jordan is not very satisfactory, but
such as it is, it does not indicate substantial
monopoly or economic inefficiency.[112] In one survey of dryland grain farmers, only 28% mentioned
marketing as a problem.[113] In El-Hurani's study of
wheat production in the Irbid district, no attempt
is made to test quantitatively the efficiency or
competitiveness of the private wheat marketing system, but his description of the system--based on
observation and interviews--depicts it as highly
competitive and efficient.[114] Typically, there were
numerous wholesale merchants and middlemen with
whom a farmer could deal, and if the farmer was un-
satisfied with the wheat price after the harvest he
could store it himself until later in the season.[115]
Thus, while the evidence available for Jordan does
not make a very strong case against the view of
marketing as monopolistic and inefficient, it certainly does not lend support to it.

Jordanian government intervention in agricultural marketing has been sporadic and inconsistent,
sometimes motivated by factors not directly connected to the system itself. Generally, development plans and policy have not subscribed to the
middleman monopsony view of agricultural marketing,
and probably rightly so. Yet briefly around 1969-
70 the Jordan Agricultural Marketing Organization
(AMO) established and operated in Amman a small
number of retail outlets for the sale of vegetables
on the justification of competing with monopolistic
retailers. The retail outlets, which were subsidized in a number of indirect ways, were unsuccessful and were ultimately halted--hardly surprising,
since if any sector of agricultural marketing is
unlikely to be monopolistic it is retail trade,
where traders are numerous and entry barriers low.
Subsequently, the AMO has played a fairly minor
role in agricultural marketing; among its activities
was a modest program of crop purchase contracts
with potato farmers, with the prospect for expansion

185

of the program to a few other minor crops.

The most important recent interventions of the
government into the agricultural marketing system
have been more an attempt to manipulate prices
than to alter the marketing system or the size of
marketing margins themselves. The adoption of
these interventions arose primarily from the sharp
rise in food prices in Jordan beginning in 1972 and
the brief army unrest in early 1974. The Department of Agricultural Economics of the MOA has the
authority to prohibit imports or exports of particular agricultural products. Each month it issues
a list of products whose export is prohibited and
others whose import is prohibited, but changes may
be made during the month as well. There seems to
be little systematic rationale for the prohibitions.
In months when domestic prices seem low and supplies high for a particular product its import
generally is forbidden and in the reverse situation
exports are likely to be banned. This may somewhat
reduce seasonal price fluctuations, which is not
necessarily a good thing. It seems likely that the
effect of these measures may be small, as they for-
bid importing at a time when it is likely to be unprofitable anyway and similarly for exports (assuming that seasonal supply fluctuations differ in
timing between Jordan and neighboring countries, as
for many crops they do).

Another measure that grew out of food price
rises and the 1974 military unrest was the creation
of the Ministry of Supply, whose single most important function has been to control the supply,
price, and marketing of wheat. The Ministry of
Supply cut the link between domestic and world
wheat prices by prohibiting the export of wheat
(except a small amount to northern Saudi Arabia)
and by buying wheat on the world market and resell-
ing it to local commercial milling companies in the
cities at a subsidized price well below the world
price. This policy had significant effects on the
marketing system. Trading in wheat by private merchants was sharply curtailed, as all wheat importing was carried out by government agencies, aid
donors, or charitable groups; wheat exporting
dropped to negligible levels, and the six large,
urban, commercial milling companies in the country
stopped purchasing domestically produced wheat in
favor of purchases at lower, subsidized prices from
the Ministry of Supply. In order to insure that
the subsidized wheat price was passed on to consumers, the Ministry of Supply controlled the price

of flour set by the commercial milling companies
and its allocation to commercial bakeries (mainly
in the cities), the price of whose bread also was
controlled. Domestically grown wheat largely was
limited to bread consumed by rural residents and
to livestock feed.[116]

The cooperative societies have not been active
in the marketing of agricultural products; their
limited marketing role has been largely confined to
input markets. In the EJV, however, it is planned
that the Farmers' Association, assisted by the AMO,
will assume a major role in the marketing of fruits
and vegetables. The Five Year Plan for 1976-80
calls for the establishment of four fruit and vegetable marketing centers to be managed by the Farmers' Association and of vegetable and fruit stor-
age facilities for the AMO. There has been no explicit statement of the rationale for these mea-
sures--whether they are intended to supplant private
traders in the performance of their traditional
functions or are to supplement them by the promotion of improved methods in such activities as
grading and the expansion of export marketing. The
latter role, that of introducing improved techniques, seems the more appropriate one, and parts
of the Five Year Plan suggest that this is the
planners' thinking. Yet the law establishing the
Jordan Valley Farmers' Association endows it with
the exclusive right to establish and operate wholesale marketing centers for the agricultural production of the Jordan Valley. This implies that the
Farmers' Association may supplant private trading.
Planners need to formulate explicitly and unambigu-
ously what the intervention of public bodies into
the marketing of EJV agricultural production is intended to accomplish, lest their measures impede
the attainment of their own unexpressed objectives.

A common picture of agricultural credit in
LDCs portrays the mass of small farmers as heavily
burdened by debt to landlords, merchants, and rural
moneylenders. Available information on the extent
of rural debt is fragmentary and dated, but what
information there is does not support this picture.
In the Jordan Valley around 1960-67, it appears
that most farmers did little or no borrowing and
that most of the borrowing which took place was
from government agencies, relatives, or friends,
rather than landlords, merchants, or moneylenders.
The 1961 survey of the EJV recorded a low level of
agricultural debt in 1960 after three successive
drought years. The total number of outstanding

short-term loans was 9% and long-term loans 7% of
the number of farm operators. Thus, at most 16%
(it will be less to the extent that operators have
more than one loan) of the total number of operators were indebted. The average loan size was
small, owner-operators did more borrowing than
tenants, and public agencies supplied more than half
the value of loans.[117]

The years 1961-65, during which the East Ghor
Canal project was completed, did not greatly change
the credit picture in the Jordan Valley, according
to sample surveys of the entire Jordan Valley in
1966 and of the East Ghor Canal project area in
1967. The proportion of farm operators using credit was greater in the 1966 and 1967 surveys than
in 1961, but it probably still was less than
half.[118] Of the total volume of credit, private
merchants, moneylenders, and landlords supplied
less than a quarter.[119] As in 1961, they were important only as suppliers of short-term credit;
long-term credit was almost exclusively the province
of public institutions.[120] The average value of
debt per farm debtor appeared significantly higher
in 1966-67, although this is partly due to substantial farmer debts to the government for land received in the land reform in the East Ghor Canal
project area.

No comparable evidence exists on agricultural
credit in the Jordan Valley after 1967 and very
little on other areas of Jordan. Since agriculture
in the Jordan Valley is very different from that
elsewhere in the country, credit conditions there
cannot simply be presumed to apply elsewhere. A
small sample survey of farmers in 1968 in a dryland area with fairly good rainfall reported that
76% of the farmers surveyed were in debt, with merchants supplying about half the value of credit,
while friends, relatives, and public agencies supplied the other half.[121] According to the 1975
agricultural census, only 11% of all agricultural
holdings in Jordan were financed by debt. However,
the way in which this was phrased--simply as
"source of finance," when many farmers must have
had several sources--casts doubt on the meaning of
these results.

If it is true that the use of agricultural
credit is low in Jordan, this is not necessarily
a good thing. A low level of borrowing may reflect
a lack of supply of credit, a lack of demand because sources of self-financing are adequate, or a
lack of demand because there are few profitable

investments available for which financing might be used. Our previous discussion of past agricultural development in Jordan suggests that the last factor probably is at least part of the explanation. The use of purchased inputs--whether financed by credit or not--is relatively limited in Jordan's agriculture and aside from newly irrigated areas and poultry production, few profitable innovations have been available for adoption. Thus, whatever insufficiency of agricultural credit may have existed cannot have been a critical bottleneck to agricultural development in the past. If Jordan's plans for accelerating agricultural development in the future are realized, agricultural credit may become a much more important component of the total development package.

The primary institutional sources of conventional agricultural credit are the Agricultural Credit Corporation (ACC), the cooperative societies, and the commercial banks.[122] Of these, the largest supplier of agricultural credit by a substantial margin was the ACC.[123] The ACC, a semi-autonomous government agency, began operations in 1960, replacing several lending institutions, whose loan portfolios it assumed. It raises funds from foreign aid donors, the government treasury, and the CBJ. Although legally permitted to accept deposits, it has not done so, on the grounds that its low interest rate on loans would not cover the interest rate needed to attract depositors from commercial banks. The ACC makes long-term, medium-term, and (since 1969) seasonal loans to farmers. Most were medium-term loans, some of which came to be long-term loans because of the ACC's policy of generous extensions and reschedulings. All its loans are intended to be supervised loans, although as a practical matter very small loans are not. Sometimes the ACC gives technical assistance with the loan, but this is generally limited and there is no direct link between the ACC and the extension system.[124]

All ACC loans are secured loans. While legally they may be secured by bank guarantees, the signatures of two guarantors, or shares of stock, in practice virtually all loans were secured by real property. In contrast, most agricultural loans from private merchants or moneylenders were unsecured.[125] Despite the security required, the repayment record on ACC loans has been poor.[126] Poor loan recovery performance has been common among institutional agricultural credit agencies in LDCs.[127]

189

The repayment record on ACC loans appears to be worse than that for similar institutions in other LDCs, but this may be explained by special circumstances. When the ACC was formed, it inherited the debt portfolio, including many bad debts, of its predecessor institutions. The 1967 Middle East war, the occupation of the West Bank, and the internal disturbances which ended in 1971 all impeded the collection of debts to the ACC, and the repayment record in recent years, although still weak, has been improving. In general, the ACC was very lenient in its treatment of overdue loans. It commonly extended loans due to special circumstances and rarely foreclosed on a mortgage.[128]

On medium- and long-term ACC loans the interest rate has been maintained at 6%,[129] which was well below the cost to farmers of borrowing from alternative sources of funds--9% on commercial bank loans and perhaps 20-30% on loans from merchants, commission agents, and moneylenders.[130] Because of the ACC's generous treatment of overdue loans and occasional forgiveness of interest on overdue loans, the true interest rate on its loans may be considered even less than 6%. Not surprisingly, demand for ACC loans on these very favorable terms greatly exceeded the supply.

In LDCs small farmers generally have less access to institutional credit than large farmers.[131] Based on the limited evidence of two surveys in Jordan, it appears that poorer farmers and tenant farmers have less access to ACC and other government-sponsored credit. One sample survey of tenant farmers in the EJV found that only 7% of those receiving credit had loans from government-supported agencies--the ACC or the cooperatives.[132] Another study surveyed 80 borrowers from institutional agricultural credit agencies (70 of which were from the ACC) and 80 borrowers from non-institutional sources (merchants, commission agents, moneylenders). It found the average farm income of borrowers from institutional sources to be almost twice that of borrowers from non-institutional lenders.[133] The primary reason that small farmers and tenants have less access to ACC credit probably is its security requirements and other criteria for creditworthiness. The red tape and long delays in ACC lending procedures[134] probably can be coped with more easily by larger farmers. In addition, it is possible that larger farmers may have greater political influence to exert on ACC loan decisions. All these conditions are common in other LDCs as well.

The fundamental approach of the ACC has been
to provide a limited supply of agricultural loans
in amounts well below the amounts demanded at the
very low interest rates it charged. Its limited
supply of credit has been rationed out among prospective borrowers in such a way as to favor larger
farmers. Because the loans are at subsidized interest rates, this amounts to a transfer of income
to larger farmers.

Like similar institutions in many other LDCs,
ACC policy, perhaps influenced by aid donors, has
overemphasized the cost of credit, when the more
important question is access to credit. When a
farmer is borrowing from non-institutional lenders
at 20-30% and then only on short term, and when he
may be able to adopt an innovation with an annual
rate of return of 20% and possibly much more, ask-
ing him to pay, say, 10% interest on loans is
hardly an unwarranted imposition, especially since
inflation in Jordan consistently has exceeded 10%
per year. Higher interest rates on loans may increase greatly the supply of credit available to
small farmers. At subsidized interest rates there
is a continual erosion of the ACC's capital, which
must be replenished by periodic infusions of funds.
Higher interest rates on loans not only could end
this erosion of the ACC's capital base, but could
allow its expansion by attracting deposits at competitive interest rates. Higher loan rates might
also divert large farmers to borrowing from other
sources, such as the commercial banks, whose
creditworthiness criteria they meet, leaving more
of the ACC's funds available to meet the credit
needs of the smaller farmer, who may not meet the
criteria of the commercial banks.

The adoption of a policy of higher interest
rates could make more resources available for lending to the smaller farmer, but the ACC should not
simply wait passively for borrowers to appear. It
needs to revise its security requirements and ease
its administrative requirements and delays, at
least on small loans, to make its facilities more
accessible to smaller farmers. Because many parts
of Jordan's agricultural sector have stagnated in
the last decade or so, agricultural credit--or lack
of it--probably has not been a critical factor.
But if the ambitious plans made for Jordan's agricultural development are to be fulfilled, improvements in the agricultural credit system may be
crucial for advance in both productivity and equity.
They may be crucial for productivity because many

of the new technologies to be adopted require substantial amounts of credit. They may be crucial
for equity because of the possibility that new
technologies will be adopted mainly by larger farmers, whose several advantages include greater
access to credit. To assure that new technologies
are adopted by small as well as large farmers, it
may be necessary to assure the access of small farmers to institutional sources of agricultural
credit.

NOTES

1. Compiled from data in Mazur thesis, pp. 63-65, 80-
82, 287-88, 292-94. Crop production data was smoothed by a
simple econometric regression to reduce the effect of rainfall fluctuations. In addition, the average for the beginning two years and the final two years of the period were
used for all data.
2. For details of the estimation of the East Ghor Canal
project's contribution to agricultural growth, see ibid.,
pp. 292-94.
3. See FAO Mediterranean Development Project, pp. 67-68;
and Oddvar Aresvik, The Agricultural Development of Jordan,
New York: Praeger, 1976, pp. 204-6.
4. See FAO Mediterranean Development Project, pp. 65-
66, 68-71; and Aresvik, pp. 192-202.
5. One indication of possible errors in the livestock
production estimates is the discrepancy between the numbers of
livestock estimated by the Department of Veterinary Services
(used in estimating national product) and the numbers recorded by the 1975 agricultural census. Compared to the census
estimates, those of the Department of Veterinary Services for
1975 were 36% greater for sheep, 47% greater for goats, and 33%
greater for cattle (JDS, Agriculture Statistical Yearbook and
Some Results of the Agricultural Census, 1975, Amman, 1976,
p. 67; and JDS, preliminary results of the 1975 agricultural
census, unpublished.)
6. The problem of overgrazing exists in much of the
Middle East. See Clawson, Landsberg, and Alexander, pp. 79-
80, 127.
7. Low slaughter weights are also due to the type of
animals raised; they are able to endure harsh conditions, but
are not of great fattening potential.
8. While some of the irrigation water in the Jordan
Valley at this time was from wells and from the Jordan River
itself, most was from perennial streams and rivers flowing
into the Jordan River.

9. JDS, The East Jordan Valley, pp. 138-39, 169-92.

10. I have computed two constant-price indices for East Bank crop production during 1967-75. Neither indicates any trend in output over the period either in the total or in the major sub-groups (grains, vegetables, fruits). Data from JDS, Statistical Yearbook, 1970, p. 108; and JDS, Agriculture Statistical Yearbook . . . 1975, p. 83. During 1967-75 there was no discernible upward trend (and there may have been a slight downward trend) in the numbers slaughtered of sheep, goats, and cattle, and the size of herds increased only modestly for cattle and goats, and not at all for sheep (ibid., p. 67; and JDS, Statistical Yearbook, 1971, p. 120).

11. Linear regressions in first differences were made with agricultural value added as the independent variable and the value added in the following sectors as dependent variables: nonagriculture; mining, manufacturing and electricity; transport; trade and banking; and public administration and defense. All variables were in current prices. In no case were statistically significant results obtained.

12. For example, imports of intermediate materials for use in manufacturing may be reduced, thereby cutting production in that sector.

13. On the statistical tests, see Mazur thesis, pp. 297-98.

14. Rural-to-urban migration cannot be determined directly because different surveys and censuses refer to populations which are not strictly comparable. One indicator of previous migration is the age-specific sex ratio. Since migration in Jordan occurs disproportionately among young and middle-age males, the proportion of males in the age group 15-54 can be taken as one rough indicator. This was 46% for the rural and nomadic population of Jordan in 1961 (computed from JDS, First Census, vol. I, pp. 58-59). For the agricultural population of the East Bank in 1975 the comparable figure was 47% (from JDS, 1975 agricultural census, preliminary results, unpublished). In both cases males outnumbered females in other age groups.

15. All numbers in this paragraph are derived from JDS, 1975 agricultural census, preliminary results, unpublished.

16. The holding may be owned, rented, or a combination of the two. The unit of holding may be smaller than the unit of ownership (e.g., if two or more tenants rented all their land from a single landlord) or it might be larger (e.g., if a small landholder increased the amount of land he cultivated by renting land). Both the unit of ownership and the unit of operation could be either in scattered parcels or a single consolidated unit.

17. It probably exaggerates the inequality of land ownership and holdings. In Jordan it appears where land quality and water supply are poor, the average area owned and operated is greater.

18. Solon L. Barraclough and Arthur L. Domike, "Agrarian Structure in Seven Latin American Countries," in Charles T. Nisbet, ed., Latin America: Problems in Economic Development, New York: The Free Press, 1969, p. 96; Doreen Warriner, Land Reform and Development in the Middle East, 2nd ed., London: Oxford, 1962, p. 30; and idem, Land Reform in Principle and Practice, London: Oxford, 1969, pp. 90, 142.

19. United Nations Development Program (UNDP)-FAO, "Dryland Farming: A Socioeconomic Study with Special Reference to Land Tenure Problems in Abu-Naseir and Mubis Villages, Baq'a Valley," report prepared for the Government of Jordan, Rome, 1970, p. 14; A. M. El-Zoobi, Socio-Economic Survey of the Operator Farmers in the Three Pilot Areas of the Project, FAO/Dryland Farming Project, Socio-Economic Studies Series No. 8, Karak, Jordan, 1973, p. 52; Ahmad Abu-Shaikha, "Land Tenure in Jordan: A Case Study of the Beni-Hassan Area," unpublished M.S. thesis, Department of Agricultural Economics, American University of Beirut, 1971, p. 58. The last study showed the distribution of ownership of only owner-operated land, but this represented 87% of the total area in the study. Since the data were presented according to different groupings in the three studies, interpolation was required to convert them to a comparable form.

20. Jared E. Hazelton, "The Impact of the East Ghor Canal Project on Land Consolidation, Distribution and Tenure," Royal Scientific Society, Economic Research Department, Amman, 1974, p. 32.

21. For details of the legislation see ibid., pp. 16-24.

22. E.g., the average size of land ownership was larger for the more arid area studied by Zoobi than the areas in the UNDP-FAO and Abu-Shaikha studies. If such an inverse relationship exists, land distribution within limited, homogeneous areas may give a truer picture of the distribution of wealth in the form of agricultural land.

23. The 1975 census was the result of an extensive data-gathering effort, which the JDS believes to have recorded nearly all agricultural holdings. Several checks were made on the farmers' estimates of holding size, including direct measurement of a random sample of holdings.

24. In the 1975 census about three-fourths of· all holdings and of the total land area were in holdings fully owned by the operator. Therefore, even though the census recorded holding units, it provides some check on the distribution of ownership units. The major discrepancy between the two sources is that the ownership data claim three times as many total ownership plots as the number of holdings recorded by the 1975 census. With three-fourths of the holdings entirely owned by the operator, these two sources could both be correct only if the remaining one-quarter of holdings were composed on average of pieces from nine different owners, which is highly implausible.

194

25. In a survey of the Jordan Valley in 1955 a positive relationship between land area owned and number of fragments was found. See FAO Mediterranean Development Project, p. 92.

26. Pranab K. Bardhan, "Size, Productivity and Returns to Scale: An Analysis of Farm-Level Data in Indian Agriculture," Journal of Political Economy, 81 (November/December 1973), 1370-86. Bardhan found decreasing returns to scale in rice production and constant returns in wheat production.

27. James A. Roumasset, Rice and Risk: Decision-Making among Low-Income Farmers, Amsterdam: North-Holland, 1976, pp. 85-96.

28. The literature is extensive. See especially William R. Cline, Economic Consequences of a Land Reform in Brazil, Amsterdam: North-Holland, 1970, ch. 2; Bardham, pp. 1379-86; Robert Mabro, "Employment and Wages in Dual Agriculture," Oxford Economic Papers, n.s. 23 (November 1971), 401-17.

29. In some LDCs measures such as subsidized credit and overvalued exchange rates with no tariffs on imported farm machinery make labor-saving machinery privately profitable where it is not economically efficient.

30. E.g., Cline (pp. 62-74) found constant returns to scale for most agricultural production in Brazil. See also footnote 26 above.

31. See Mohamed Haitham Mahmoud El-Hurani, "Economic Analysis of the Development of the Wheat Subsector of Jordan," unpublished Ph.D. dissertation in Economics, Iowa State University, Ames, Iowa, 1975, pp. 19-23, 102, 319-22, 326-27. El-Hurani surveyed the area around Irbid, Jordan's principal grain-growing region. Of the farmers he interviewed, 92.5% hired custom tractor operators (ibid., p. 102). He estimated that combine harvesters were used on 90% of the land which was sufficiently level for the efficient use of combines and that all the combine harvesting was done by custom operators (ibid., pp. 326-27). Since the timing of farm operations varies geographically, custom operators, especially of combines, sometimes operate in different parts of the country at different times of the year.

32. Abu-Shaikha (p. 68) performed simple correlations between land fragmentation and labor and seed costs, gross income from field crops per dunum, making fences around plots, land disputes with neighbors, and use of machinery on land. In no case did he find a significant correlation.

33. JDS, 1975 agricultural census, preliminary results, unpublished. The averages are approximate because I have calculated them from size distributions for a range using the midpoint of the range.

34. Hazleton, p. 37. Note, however, that this is not precisely comparable to the averages of fragments per holding in the previous paragraph.

35. UNDP-FAO, p. 5 and Table 7, p. 19. Of the landowners surveyed by Abu-Shaikha (p. 70) about half were unwill-

ing to exchange plots with other farmers in the area.

36. El-Hurani, pp. 130-36.

37. On the relative importance of sharecropping in different areas see UNDP-FAO, p. 13; El-Zoobi, p. 55; Abu-Shaikha, p. 37; Maurice B. Issi, "Socio-Economic Aspects of the Wadi Dhuleil Area of Jordan, 1973-1974," Economic Research Department, Royal Scientific Society, Amman, 1975, pp. 2-3; JDS, Social and Economic Survey of the East Jordan Valley, 1973, Amman, 1973, p. 144.

38. The pioneer was Stephen N. S. Cheung in "Private Property Rights and Sharecropping," Journal of Political Economy, 76 (November-December 1968), 1107-22, and The Theory of Share Tenancy, Chicago: University of Chicago Press, 1969. Among other supporters of the "sharecropping is efficient" hypothesis see Joseph D. Reid, Jr., "Sharecropping and Agricultural Uncertainty," Economic Development and Cultural Change, 24 (April 1976), 549-76, and Roumasset, pp. 69-79.

39. Risk may also be shifted from farmer to landowner if the landowner hires the farmer as a wage worker. However, inefficiencies of managing wage labor in agriculture often make this option unattractive.

40. Reid, pp. 570-73.

41. E.g., P. K. Bardhan and T. N. Srinivasan, "Crop-sharing Tenancy in Agriculture: A Theoretical and Empirical Analysis," American Economic Review, 61 (March 1971), 48-64.

42. Royal Scientific Society (RSS), Economic Research Department, "Agro-Economic Aspects of Tenancy in the East Jordan Valley, 1975," Amman, 1975, pp. 38-41. In another study (Abu-Shaikha, p. 76), which examined only three variable inputs—plowing, seeds, and labor—the tenant usually paid the entire cost of all three.

43. RSS, "Agro-Economic Aspects of Tenancy in the East Jordan Valley," pp. 41-46, 53-54.

44. Issi, pp. 18-28.

45. RSS, "Agro-Economic Aspects of Tenancy in the East Jordan Valley," pp. 55-76.

46. They failed to standardize for other variables (such as farmer's age or education or the size of the holding), which might affect net returns per dunum. They computed net returns per dunum on a crop-by-crop basis without allowing for the possibility of different crop mixes on different farms. However, the study by Issi (p. 59) shows the crop mix by tenancy form and it is evident there that different crop mixes do not alter his findings.

47. These are derived from totals for the East Bank and therefore include both rainfed and irrigated production. However, most production of each of these crops is under rainfed conditions.

48. For each crop regressions of output on time and rainfall were made for two alternative functional forms. In no case was the coefficient on time significantly different

from zero and in five of six cases the coefficient was less than its standard error. The estimated growth rates, although statistically insignificant, were all positive, ranging from 4-9% per year.

49. For a pioneering and classic statement see Theodore W. Schultz, Transforming Traditional Agriculture, New Haven: Yale University Press, 1964.

50. E.g., combine harvesting may reduce crop loss and produce a harvest of cleaner seeds, unmixed with dirt and weed seeds.

51. On the experience of improved wheat varieties in (mostly unirrigated) production in Lebanon see Brook A. Greene, "Mexipak Wheat Performance in Lebanon, 1970-71," Middle East Journal, 28 (Autumn 1974), 437-40.

52. El-Hurani, pp. 182-186b.

53. Eugene P. Winters, "Wheat Research and Extension Program in Jordan: Phase II," pp. 132-34; and Norman Geotze and David P. Moore, "Constraints of Adoption of Improved Wheat Production Practices in Jordan," pp. 196-97, both in Jordan Wheat Research and Production, final report of contract AID/sa-C-1024 between Agency for International Development and Oregon State University, 1976.

54. On the points in this paragraph see three papers in ibid.; David P. Moore, "Soil Fertility Research on Wheat in Jordan," pp. 55-68; W. E. Schmisseur, "Economic Evaluation of Dryland Wheat Technologies Introduced in Jordan," pp. 79-124; and Goetze and Moore, pp. 193-205.

55. Aresvik, pp. 229-35.

56. In this technique shallow tillages are used to control weeds and conserve moisture during a fallow year.

57. El-Hurani, pp. 253-61, 294-95; John D. Hyslop, "The Dryland Subsector of Jordanian Agriculture: A Review," Agriculture Division, USAID, Amman, Jordan, 1976, pp. 38-45, citing Schmisseur.

58. See Goetze and Moore, pp. 195-96; and Hyslop, pp. 46-47.

59. Compare tables 5.3 (p. 270), 5.7 (p. 287), 5.11 (p. 301) and 5.15 (p. 312) in El-Hurani.

60. Hyslop, pp. 38-41, 46-50; and Schmisseur.

61. For males 15 and over, 63% in the East Jordan Valley were illiterate, compared to 56.5% for rural (excluding nomads) Jordan in the 1961 census. JDS, The East Jordan Valley, pp. 47, 63; and JDS, First Census, vol. I, p. 124. If the East Jordan Valley could be compared with East Bank farmers only, the unfavorable comparison might not stand up, as West Bank farmers probably were better educated than those in the East Bank. In general, literacy figures for LDCs should be treated with caution.

62. Hyslop (pp. 60-61), citing El-Zoobi, has made this observation. In addition to El-Zoobi's study, Abu-Shaikha's study (p. 40) also found farm operators to be predominantly

old (65% over 40) and illiterate (about three-fourths).

63. Carl H. Gotsch, "Wheat Price Policy and the Demand for Improved Technology in Jordan's Rainfed Agriculture," Discussion Paper No. 2, Studies of Dryland Agriculture, The Ford Foundation, Amman, Jordan, 1976.

64. The retail price of bread remained constant from 1966 until 1975.

65. The Ministry of Supply established a support price for domestically produced wheat in 1974, but at a level well below world market prices. Sales of domestically produced wheat to the Ministry of Supply were small, probably because the support price (allowing for the unattractive arrangements under which the wheat had to be sold to the Ministry) was not much different from the domestic equilibrium price. It is questionable whether the price support program had any significant effect on the price of domestically produced wheat.

66. Gotsch, pp. 9-15.

67. El-Hurani, pp. 18-27, 318-27; and Schmisseur, p. 104.

68. El-Hurani, pp. 327-34; Schmisseur, pp. 104-5; Leonard Haldorson, "Availability of Goods and Services for Improved Wheat Production in Jordan," in Jordan Wheat Research and Production, pp. 162-92; and Hyslop, pp. 62-71.

69. For the Middle East generally, the package approach has been stressed by Clawson, Landsberg, and Alexander, especially pp. 162-63.

70. See El-Hurani, Chapters IV and V.

71. Ernest J. Kirsch, "Report to the Government of Jordan on Dryland Farming Extension Programs in the Irbid Project Area," draft, UNDP/FAO Project JOR/75/011, Amman, 1975 (mimeographed), pp. 12-13.

72. Goetze and Moore, pp. 200-201.

73. Kirsch, pp. 9, 24-25; Wael Kanaan and Yousef Attieh, Jordan: Agricultural Development, Jordan Ministry of Culture and Information, Amman: Jordan Press Foundation, 1974, p. 35.

74. El-Zoobi (p. 83) found that only 14.3% of the farmers he interviewed in the Karak area could identify their extension agent. The ratio of agents per farm in this area is somewhat lower than that for the country as a whole, however.

75. Uma Lele, The Design of Rural Development: Lessons from Africa, Baltimore: Johns Hopkins, 1975, Chapter IV; and E. B. Rice, Extension in the Andes: An Evaluation of Official U.S. Assistance to Agricultural Extension Services in Central and South America, Cambridge, Mass.: The MIT Press, 1974.

76. Number of extension workers from the Agricultural Extension Division of the Jordan Ministry of Agriculture, number of farms from the 1975 agricultural census, and comparative figures for other LDCs from Robert E. Evenson and Yoav Kislev, Agricultural Research and Productivity, New Haven: Yale University Press, 1975, p. 18.

77. Ibid., pp. 99-103, 157-61.

78. One piece of evidence is the reported fact that some farmers whose lands were used for demonstrations of new practices abandoned the new techniques when the demonstrations (paid for by the government) were terminated.

79. NPC, Five Year Plan, p. 146.

80. For a good discussion of agricultural cooperatives up to the 1967 war see FAO Mediterranean Development Project, Chapter 10.

81. While there was little net change in the number of societies, a number of new societies were formed, while some existing societies were consolidated, dissolved, or inactivated. Thus, one of the long-standing deficiencies of the system--the existence of small and weak societies--was ameliorated.

82. Another price incentive to farmers joining cooperatives was the cooperative system's purchase of seed from them for a price above the market level.

83. Haldorson, pp. 189-90.

84. Ibid., p. 190.

85. El-Hurani, pp. 336-38.

86. See Shawki Barghouti, "The Role of Agricultural Cooperatives in Improving Wheat Production in Jordan," working draft, The Ford Foundation, Amman, 1976, (typescript), pp. 24-27. Barghouti interviewed 199 farmers from 41 villages in the rainfed areas, 87 of whom were cooperative members. The sample was not a statistically random one, however.

87. Rice, p. 119.

88. On the problems of autonomous rural development projects in the rather different context of Africa, see Lele, Chapter 8.

89. Barghouti's preliminary work is directed at the question of the communication role of cooperatives. See especially pp. 15-19.

90. Haldorson (p. 172) believes that the fact that cooperatives are more active in areas distant from Amman (the primary source of inputs) suggests that input availability may be one of their important functions.

91. At the end of 1975 nonagricultural cooperative societies made up over half of the total number of cooperative societies and over two-thirds of the total number of cooperative society members.

92. The term was used by Clawson, Landsberg, and Alexander (p. 127) to describe only one aspect of the changes needed to achieve proper pasture management in the Middle East generally.

93. For an analysis of these matters related to the Middle East generally, see ibid., pp. 79-80, 125-27.

94. Ibid., p. 127.

95. F. Qushair and J. Hyslop, "Brief Analysis of Feedgrain Requirements for Livestock and Poultry Industry in

Jordan," [Amman] USAID/Jordan, November 3, 1975 (typescript). As the authors acknowledge, the calculations are very rough.

96. FAO Mediterranean Development Project, pp. 70-71; Aresvik, pp. 193-94, 202.

97. One project evaluation--of a proposed combination dairy-beef-forage production complex--estimated low prospective rates of return (7% on the most favorable assumption). FMC International, S.A., Executive Summary: Integrated Dairy-Beef Complex, Jordan, presented to National Planning Council, Amman, Jordan, 1975.

98. Aresvik, pp. 195-96, 200; Kirsch, p. 19.

99. Abdul Wahhab Jamil Awwad, "Agricultural Production and Income in the East Ghor Irrigation Project: Pre- and Post-Canal," Amman: United States Agency for International Development, 1967; Hisham Awartani, "Progress Appraisal of the East Ghor Rural Development Project," Cooperative Institute, Jordan Cooperative Organization, Amman, 1968; and Jordan River and Tributaries Regional Corporation (JRTRC), Jordan Valley Project: Agro- and Socio-Economic Study, Final Report, Dar al-Handasah, Beirut, and Netherlands Engineering Consultants, The Hague, 1969, especially Volume III, annexes E-H. The first two cover the East Ghor Canal project area only, whereas the last surveys the entire Jordan Valley, both East and West Banks, but with relatively heavy representation in the sample from the project area. The last study is particularly detailed.

100. Ibid., Annex E, pp. 17, 20-28, 69, 75, 85, and Annex H, p. 8; Awwad, pp. 19, 23.

101. JRTRC, pp. 40-46.

102. The original detailed plan for the Yarmouk Project was drawn up by two American engineering firms and presented in an eight-volume report: Yarmouk-Jordan Valley Project, Master Plan Report, Michael Baker, Jr., Inc., Rochester, Pa., and Harza Engineering Co., Chicago, Ill., 1955.

103. JDS, Social and Economic Survey, p. 8. An estimate of 100,000 for the prewar population is suggested in Jordan Valley Commission (JVC), The Jordan Valley Social Development Program: A Supplement to the Jordan Valley Rehabilitation and Development Plan, n.p., 1974, p. 4, but this may be on the high side.

104. JVC, Summary: Jordan Valley Development Plan, 1975-1982, Amman, May 1976, pp. 4-5, 35. On the 1975 status of major projects in the 1973-75 plan see JVC, Jordan Valley Development Plan, 1975-1982, n.p., November 1975, pp. A21-25.

105. See ibid. for the original document. Some subsequent revisions are incorporated in the less detailed JVC, Summary: Jordan Valley Development Plan. These two documents are the source for the succeeding discussion of the 1975-82 Jordan Valley Development Plan.

106. Good schools, health centers, and subsidized housing may be needed to attract migration into the EJV. Since such

migration is required to achieve the production goals of the plan, a part of these costs may be attributable to productive activities and should be included in rate-of-return estimates.

107. A new technique that began to spread rapidly and spontaneously in the EJV beginning around 1975 was the use of plastic greenhouses for vegetable production--a technique which had already proven successful in other countries.

108. See above, p. 177.

109. In the first election for the board of directors of the Farmers' Association in 1976, eight of ten members elected were officers of cooperative societies.

110. E.g., the Farmers' Association requires membership by all farmers in EJV irrigated areas; it is to engage in planning of cropping patterns and rotations and may have sub-stantial control over techniques as well; it may play a large role in marketing of inputs and outputs.

111. See, inter alia, Yujiro Hayami and Vernon W. Ruttan, Agricultural Development: An International Perspective, Balti-more: Johns Hopkins, 1971, pp. 264-69; and Uma J. Lele, "The Roles of Credit and Marketing in Agricultural Development," in Nurul Islam, ed., Agricultural Policy in Developing Coun-tries, New York: John Wiley & Sons, 1974, pp. 430-31; and the sources cited in these two studies.

112. See also pp. 73-5, above.

113. Abu-Shaikha, p. 99.

114. El-Hurani, pp. 28-32, 343-58.

115. The area studied by El-Hurani is the most highly developed wheat-producing area of the country. What he finds there may not be true of the more arid and less developed areas in the south, for example. But in such areas most grain is produced for home consumption in any case.

116. For a good discussion of these various measures see El-Hurani, pp. 39-44, 358-82.

117. JDS, The East Jordan Valley, pp. 268-75.

118. It is impossible to give a precise figure for the proportion of farm operators using credit, because both sur-veys report results for different categories of loans (e.g., short-term and long-term) only. Since some farmers doubtless borrow in more than one category, the correct proportions can-not be ascertained from the published reports. In the survey taken in 1966 the proportion of farmers borrowing in three different categories was 25%, 27%, and 39% (calculated from JRTRC, Annex E, pp. 119-20, 122). In the survey taken in 1967 the proportions in two categories were 25% and 35% (Awartani, pp. 78, 81).

119. Calculated from JRTRC, Annex E, pp. 119-21; and Awartani, pp. 79, 82.

120. JDS, The East Jordan Valley, pp. 270, 272; and Awartani, pp. 79, 82.

121. UNDP/FAO, p. 27.

122. This does not include credit from friends, rela-

tives, landlords, merchants, or individual moneylenders, nor the farmers' liabilities to the government for unpaid taxes or for land received in the Jordan Valley land reform area.

123. Of the total agricultural loans outstanding from these three sources at the end of 1974, 65% were from the ACC, 31% from the commercial banks, and 4% from the cooperative societies. CBJ, Monthly Statistical Bulletin, 13 (March 1977), Tables 12, 17; and Jordan Cooperative Organization.

124. For a good discussion of the ACC on which much of this paragraph is based see Thomas Stickley and Marwan Hayek, Small Farmer Credit in Jordan: A Country Program Paper on the Agricultural Credit Corporation of Jordan, Faculty of Agricultural Sciences, American University of Beirut, Beirut, Lebanon, 1972.

125. Of 80 loans from non-institutional sources surveyed by Dabbas, only 4% were secured by land mortgage, another 6% by a signed note only, and the remaining 90% by reputation only. Adnan Dabbas, "Lending Procedures Followed by the Institutional and Non-Institutional Sources of Credit in the Balqa District of Jordan," unpublished M.S. thesis in agricultural economics, American University of Beirut, September 1973, p. 42. Another survey found that only 28% of 29 farm loans from merchants were secured by land mortgage (UNDP-FAO, p. 29).

126. If repayments in advance of due dates are counted as receipts of payable amounts, then in the two years 1974-75 about 61% of total payable amounts were received by the ACC. For years the loan repayment rates published by the ACC were calculated in an erroneous way. Measured by this erroneous method, the figure for 1974-75 would be only 31%. I am grateful to Nureddin Taquieddin of the ACC, who discovered the error, for providing me with these data.

127. Lele, "The Roles of Credit and Marketing," pp. 422-23.

128. Stickley-Hayek, pp. 35-36; and Burhan Abu-Howayej, "Factors Affecting Delinquency in Repayment of Agricultural Institutional Loans in Jordan," unpublished M.S. thesis in agricultural economics, American University of Beirut, Beirut, Lebanon, September 1970, pp. 73 ff.

129. On seasonal loans the rate was 0.7% per month, with a small discount for repayment on schedule.

130. Little is known about interest rates on non-institutional loans in Jordan. An estimate of 20-30%, sometimes up to 40%, made by the Jordan Department of Lands and Surveys in the 1960s is commonly cited (see FAO Mediterranean Development Project, p. 100). Such rates would be roughly comparable to rates common in other LDCs.

131. See, e.g., Lele, "The Roles of Credit and Marketing," pp. 417-18, 425-28.

132. RSS Economic Research Department, "Agro-Economic Aspects," pp. 47-50. Less than 3% were from the ACC and a little over 4% were from the cooperatives.

133. Dabbas, pp. 36-37.

134. See ibid., pp. 39-42.

8
Industry

Although industry has always accounted for a
small share of total output or employment, it has
contributed significantly to growth during some
periods, particularly 1959-66. Nonetheless, the
industrial sector in Jordan remains more important
for its potential than its past or current role in
the economy. This chapter begins with a survey,
using statistical data where appropriate, of the
evolution of the industrial sector in Jordan, which
has occurred in four distinct phases since the formation of the country. Subsequently, it reviews
major policy measures which have affected the course
of industrial development and some prospects for the
future.

1. THE COURSE OF INDUSTRIALIZATION

a. 1948-58

When Jordan was formed after the partition of
Palestine, it was relatively underindustrialized
compared to other LDCs at a comparable level of income per head. During the 1950s, the growth of the
industrial sector did not quite keep pace with the
rapid growth of the economy as a whole, although it
might ordinarily have been expected to grow considerably faster. Throughout the 1950s the industrial sector was miniscule and its growth was of
marginal significance. This situation and some of
its causes (political instability, underdevelopment
of transport facilities and other infrastructure)
were discussed above in Chapter 4 (pp. 75-76). By
the late 1950s comparative political stability was
established and major improvements in infrastructure, especially in the road network and Aqaba port,
had been carried out. The stage was set for a

period of rapid industrialization, ultimately to be cut short by war in the Middle East in 1967.

b. <u>1959-66</u>

The growth of output in mining and manufacturing accelerated to an average annual rate of over 15% during 1959-66--almost twice the growth rate for GDP at factor cost during the same period. Although mining and manufacturing value added was only 7-1/2% of GDP at factor cost in 1959/60, it accounted for about 18% of the total growth in GDP between 1959 and 1966. By 1965/66 the share of mining and manufacturing in GDP had risen to about 11%. Compared to the typical pattern in LDCs, the rate of growth in mining and manufacturing in Jordan during 1959-66 was considerably greater than what would have been expected on the basis of increased per capita income alone.[1]

Table VIII.1, which is derived from data in current prices, presents sector-by-sector details of Jordan's manufacturing industry during the 1959-66 period. Presentation in this way, according to the International Standard Industrial Classification (ISIC) can be quite misleading. It is common to think of certain industries (most often ISIC sectors 30-38) as technologically advanced. On this basis, Jordan's manufacturing industry, which had a high concentration of manufacturing value added in these sectors compared to the average country of similar per capita income and a similar share of manufacturing in GDP [compare columns (2) and (3)], would be judged relatively advanced technologically and might be expected to be relatively capital-intensive. Yet if we look at the composition of these industrial sectors in Jordan, it is clear that they were mainly small-scale and did not involve technologically complex processes nor much capital equipment. Thus, "rubber and products" was simply tire retreading, "chemicals and products" was mainly production of soap and detergents, and "basic metals and products" included many small metal-working shops and goldsmiths. In 1966 average value added per establishment was less than $3,000 in rubber and products, basic metals and products, and machinery.[2] In ISIC sectors 20-29 also, small-scale, labor-intensive production prevailed. Value added in food manufacturing was mainly contributed by grain mills, olive oil presses, small bakeries, and confectionery shops. Most establishments in "clothing and footwear" and "wood

205

TABLE VIII.1. PERFORMANCE IN MANUFACTURING BY SECTOR, 1959-66

ISIC No.	Sector	Share in Manufacturing Value Added (percent)			Growth of Value Added, 1959-66	
		Jordan, 1959 (1)	1966 Jordan (2)	1966 Typical Country (3)	Average Growth Rate (percent per year) (4)	Share in Total Manufacturing Growth (percent) (5)
20-21	Food & Beverages	22.7	18.5 }24.3	49.3	12.5	16.1
22	Tobacco Products	5.3	5.8	6.6	17.2	6.1
23	Textiles	4.2	5.2	8.8	19.6	5.8
24	Clothing & Footwear	18.3	9.5	5.1	5.4	4.6
25-26	Wood & Products	11.4	9.2	.8	12.3	8.0
27	Paper & Products	.4	.7	3.9	27.6	1.0
28	Printing & Publishing	2.7	2.2	1.7	13.0	2.0
29	Leather and Products	.4	1.7	1.9	43.4	2.4
30	Rubber and Products	1.0	.3		0	0
31	Chemicals and Products	1.3	5.5 }19.5	6.3	41.9	7.9
32	Petroleum & Products	-	14.0		-	21.8
33	Nonmetallic Minerals	16.6	14.7	7.0	13.9	13.7
34-35	Basic Metals & Products	5.7	6.7 }11.2	6.7	18.6	7.3
36-37	Machinery	1.3	1.5		17.8	1.6
38	Transport Equipment	3.2	2.9		14.2	2.8
39	Miscellaneous	5.5	1.4	1.9	-5.2	-1.0
20-39	Total	100.0	100.0	100.0	15.9	100.0

NOTES

Columns (1), (2), (4), and (5) are calculated from current-price data in JDS, The National Accounts, 1959-1967, p. 34. Column (5) was calculated in the following way: For each sector, the absolute increase in value added in that sector between 1959 and 1966 was divided by the absolute increase in total manufacturing value added between 1959 and 1966.

Column (3) is calculated from equations in UN Department of Economic and Social Affairs, A Study of Industrial Growth, New York, 1963, p. 7. These equations give sectoral value added in 1953 U.S. dollars as a function of per capita income, population, and the relative degree of industrialization. The relative degree of industrialization measures the degree to which a particular country's industrial value added diverges from that predicted by its per capita income and its population. The calculations were made assuming the levels of per capita income, population, and relative degree of industrialization prevailing in Jordan in 1966.

and products" (mostly furniture) were small-scale, virtually handicraft, producers.

Although most manufacturing firms were very small (over 90% of the total number of establishments in 1966 employed fewer than 10 persons), a few firms dominated the sector in terms of production and value added. In 1966 two firms producing almost solely for the domestic market--the petroleum refinery and the cement plant--jointly accounted for 26% of value added in manufacturing. Another 10% originated in a vegetable oil firm, four cigarette plants, a tannery, and a firm producing batteries. Petroleum refining and cement production, two industries that are frequently important in early stages of the industrialization of LDCs, accounted for about one-third of Jordan's rapid growth in manufacturing value added between 1959 and 1966.[3]

Most of Jordan's manufacturing output (64% in 1966) was for final consumption. Only 31% went into intermediate uses, mostly outside the manufacturing sector. Jordan's inter-industrial relationships were few and of the most elementary kind, such as the sale of leather to the shoe industry. Neither production for investment nor production for export was important in manufacturing. In 1966 only 1% of the value of manufacturing output went directly into investment uses and 4% into exports.[4] Only for the battery company, and to a much lesser degree the cigarette plants, was production for export of any importance relative to production for domestic use.[5]

In Table VIII.1 the greatest discrepancy between Jordan and the typical LDC appears in the subsector of food and beverages. Although this subsector contributed over 16% of total growth in manufacturing value added between 1959 and 1966, this was not because the sector grew especially rapidly, but rather because it formed a large part of the total at the beginning of the period. Compared with the average LDC of similar per capita income and level of manufacturing development, however, the share of food and beverages in total manufacturing value added was exceptionally low in Jordan.[6] This is partly because of the small share of agriculture in the economy.[7] In addition, there is less need for preserving and canning of fruits and vegetables because of the availability of fresh produce from Jordan and nearby countries over much of the year. The disparity between Jordan and the normal country proportion seems too large to be accounted

for by these factors, but that is just a speculative judgment.[8]

The rapid growth of manufacturing value added
during the 1959-66 period was the consequence both
of increased domestic demand and of import substitution, but not of an increase in exports. The increased demand is the direct result of the 7% average annual growth rate of real GDP during the period.
There are several measures of import substitution,
and they sometimes give different results. Choice
between them is largely arbitrary.[9] One indicator
of import substitution is the change in the ratio of
domestic production to total available supplies.[10]
The increase in this ratio over time may be taken as
an indicator of import substitution. Table VIII.2
presents ratios of domestic production of manufactured goods to net domestic supplies (the value of
total sales plus imports minus exports). Comparison of columns (1) and (2) gives some indication of
the degree of import substitution in Jordan during
the period 1959-66. In all but the relatively unimportant paper and printing sector, the ratios
rose, generally by significant amounts. The ratios
for the foodstuffs sector probably should not be
taken as indicators of the role of Jordan's food
manufacturing industries; rather, the low ratios
may be more the effect of developments in the agricultural sector.[11] The tobacco products sector produced a surplus for export (as indicated by a ratio
exceeding 100%), so that the rise in that ratio denotes export expansion rather than import substitution.

In column (3) are presented ratios for the
average country at Jordan's 1966 level of per capita income and population, derived from cross-
country regression equations. Although there are
significant variations from sector to sector, overall Jordan appears fairly typical, even allowing
for the fact that the ratios in column (3) are
slightly understated.[12]

Some idea of the degree of import substitution
possible for a country with Jordan's population and
natural resources may be given by the ratios for
Israel in 1958 given in column (4). Jordan and
Israel were comparable in many respects. Both had
small populations (2.0 million for Jordan and 2.7
million for Israel in 1966; 2.1 million for Israel
in 1958), sparse mineral resources, and rather similar agricultural resources. Their locations are,
of course, similar, with Israel having better access
to the west. Both have had rapid population growth,

TABLE VIII.2. SHARE OF DOMESTIC PRODUCTION IN NET DOMESTIC SUPPLIES OF MANUFACTURED PRODUCTS, 1959, 1966 (percent)

ISIC No.	Sector	(1) Jordan 1959	(2) Jordan 1966	(3) Typical Country	(4) Israel 1958
20	Foodstuffs	41.4	48.3 ⎤ 61.6	85.5	87.2
21	Beverages	76.2	87.0 ⎦		102.8
22	Tobacco Products	102.3	109.1		98.0
23	Textiles	8.0	22.5	30.3	93.1
24,29	Clothing, Shoes, & Leather	40.6	63.1	69.8	102.4
25-26	Wood and Furniture	72.4	76.7	66.2	99.5
27-28	Paper and Printing	43.4	38.0	46.1	87.8
30-31	Rubber, Chemicals, and Products	15.7	25.1	35.6	78.2
32	Petroleum and Products	0	85.7	3.0	76.3
33	Nonmetallic Mineral Products	54.8	77.3	60.5	99.0
34-35	Basic Metals & Products	14.1	25.5	34.0	69.9
36-38	Machinery & Vehicles	5.9	9.6	10.8	54.1

Net domestic supply is defined as the value of all sales (including sales to intermediate users) of domestically produced and imported goods minus the value of exports. All values used are in current prices. Domestic production and exports are valued at producers' prices and imports c.i.f. Two manufacturing sectors are omitted from the table: miscellaneous manufactures and (for Israel) diamond polishing.

The ratios for Jordan were calculated from data in unpublished worksheets of the JDS Economic Section. The data for Israel are from Michael Bruno, Interdependence, Resource Use and Structural Change in Israel, Jerusalem: Bank of Israel, 1962, pp. 36-39 and Tables M-1 and M-2.

The typical country ratios are calculated from equations in Chenery. In Table 6, column (8), Chenery presents estimates of u, the proportion of imports in total supplies, calculated from cross-section regression equations for a country with $100 per capita income and population of 10 million. Using the same equations, I have estimated a new u (call it u*) for per capita income of $200 and population of 2 million. The ratios in column (3) are then 1-u*. Conceptually, this differs slightly from the ratios of the other three columns in that the Chenery equations exclude exports. Since manufactured exports are very small in most LDCs, the difference is undoubtedly of negligible importance.

211

large import surpluses, heavy defense burdens, and
unusually large service sectors. The major difference was in per capita income: Israel's GDP at factor cost was about $700 per capita in 1958, compared
to $200 for Jordan in 1966. The ratios for Israel
in 1958 may give some idea of the share of domestic
production in total supplies of manufactures attainable by a country like Jordan on the basis of supplying the domestic market alone. As measures for
this purpose, the ratios shown for Israel may be
slightly overstated; first, because exports are
netted against imports,[13] and second, because some
industries in Israel may have been overexpanded.[14]
These qualifications cannot affect the general conclusion from comparison of columns (2) and (4):
that Jordan in 1966 had by no means reached the
limits of import substitution in manufactures and
that further growth in manufacturing output based
on import substitution was possible.

Besides manufacturing, the industrial sector
includes mining, which contributed 15% of industrial value added in 1965/66. Of the mining total,
56% was attributable to stone crushing and quarrying, the remainder to the mining of phosphate, the
only industrial export of much significance. Although the phosphate was to increase in importance
when the world price soared in the 1970s, at this
time it was less important than either the petroleum
refinery or the cement plant, in terms of value of
production or value added.[15] A single company, with
majority government ownership, mined phosphate at
two sites, virtually all of it for export. Jordanian phosphate was exported both on ordinary commercial agreements and through government-to-government
bilateral trade agreements with such countries as
India and Yugoslavia.[16]

c. 1967-71

For the industrial sector the period 1967-71
was one of little overall development but of cycles
induced by changing political circumstances. Recession in the aftermath of defeat in the 1967 Middle East war was followed by recovery in 1968-69,
then cut short by civil war in 1970-71, with recovery beginning again in 1971. By 1971 the value
of East Bank industrial production probably was not
much different from its 1966 level when measured in
constant prices.[17]

The immediate impact of the 1967 war on East
Bank manufacturing was to cut off the West Bank

market. The imposition of high Israeli tariffs on
West Bank imports from the East Bank plus the elimination of barriers to trade in manufactures between Israel and the West Bank both diverted West
Bank purchases of manufactures away from the East
Bank toward sources in Israel. The effect is the
classic trade-diversion effect of the formation of
a customs union upon the trade of outsiders with
members of the union, here compounded by the exceptionally high level of tariff protection imposed on
the West Bank by the union. Of course, since about
30% of the prewar West Bank population fled to the
East Bank, not all the original West Bank market
was lost to East Bank industry, but those who fled
must have been mainly the more impoverished of the
West Bank population. The effect of the loss of the
West Bank market must have been most severe upon
those East Bank industries (such as the petroleum
refinery and the cement plant) with substantial
scale economies and limited prospects for exporting
their output. However, the domestic boom of 1968-
69--a largely aid-induced and somewhat artificial
one--picked up the slack in most manufacturing industries.

The civil war which broke out in September 1970
halted virtually all industrial production for a
month, and some industrial establishments suffered
physical damage. Manufacturing began to recover in
1971, despite the hindrances posed by closure of
the Iraqi and Syrian borders in that year. Phosphate mining did not begin to recover until 1972.
Although statistics on industrial capacity utilization are not collected on a consistent and unambiguous basis, there seems little doubt that most industrial firms were operating well below capacity
around 1970-72.[18] Viewed as a whole, the period
from 1967 to 1971 must be considered one of lost
time for industrial development.

d. 1972 and Beyond

As internal and external political conditions
returned to near normal in 1972, the growth of the
industrial sector began to accelerate. Between
1972 and 1975 current-price value added increased
at an average annual rate of 35%.[19] Much of this
represented increased price levels, rather than real
growth. The cost-of-living index for the four largest cities in the East Bank rose by an average
annual rate of 14.1% during the same period.[20]
Between 1972 and 1975 the average price of

213

phosphate exports (not included in the cost-of-living index) rose by 379%, while the actual tonnage exported rose by only 18.5%. Thus, the increase of 468% in the current-price value of phosphate was largely due to price increases, not increased production. If the tonnage of phosphates exported in 1975 had been sold at 1972 prices, the value of 1975 phosphate exports would have been J.D. 15.7 million less in 1975 than it actually was.[21] The recorded increase in current-price mining and manufacturing value added between 1972 and 1975 was only J.D. 29.0 million. Thus, higher prices for phosphates account for over half of the 1972-75 increase in industrial value added.

The rapid growth of current-price industrial value added between 1972 and 1975 cannot serve as a guide to future prospects. Much of the increase represented not real growth but inflation. While the rise in price of an export such as phosphate is favorable to Jordan in a way that price rises in a good produced and consumed at home are not, much of the phosphate price rise was only temporary, as a sharp decline in world phosphate prices began in the latter part of 1975. Of the 1972-75 industrial growth not attributable to inflation, a part--probably an important part--was due to a factor that could not be sustained after 1975, viz., the fuller utilization of existing capacity. Although no precise estimates are available, there is no question that there was considerable excess industrial capacity in 1972 and that little remained by 1975. Subsequent growth would have to be based on increasing the potential output of the industrial sector rather than utilizing the existing potential more fully.

It would be futile to compare in absolute terms the industrial sector in the mid-1970s with the 1960s. The intervening inflation, and the lack of data to adjust for it, make absolute comparisons in current prices meaningless. Comparisons must be limited to relative terms, which unfortunately do not tell so complete a story. Table VIII.3 shows the relative importance of different manufacturing sectors in total manufacturing value added for all Jordan in 1966 and the East Bank alone in 1967 and 1974. It should be remembered that East Bank production in 1967 was significantly affected by the war in that year. The censuses vary somewhat in their coverage and sectoral definition, which accounts for the low 1974 figures for footwear, wood and furniture, and perhaps rubber and products. When such statistical aberrations are allowed for,

214

TABLE VIII.3. SHARE OF MANUFACTURING SECTORS IN TOTAL MANUFACTURING VALUE ADDED, 1966, 1967, 1974 (percent)

	Jordan 1966	East Bank 1967	East Bank 1974
Food Manufacturing	16.0	19.1	16.8
Beverages	2.4	2.1	1.8
Tobacco	5.8	6.6	6.0
Textiles	5.2	7.4	8.4
Clothing	5.6	4.6	4.9
Footwear	3.8	3.6	.7
Wood and Furniture	9.2	8.3	3.4
Paper and Products	.8	.9	1.1
Printing and Publishing	2.2	3.7	1.8
Leather and Products	1.7	.4	2.7
Rubber and Products	.3	.4	–
Chemical Products	5.5	5.8	6.7
Petroleum Refinery	14.5	13.8	14.5
Nonmetallic Mineral Products	14.6	9.9	11.4
Basic Metal Products	6.7	7.5	14.7
Electrical Machinery	1.4	1.1	2.3
Transport Equipment	2.9	1.9	1.7
Miscellaneous	1.5	3.0	1.0

NOTES

Sources: 1966 from JDS, The National Accounts, 1959-1966, p. 78; 1967 from JDS, Manufacturing Industrial Census, 1967, p. 13; 1974 from JDS, 1974 industrial census, preliminary results (unpublished).

the overall pattern of the manufacturing sector
does not look much different in the three cases.
The smallness of the difference between all Jordan
in 1966 and the East Bank alone in 1967 and 1974 is
partly because the East Bank accounted for most of
the manufacturing production in Jordan as a whole,
so that the figures for prewar Jordan as a whole
reflect mainly the East Bank pattern. Since there
was relatively little industrial development from
1967 to 1974 little change could be expected between those years, and the differences shown may
largely reflect different degrees of underutiliza-
tion in 1967. The biggest change between 1974 and
the earlier years was in basic metal and products,
as a result of the establishment of a company fab-
ricating iron products.

Table VIII.4 indicates the relative share of
domestic production in 1974 total domestic supplies
of manufactured products. Trade with the West Bank
was negligible in all but two sectors, for which
two alternative estimates have been made. The "a"
estimates in Table VIII.4 are calculated by treat-
ing the West Bank like any foreign country. From
an economic, if not a political, viewpoint, this is
probably the more logical approach. Alternatively,
the "b" estimates are calculated by imagining that
imports (net of exports) from the West Bank were
actually produced in the East Bank. This is obviously untrue, but some supplementary measure is
needed to take account of the unique status of the
West Bank and its continuing relationship (especially nonapplicability of Jordanian tariffs) with
the East Bank.

Table VIII.4 may be compared with the similar
estimates for prewar Jordan as a whole in Table
VIII.2. Perhaps surprisingly, the overall degree
of import substitution, as indicated by the ratios
in these tables, was not much different for all
Jordan in 1966 and the East Bank in 1974. The
biggest difference, in nonmetallic mineral products,
was the consequence of unusual and temporary cir-
cumstances--exports of cement to neighboring oil-
rich countries undergoing a construction boom. The
ratios for the typical country comparable in income
and population are very similar in Tables VIII.2
and VIII.4 because the levels of population and per
capita income were similar for all Jordan in 1966
and the East Bank in 1974.

In conclusion, Tables VIII.2-4 indicate that
the overall profile of manufacturing in the East
Bank in 1974 was very similar to that of Jordan as

TABLE VIII.4. SHARE OF DOMESTIC PRODUCTION IN NET DOMESTIC SUPPLIES OF MANUFACTURED PRODUCTS, 1974 (percent)

Sector	East Bank 1974			Typical Country
Foodstuffs				
	a 50.3	a	58.5	
Beverages	b 62.0	b	68.6	85.0
	81.0			
Tobacco Products	128.3			
Textiles	32.9			29.8
Clothing, Shoes, & Leather	65.7			69.8
Wood and Furniture	64.7			65.8
Paper and Printing	32.7			46.5
Rubber, Chemicals, and Products	a 27.8			37.7
	b 33.3			
Petroleum and Products	87.3			2.8
Nonmetallic Mineral Products	107.6			61.4
Basic Metals and Products	29.9			34.5
Machinery and Vehicles	7.5			15.5

NOTES

See the Notes to Table VIII.2 for definitions and the method of calculation. The ratios for the typical country are calculated in the same manner as in Table VIII.2, but using a per capita income of $230 (in 1953 dollars) and a population of 1.75 million.

The ratios for Jordan were computed from data in JDS, 1974 industrial census, preliminary results (unpublished); UN Department of Economic and Social Affairs, Statistical Office, Year-book of International Trade Statistics, 1974, vol. I, New York, 1975, pp. 510-15; JDS, External Trade Statistics, 1974, and Israel Central Bureau of Statistics, Quarterly Statistics of the Administered Territories, VI (May 1976), 18.

a = net imports from West Bank treated as imports from abroad.

b = net imports from West Bank treated as domestic production.

a whole in the immediate prewar years. In part, this may be because postwar developments offset the effects of partition. Perhaps to a great degree it was because the pattern for all prewar Jordan was dominated by that for the economically more developed and industrialized East Bank and because there was little change in the manufacturing sector between the 1967 war and 1974. For industry as a whole, there was one major change: the expansion of phosphate earnings, due partly to output expansion but mainly to transitory price increases.

This was the state of Jordan's industrial sector when the NPC presented its Five Year Plan for 1976-80. It projected a five year growth rate in industry that far exceeded any previous Jordanian experience or the experience of almost any other country as well. Constant-price value added in mining and manufacturing was projected to increase by 220% between 1975 and 1980, or at an average annual growth rate of 26.2%.[22] The plan projections imply a gross ICOR for mining and manufacturing of 2.3 during the plan period--an extremely optimistic figure when it is realized that many of the planned new projects were highly capital-intensive and some projects would not begin production until after the end of the plan period.[23] The sheer volume of investment to be undertaken during the plan--29.2% of GNP, of which 30% was to be in the industrial sector--makes it unlikely that all the planned investment could be carried out and even if it were, the inevitable bottlenecks and shortages would elevate the ICOR above the usual level expected. The aggregative plans for the industrial sector are implausible. They are only a part, albeit a critical part, of an overall development plan which was overambitious and implausible. Further discussion of this question will be continued in Chapter 9, where the plan as a whole will be surveyed.

The Five Year Plan's ambitious aims for the industrial sector rested on a small number of relatively large projects. Most important was the expansion of phosphate exports from 1.1 million tons in 1975 to 7 million tons in 1980 while the price of phosphates (measured in dinars of constant purchasing power) was to remain near the unusually high level of 1974.[24] Assuming that value added in phosphate remains about half the value of total sales, this increase in phosphate export sales by itself accounts for almost two-fifths of the 1975-80 increase in industrial value added projected by

218

the plan. It was, however, based on extraordinarily optimistic projections of the future world demand for phosphates with no attention to the problem of marketing such an increase in output--an
area in which Jordan has been weak.

The single largest industrial investment
planned was a chemical fertilizer project to utilize lower-grade Jordanian phosphate to produce
triple superphosphate and monoammonium and diammo-
nium phosphate, mostly for export. On the face of
it, this would appear to be a very sensible investment. These are among the fastest-growing forms
in which phosphatic fertilizer is used. Because a
significant amount of bulk is lost in the course of
processing, production close to the source of phosphate rock is generally most efficient because it
saves on transport costs. The fertilizer project
was to be located at the southern tip of Jordan's
coastline near Aqaba. A possible danger is that
pollution from the plant might endanger the potential of Aqaba as a resort area.

Another project in the Five Year Plan was for
the production of potash from the Dead Sea. This
project had been bruited about for decades, but
when the plan was presented its economic feasibility still had not been firmly established. If undertaken, it would not begin production before 1982.
Other major industrial projects in the plan included major expansions of the cement plant and the
petroleum refinery, a textile factory, and a new
cement plant in southern Jordan producing mainly
for export.

In 1976 an Australian consulting team com-
missioned by the Jordanian government issued a report proposing a number of additional feasible
investment projects. These included poultry freez-
ing, sugar refining, a glass factory (which was already under consideration), lime products (viz.,
sand lime bricks and ready-mix concrete), and an
integrated, multi-product wood complex at Aqaba
using imported logs.[25] These represented the results of preliminary feasibility studies and would
require more thorough feasibility studies before
adoption.

2. INDUSTRIAL DEVELOPMENT POLICY[26]

To promote and shape the growth of the industrial sector, the government has used protection
from import competition, fiscal and credit incentives, and a limited degree of government share-

holding and direct regulation. Its approach may
be described as paternalistic free enterprise, more
paternalistic (and regulated) for larger enterprises than small. Paternalism has included protection
of domestic enterprises from foreign competition
by tariffs or import prohibitions. Further, the
government sometimes shielded existing firms from
domestic competition by granting monopolies or by
declining to issue investment licenses to potential
competitors. In the early and mid-1970s industrial
development policy swung perceptibly toward promoting more competition, and these protective
measures were eased.

a. Investment and Import Licensing

In a few cases the government's role in an industrial enterprise begins at its conception. For
some prospective industrial investments, generally
relatively large ones, the government may sponsor a
feasibility study, typically carried out by a foreign consulting firm and financed by foreign assistance agencies, such as the United Nations Industrial Development Organization (UNIDO). For most
industrial projects, however, the investor's first
official contact with the government's apparatus
of industrial promotion and control is the application for an industrial license from the Ministry of
Industry and Commerce (MIC).[27] Investments establishing new industrial firms or expanding existing
firms into new production lines require a license
from the MIC. Applicants for a license are required to submit accounting data on the prospective
investment, including financing, purchased inputs,
price and quantity of output, number and salaries
of employees. For large investments the MIC may
require the prospective investor to submit a feasibility study by a reputed consulting firm.
Until the early 1970s the licensing of new industrial investments was commonly used to restrict
the number of enterprises established. It had been
common to deny licenses on the grounds that the
sector in which investment was sought was "saturated." In practice, this can lead to excess profits and competitive slack among the existing firms
in the industry. Around 1971-72 the government began to approve nearly all license applications without regard to the number of firms currently in existence. Since then investment in "saturated" sectors has been discouraged only by granting it less
generous tax incentives under the Encouragement of

220

Investment Law (see below). Investment licenses
generally have been granted to small investment
projects within a day and to large investments projects within two weeks. The new policy, besides
promoting competition in domestic markets, was intended to stimulate exports by industries for which
the domestic market was "saturated."

Since the adoption of a policy of liberal approval of applications for licensing new industrial
investment projects, the effect on the economy of
the investment licensing process has been diminished. It is now rationalized as a form of manda-
tory technical assistance to prospective investors.
MIC spokesmen claim that their advice to prospective investors has dissuaded some from projects
which would have been unprofitable and persuaded
others to improve the design of their projects.
In the MIC's review of an application for an investment license, the primary consideration is the
likely future profitability of the project. In
this the MIC is in part trying to extend technical
assistance and in part trying to guard against the
danger that future losses by the new enterprise
will lead to pressures for government rescue, perhaps in the form of increases in tariff protection
or government purchase of shares. As a source of
technical assistance from the MIC, the investment
licensing process can be at best useful at early
stages of industrialization, when the economy is
simple and many investors unsophisticated. For the
future Jordan probably will require a more selective approach; a method of technical assistance
which tries to help all prospective investors
through a routine screening process may in the end
be of little help to any.

Prospective investors in industry are required
to obtain from the MIC import licenses for the import of capital equipment.[28] This requirement
applies both to investments not subject to investment licensing (expansion of an existing activity)
and those that are. The import licenses generally
are readily granted and once they are obtained the
required foreign exchange permits are granted automatically. According to the MIC, the primary reason for requiring investors to submit applications
for imports of industrial machinery is to provide
the government with information on industrial investment and production capacity that might assist
in the planning process. In practice, however, the
MIC made virtually no use of the information
gathered in this way and did not even compile it

in a systematic fashion.

The prospective investor in a new industrial activity must submit information on his investment to the MIC when he applies for an investment license and again when he applies for a license to import the necessary machinery. In addition, if it is a new company, the firm must be recorded with the Registrar of Companies in the MIC. Also, the typical investor will apply through the MIC for benefits under the Encouragement of Investment Law, for which he is required to submit information similar to that required for an investment license. In all, similar information is demanded repeatedly, and much of it is not used in any case. These requirements could be readily streamlined. Nonetheless, the requirements as they have existed cannot have been a very serious obstacle to industrial investment in Jordan, for the cost in unnecessary time and expense to most investors would appear to be modest. A more important cost may be the diversion of the efforts of civil servants to bureaucratic red tape from potentially more productive activities, such as expanded technical assistance to investors or more effective implementation of other regulatory measures.

b. Protection, Regulation, and Fiscal Incentives

The general level of tariffs in Jordan is low compared to many LDCs.[29] However, for Jordan the overall average tariff level may not accurately represent the level of protection accorded to Jordanian industry for two reasons: First, since industry in Jordan is underdeveloped, only a relatively small fraction of imported industrial goods competes directly with Jordanian industrial production. It is the duties on these goods which determine the level of tariff protection, and for some domestic industries (e.g., footwear, batteries, detergents, woolen worsted) the rates have been sizable (50% and more). Second, some of the most important industries have been protected by direct restrictions on imports, rather than customs duties. In some cases this is accomplished by forbidding imports except with special permission from the MIC; in other cases (e.g., the cement plant, petroleum refinery, and tannery) the single local firm in a product category has been granted a government monopoly over imports in that same category.[30] In the 1960s the degree of protection to domes-

222

tic industry tended to increase as protection was granted to newly established industries. In the straitened circumstances following the 1967 war customs duties were increased mainly to raise revenue. This did not always increase protection to domestic industries correspondingly because excise or production taxes on some domestically produced goods were also increased.

LDCs increasingly are coming to realize the high costs and other disadvantages of excessively high import protection, especially when it is achieved by direct quantitative restrictions on imports.[31] In the early and mid-1970s Jordanian policy moved somewhat haltingly toward lower protection and more reliance on tariffs rather than direct import restrictions.[32] This may be viewed as the international counterpart of the contemporaneous shift in investment licensing toward promoting more domestic competition. An important step in the policy of increased liberalization occurred in July 1976, when substantial tariff reductions were mandated on imports competitive with important domestic industries, including confectionaries, paints, batteries, toilet soap, textiles, woolen clothes, and footwear.[33]

In a few--but important--industries, price regulation, rather than the degree of protection, determines the domestic price. Any industry which is protected by an import ban or monopoly control over imports is subject to price control, and industries enjoying very high tariff protection may also have their prices regulated.[34] For industries subject to price control, the MIC carries out a detailed cost accounting and tries to set prices that will allow the domestic industry a rate of return on investment between 7% and 12%, over which there may be negotiation with the domestic industry.[35]

Economists studying regulated industries in the developed countries have identified a number of problems, including the difficulty of regulators accurately estimating industry costs and the incentives regulation often gives to the industry to adopt inefficient methods. There is no reason to think that Jordan has solved these problems where the developed countries have not. The policies adopted in the 1970s--less restrictive licensing; greater reliance on tariffs, rather than quantitative import restrictions, for protection; lower levels of protection--can, by stimulating greater competition, eliminate the need for regulation of some industries and alleviate the problems of regulating other industries. Nonetheless, in an economy such as Jordan's problems cannot be avoided simply by abolishing regulation. Even if the government does not directly regulate prices, it inevitably will determine domestic prices of many industrial products by its tariff and import restriction policies. In numerous Jordanian industries efficient scale of plant is large relative to the size of the domestic market, so that natural monopoly or oligopoly prevails. In such cases increases in protection beyond a certain point would simply increase monopoly profits at the expense of the consumer while decreasing domestic production.[36] Thus, an analysis of industry costs is unavoidable to determine an appropriate level of import protection.

Excise taxes are imposed on many of the most important domestically produced industrial products. They are levied largely for revenue reasons, for the excise tax pattern that has prevailed shows no consistent rationale in terms of resource allocation. While some goods commonly subject to excise taxes in other countries are also taxed in Jordan (petroleum products, alcoholic beverages, cigarettes), Jordan taxed some capital goods inputs (iron cable and bars, cement) and goods consumed by low-income groups (matches, soap, vegetable oil). The rationale sometimes given is that excise taxes are to make up for tariff revenue lost when domestic production replaces imports. However, there is no necessary reason why revenue lost on imports of one commodity must be replaced by taxes on domestic production of that same commodity; increased tax revenue from any source can accomplish the same objective.

Under Jordan's Encouragement of Investment Law potential investors in industry could apply to the government for tax exemptions.[37] If the project was granted the status of an Approved Economic Project, it was exempted from customs duties and all other charges on imported fixed assets, from income and social services tax on profits for a temporary period, and from building and land taxes for a temporary period. If the project was granted the lesser status of an Economic Project, it was exempted only from duties and other charges on its imported fixed assets.[38] In both cases expansion of an existing enterprise was also eligible for tax exemptions, although the temporary tax exemptions allowed were for a shorter period than in the case of a new project. Somewhat longer exemptions were given if the applicant was a publicly held corporation or if the project was located outside the Amman Governorate, in which most industry was concentrated.

The prospective investor seeking exemption applied to the Encouragement of Investment Office of the MIC, to which he supplied details of the project and documentation (including invoices and catalogs for the imported machinery for which exemption from import charges was sought). This was reviewed by technical staff of the Office, and perhaps after revision in the investor's application, the Office made a recommendation to the Encouragement of Investment Committee, composed of seven high-level government officials and four representatives of the private sector. The Committee, which met at least once a month, would decide the exemptions to be awarded. Its decisions, in turn, required ratification by the Council of Ministers. The recipient of any exemptions was required to submit annual financial statements to the Committee and to keep a record of all fixed assets imported under the exemptions.

The 1972 Encouragement of Investment Law is ambiguous and misleading about the criteria used to determine the award of exemptions under the law, but from the accounts of representatives of the Encouragement of Investment Office and Committee it is evident that some consistent criteria have been applied.[39] Perhaps the most important one was the size of the project. A large project was more likely to be awarded the status of Approved Economic Project, while a smaller project was more likely to receive the less lucrative status of Economic Project.[40] While most applicants under the Encouragement of Investment Law received at least the lesser status of Economic Project, investors with small projects generally did not apply at all, perhaps partly because they were deterred by the application requirements and partly because it was evident to them that very small projects were unlikely to be given exemptions.

The second important criterion in the awarding of tax exemptions has been the degree to which existing domestic firms already were supplying the local market. If the project represented an industry new to Jordan, it was virtually certain to receive the status of Approved Economic Project. On the other hand, if the domestic market was considered "saturated" by domestic producers, the project was likely to receive no more than Economic

225

Project status unless it was expected to export a substantial portion of its output. Expansion of an industry already highly profitable or renovation of an existing industry was unlikely to receive Approved Economic Project status and might receive no exemptions at all. Finally, status as an Approved Economic Project was more likely to be granted if the project was located outside the Amman Governorate or was undertaken by a publicly held corporation.

A system of tax exemptions for new investments may be administered in either of two alternative ways: (1) by automatic means, such as low or zero tariffs on capital goods regardless of the use to which they are put or by awarding exemptions automatically to investments that meet certain clearly specified and fairly objective criteria; (2) according to the discretion of officials, who attempt to distinguish between different investments according to subjective judgments based on more complex criteria. The actual system chosen may be anywhere on a continuum between these two polar cases. It is evident that in its Encouragement of Investment Laws Jordan has adopted a position close to option (2). This may be seen as another manifestation of Jordan's generally paternalistic approach to the promotion of industrial development.

Potentially, a system of awarding exemptions according to administrative discretion may permit more precise fine-tuning in promoting some actions and deterring others. Among its disadvantages are its more cumbersome administrative features and the greater possibilities for human error or favoritism. In the case of Jordan it is doubtful whether a discretionary system of awarding tax exemptions can be expected to realize the potential advantages such an arrangement might at best achieve.

In practice, the decision to award tax exemptions has been based partly on objective criteria: the size of the investment, whether it was outside the Amman Governorate, whether it was undertaken by a publicly held corporation. Where finer distinctions might have been made, there was little information on which to base them and they sometimes may have been myopic. There appears to have been a tendency to award exemptions more generously to investments in industries where there currently appeared to exist shortages or prices were rising rapidly. However, new investors in such sectors may receive supra-normal short-run profits on new investments, and additional tax incentives may

226

simply make more profitable, investments that
would have been undertaken in any event. Since
income tax exemptions under the law were for a
temporary period only, the exemptions would be particularly rewarding to new investors in an industry with temporarily high short-run profits. Yet
an industry with a more extended time profile of
profits may be more deserving of fiscal encouragement, because investment may be deterred by investor myopia, risk aversion, externalities of the
learning process, or capital market imperfections.

In a highly discretionary system of awarding
fiscal incentives, the decision-makers require a
substantial volume of reliable information about
the present and future shape of the economy as well
as the investment projects under consideration. In
Jordan much of the needed information has been
lacking and the deficiency is likely to continue
into the future. Especially since the 1967 war,
very little reliable statistical information on the
economy has existed. Nor do Jordan's development
plans supply reliable projections of the future
course of the economy.[41] Finally, because of the
openness of the Jordanian economy--its reliance on
foreign trade, foreign aid, and employment abroad--
its future development is highly dependent on unpredictable events abroad. For all these reasons
a high degree of discretion in the awarding of fiscal incentives seems inappropriate for the Jordanian economy.

If Jordan wishes to use tax incentives to promote investment, a simpler, less discretionary system may be preferable to the existing arrangements.
Instead of exempting certain users of capital
equipment from customs duties, it would be much
simpler to reduce or eliminate tariffs on different types of capital equipment regardless of the
user. This would allow small firms, which receive
almost no assistance from the government, to share
in the tax exemptions as well as large firms. It
would eliminate the necessity for procedures--ap-
plied under the current system--to verify that imported capital equipment was put to the uses originally designated in the application for exemptions. Under the existing system, the government
could tax a truck used by a merchant while exempting a truck used by a factory. This possibility
would be lost if the existing system were eliminated, but it is not evident that this would be
harmful. It is questionable whether any official
body in Jordan (or most other LDCs) can have the

information to make very informed distinctions of this nature between more and less deserving investments.

If temporary exemptions on income tax, social services tax, and land and building tax are to be retained, the criteria for qualifying for exemptions could be made more objective. They could be extended to all new firms, or a variety of benefits could be made conditional upon such objective criteria (currently used in a discretionary manner) as size, sector, and location of the investment. No judgments by high-level officials would be needed. For administration of such an incentive system, it would only be necessary to verify that the objective criteria were met.

c. Industrial Financing

Public policy measures directly affect industrial financing in several ways, most significantly through government purchase of shares, loans by the semi-public Industrial Development Bank, banking regulations channelling commercial bank lending to the industrial sector, and government assistance in arranging financing from domestic and foreign institutions. Other measures, such as the grant of monopoly or of tariff protection, indirectly may have a great effect on the ability of a firm to raise funds.

The Jordan government holds shares in industrial enterprises, hotel, transport, and tourism companies, electric utilities, and semi-public institutions such as the Housing Bank and the Industrial Development Bank. In the industrial sector its shareholdings ranged from a small minority share to nearly total ownership. Most commonly, government shareholding in an industrial firm originated with the inception of a new firm and was only one of several protection and incentive measures bestowed on the firm. It was generally believed that government equity participation made private investors more willing to subscribe to shares in the company.

As a matter of policy, government shareholdings are intended to be in industries with a significant impact on the economy and large capital requirements. In practice, however, the volume and distribution of government shareholding has been determined on a somewhat haphazard basis. In some cases the government has initiated or increased its equity ownership in order to assist firms in finan-

cial difficulty.[42] While many of the largest firms
had some government ownership, the government's
share varied greatly (e.g., 6% of paid-in capital
for the refinery, 45% for the cement company and
89% for the phosphate company in 1975) with no
consistent rationale evident, and some important
firms (e.g., in brewing, cigarettes) had no government equity participation at all.[43] A 1969 study
of industrial firms with government equity participation found no correlation between the government
share in ownership, on the one hand, and employment,
capital stock, exports, or value added, on the
other.[44]

The relationship between the government and the
firms in which it owns shares is necessarily somewhat equivocal. In some cases, the government
finds itself in the position of regulating the
prices of firms in which it owns shares. It is
common for government shareholding to be accompanied by other assistance, such as arranging loans
from other sources. In cases where there exist
competing firms, there may be understandable re-
sentment. Government participation can be, and
sometimes has been, used to benefit politically
influential private groups and to preserve incompe-
tent management or inefficient firms.[45]

The strongest justification for a policy of
government equity participation is based on the
infant industry argument: that despite more-than-
compensating social gains in the later years of a
project, losses in the early stages may deter investment because of insufficient investor foresight,
externalities in the learning process, risk aversion, or capital market imperfections. These justifications for government assistance may be valid
in the early stages of a project, but have little
force once the project is well established. The
appropriate government policy would be to sell off
shares in firms once they become established. However, the Jordan government had never (as of 1976)
sold any of its shares in private firms, partly
because of political pressures from private holders
of shares in the same companies, who feared a decline in the value of their shares. The Ministry
of Finance also resisted the sale of shares because
of the resultant loss of dividend revenue to the
government budget--a narrowly financial view of the
function of public finance, which also ignores the
alternative uses to which funds raised from the
sale of government shares could be put.

Jordan's semi-public industrial lending institution, the Industrial Development Bank (IDB), was established in 1965. It succeeded the Industrial Development Fund, a lending agency, founded in 1957, which had suffered from a poor collection record and whose loan portfolio was taken over by the IDB.[46] The IDB is a semi-autonomous institution with both public and private ownership. Since its employees are outside the civil service system, the IDB is able to attract able employees with relatively attractive salary scales. The government holds a little less than half of the value of paid-in capital in the form of ordinary shares (on which no dividends have been paid), while the remainder--in the form of preferred shares guaranteed a minimum 6% tax-free return by the government--is held by the private sector, primarily local banks, insurance companies, other firms, and pension funds.[47] Representatives of the government on the IDB's board of directors have been limited to a maximum of a third of the votes cast on any measure.

In addition to share capital, borrowing has since 1970 provided an additional source of funds for the IDB. Discounting by the CBJ was the largest single source of borrowed funds and financed a third of total IDB assets in 1975.[48] Foreign aid agencies, particularly those of West Germany and Kuwait, also were important sources of borrowed funds. The IDB has not accepted deposits, which would place it in competition with commercial banks, some of which are important shareholders in the IDB. Nor has the IDB sought to sell bonds to the public, since the interest rate it would need to pay would not be covered by its net earnings on the loans it extends.

The IDB is authorized to supply both debt and equity capital to firms in both industry and tourism. Debt capital extended to the industrial sector has been much the most important. IDB ownership of shares represented only about 5% of the total financing extended at the end of 1975; in that year it held shares in only six firms. Of all IDB loans extended during 1965-75, 85% were to the industrial sector, the remainder to tourism.[49]

The IDB has concentrated on medium-term lending; during 1965-74 83% of the amount of loans approved were for 5-15 years.[50] The interest rate charged on its loans was 7% until mid-1976, when it was raised to 8%. This compares to 9% on commercial bank loans.[51] It is evident that loans from the IDB and from commercial banks are closely competitive in terms of cost. IDB loans generally are of

230

longer maturity than commercial bank loans to industry, but many commercial bank loans are repeatedly rolled over to provide a continuing source of credit.

The relatively high interest rates of the IDB--not greatly below those of alternative sources of funds--are in contrast to the operation of the Agricultural Credit Corporation. The ACC's interest charge of 6% is well below the cost of funds from alternative sources (often local merchants or moneylenders) to its potential borrowers. As a result, the demand for loans greatly exceeds the ACC's supply. Because of its relatively low interest rates, the ACC in effect has been an agency for extending fiscal subsidies as much as a financial institution. There is an element of subsidy in the IDB's lending, paid for mainly by low-interest (4%) loans from the CBJ and by the government's holding IDB ordinary shares, which have never paid dividends. However, this subsidy is comparatively small (except for the IDB's Small Industries and Handicrafts Loan Fund, to be discussed below).[52] The IDB performs primarily a financial, rather than a fiscal, function.

For ordinary IDB loans application procedures are comparatively lengthy and involved, and after the loan is granted the IDB staff monitors the project fairly closely, especially if it is experiencing difficulty. As a result, the repayment rate has been comparatively good.[53] Another consequence has been the limited use of the IDB for fairly small loans.[54] It is a common phenomenon among institutional development finance agencies in LDCs that administrative procedures considered necessary for effective administration tend to exclude the small borrower. In 1975 the IDB began to address this problem.

In early 1975 the Small Industries and Handicrafts Loan Fund was established within the IDB to make small loans with a minimum of administrative formality.[55] The loan application requires only a single visit to the site by a loan officer, who fills out a simplified form on behalf of the applicant. Security may be in the form of real estate, machinery, or a co-signer. The process is expected to take normally one week. The interest rate charged is 7%, which represents a subsidized rate to most borrowers, for whom the cost of funds from alternative sources is considerably higher. Since the maximum loan allowed is very small, the subsidy to any individual is minor. The Small Industries

231

and Handicrafts Loan Fund represents an imaginative experiment; its performance in the future may have lessons for other LDCs as well as Jordan.

The Small Industries and Handicrafts Loan Fund is one manifestation of a generally resourceful and enterprising approach to development finance on the part of the IDB. In contrast to specialized credit institutions in many LDCs, which generally overemphasize the security of the prospective borrower, the IDB has given due weight to the profitability and earning potential of the enterprise.[56] Rather than waiting passively for borrowers, the IDB does make a limited attempt to bring its resources to the attention of prospective borrowers.[57] The IDB considers the provision of technical assistance an important part of its task. In the past this has been provided solely to actual or prospective borrowers as part of the loan process, but it could develop into a partly separate activity in the future.

The primary function of the IDB has been a modest, but useful one: to provide medium-term loans to medium-sized industry. It supplements the commercial banks, which lend to industry primarily on shorter terms. The IDB has not been the primary source of finance for major projects by Jordan's largest firms, such as phosphate, cement, or petroleum refining, because their capital needs were too great for the IDB's limited resources. Until the establishment of the Small Industries and Handicrafts Loan Fund in 1975 small borrowers were effectively excluded by the IDB's administrative procedures. In the future the IDB may be successful in reaching the small borrower. Nonetheless, because of its limited resources, its function as a financial institution will continue to be a modest one as one of several sources of finance for industry and tourism. It may, however, expand its role in other areas, such as technical assistance.

Of the two domestic institutional sources of loans for mining, manufacturing, and tourism--the IDB and the commercial banks--the commercial banks have been quantitatively the more important. Since 1968 the commercial banks accounted for roughly two-thirds to three-fourths of outstanding loans to the sectors from these two sources. The commercial banks' share fell from 1968 to 1972 and increased thereafter. The commercial banks were predominant as lenders to mining, manufacturing, and tourism even though only 11-14% of their outstanding loans went to these sectors.[58]

232

After 1972 commercial banks increased their
loans to industry as a proportion of their total
lending. In the mid-1970s the CBJ began to coerce
commercial banks to increase the share of their
loans to "productive" activities, such as agriculture and industry, and away from financing such
activities as commerce. The CBJ began with moral
suasion in 1973 and beginning in late 1974 imposed
ceilings on the expansion of commercial bank lending, with exemptions for agriculture, industry,
and public projects. Since the major expansion in
the share of industry in commercial bank loans
occurred between 1972 and 1974, while strong CBJ
measures did not take effect until the latter half
of 1974, it is difficult to connect the two. Nonetheless, the new CBJ policy of attempting to influence the sectoral allocation of bank loans may
have implications for the future.

d. Other Policy Measures

Government measures to promote industrial exports have been comparatively limited. Joint
government-industry trading centers have been established in a few neighboring countries to promote Jordanian products. Customs duties are re-
bated on imported materials used in the production
of exports. For the Department of Standards and
Specifications of the MIC, established in 1972,
helping industrial exporters to meet the quality
requirements of foreign markets may come to be one
of its most important functions. Indirectly,
measures to promote greater competitiveness of industrial firms, such as more liberal licensing of
industrial investments and fewer barriers to import competition, ultimately could significantly
increase the competitiveness of Jordanian industrial products in foreign markets.
Measures to reduce trade barriers between Arab
countries could stimulate exports, particularly
of industrial products, but there have been limitations to the effectiveness of such measures. Some
Arab countries, particularly Kuwait and Saudi
Arabia, have sufficiently low trade barriers that
relatively little in the way of special measures
is needed. Jordan has sought to reduce barriers to
trade with Egypt, Syria, and Iraq through the Arab
Common Market. However, since all three countries
had government-controlled foreign trade systems, in
which imports were regulated primarily by non-
tariff means, the Arab Common Market arrangements,

which in practice were largely limited to tariff cutting, were relatively fruitless.[59]

In 1975 Jordanian and Syrian officials signed initial economic agreements which were intended to be the first step in an ambitious program of economic integration between the two countries. By 1976 all trade barriers (both tariffs and direct controls) between the two countries ostensibly had been lifted and tariffs unified on most imported inputs used by similar producers in both countries.[60] Long-range plans included an ambitious array of cooperative undertakings, including joint planning of major industrial investments; joint Syrian-Jordanian companies in mining, industry, transportation, and banking; linking of electricity systems; and a common free industrial zone. It probably will be years before the outcome of these integration measures can be adequately assessed. Skeptics point to the historical instability of Middle East alliances and the marked disparity between the comparatively free-enterprise Jordanian economic system and the more controlled Syrian system.[61]

The government is empowered to grant land to private industrial firms, but this power has been seldom used. As do most countries, Jordan gives preference to local firms in government purchases--a measure of some consequence in Jordan because of the relatively large size of its armed forces. Labor legislation permits the existence of unions, but the conditions under which strikes are allowed are sufficiently restrictive that strikes are largely unknown.

A variety of government measures may have substantial impact on the industrial sector even though they were undertaken primarily for other purposes. For example, the measures adopted in the mid-1970s to hold down the urban price of bread, a major wage good, acted to hold down the real price of labor to industrial and other urban employers. Also, the financing of relatively high levels of education must have a significant effect on industry, as well as other modern sectors. Another important instance is the provision of infrastructure, such as transport and power facilities.

Jordan's transport network was greatly advanced by investments in road and Aqaba port development during the 1950s. For most manufacturing industry the effect of the new transport investments probably was fairly minor; the lower cost of imported materials would have been counteracted by the reduction in barriers to import competition arising from

234

transport costs. However, for the phosphate industry, which exported its output through Aqaba and
Beirut, the impact was substantial. Electricity
costs in Jordan have been relatively high, and
large industrial companies generally generated
their own supply.[62] Further development of the
electric power system was given a high priority in
the 1976-80 development plan.[63]

e. Conclusions

It is not difficult to discern a unifying theme
in many of the Jordanian government's industrial development policies. Its original approach was a
fundamentally free-enterprise philosophy shaped by
a government attitude of benevolent paternalism.
This theme manifested itself in frequently high
levels of protection from import competition, investment licensing procedures which often protected
existing firms from the entry of new firms and attempted to protect prospective investors against
their own mistakes, government shareholding and
financial measures that were sometimes used to rescue firms in trouble, and occasional government
initiative in starting new firms by commissioning
feasibility studies, buying shares, and arranging
other financing. The high degree of administrative
discretion permitted in the administration of investment licensing and especially the Encouragement
of Investment Law may be seen as a more indirect
manifestation of this same approach.
The highly discretionary, paternalistic system
embodied an implicit perception of the economy as
extremely simple (hence the presumed competence of
officials to make discretionary judgments despite
a dearth of statistical data) and of Jordanian industry as a fragile flower in a harsh environment
(hence the presumed need for paternalism). In the
1950s and 1960s, when industrial development began
to take root in Jordan, these assumptions probably
were close to reality. When educational levels
were low and entrepreneurs experienced in industry
were few (most entrepreneurs coming from the merchant class), a paternalistic arrangement partly
designed to protect investors against their own
mistakes may have been appropriate. The deterrence
effect on potential industrial investors of the
extraordinary political uncertainty at this time
constituted another justification for an especially
solicitous government role in promoting industry.
The policy of paternalistic nurturing of industrial

development is best suited to a strategy of import-
substituting industrialization. As is evident from
section 1 of this chapter, the development of manufacturing industry has been heavily concentrated
in producing substitutes for previously imported
manufactures. Except for phosphates, exporting was
a comparatively minor source of industrial growth.

After the rapid development of Jordanian industry up to 1967 and the resolution of internal tensions in the 1970-71 civil war, the assumptions on
which industrial development policy had been based
began to be progressively less appropriate. The
population was more educated, industrial entrepreneurship more experienced, the economy more complex,
and the political situation apparently more secure.
While there was still room for import substitution,
there was much less room in 1966 than in 1959, and
after the great increase in Middle East oil revenue
the potential payoff to Jordan from industrial exports was much enhanced.

Jordanian industrial policy has begun to adapt
itself to the changing economic environment. In
the early and mid-1970s there was an increasing
emphasis on promoting competition through licensing
investments more liberally, reducing the use of
monopoly grants and other quantitative restraints
on imports, and lowering levels of tariff protection. Besides continuing these desirable measures,
the government could adapt to the changed environment in several other areas of its industrial policy. It was suggested in section 2.b above that
Jordan's policy of investment incentives appeared
too discretionary for an increasingly complex economy with increasingly sophisticated entrepreneurs,
particularly in view of the dearth of reliable
statistical information available to administrators
and policy-makers. Also, it would be logical for
the government to sell its shares in companies as
those firms mature, although the political obstacles to this should not be minimized. In the past
government financial and international trade policies have been used to prevent any sizable industrial firm from going bankrupt. As Jordanian industrial entrepreneurship becomes more robust,
this policy can become counterproductive, maintaining uncompetitive firms at considerable cost to the
economy. Paradoxically, one indicator of a matur-
ing industrial policy may come the first time the
government allows a firm of some size to fail.

In Jordan many of the policy measures applied
to industry are applied equally to tourism invest-

ments, such as hotels and tourist busses. Tourism projects require an investment license from the Ministry of Tourism and Antiquities, as do industrial projects from the MIC. Like industrial projects, tourism investments are eligible for tax incentives under the Encouragement of Investment Law and for loans from the IDB. The government holds shares in hotel, transport, and tourism companies as well as in industrial firms. It is not evident what the two sectors of industry and tourism have in common that would justify this similarity of treatment. The strongest economic arguments for special treatment of industry generally center on its technical novelty and frequently large scale economies and on the associated problems of risk, investor ignorance, externalities of the learning process, and capital market imperfections that may inhibit unassisted free enterprise from achieving an optimal allocation of investment. It does not seem that most tourism investments would share these characteristics of large scale economies and especially of technological novelty. It would seem appropriate to design a separate strategy for tourism rather than attaching it to measures designed primarily for the industrial sector.

NOTES

1. See note 36 of Chapter 4 above, p. 79.
2. JDS, The National Accounts, 1959-1967, p. 78.
3. Ibid., pp. 34, 75-80.
4. From the 1966 input-output table in JDS, The National Accounts, 1959-1966, pp. 85-86.
5. Over the two years 1965 and 1966 the battery factory exported about 37% of the value (ex-factory) of its output. The corresponding figure for the cigarette industry was 12%. Calculated from unpublished worksheets, JDS Economic Section, and the 1959-65 and 1959-66 issues of the JDS national accounts.
6. Compare columns (2) and (3) of Table VIII.1. Although it is necessary to include tobacco products with food and beverages, the disparity was undoubtedly in food and beverages, not in tobacco products, since Jordan was a net exporter of the latter.
7. But Jordan did import large quantities of unprocessed food products, which were sometimes then processed in Jordan.

237

For some products, however, the processing took place abroad; in particular, a large share of wheat imports were in the form of wheat flour.

8. There has been some suggestion that fruit and vegetable canning was especially underdeveloped in Jordan. See FAO Mediterranean Development Project, p. 88.

9. See Padma Desai, "Alternative Measures of Import Substitution," Oxford Economic Papers, n.s. 21 (November 1969), 312-24.

10. This and most other measures of import substitution involve measures of the value of sales of imported and domestic products. A preferable measure would be some indicator of value added of imported and domestic products. Lack of the necessary data prohibits such a calculation, however.

11. For example, usually a significant proportion of supplies of flour was imported. This does not indicate that grain mills in Jordan could not process an amount of flour that would supply all Jordan's needs (in very good crop years, when Jordan was self-sufficient in grains, they did). Rather, it was because shortages of wheat were mainly met by the importation of wheat flour, not unmilled wheat. Perhaps this saved on transportation charges or perhaps it was simply because U.S. food aid came in the form of wheat flour.

12. The understatement is due to the fact that the estimates of column (3) omit exports rather than netting them against imports, as is done in deriving the ratios of the other three columns.

13. In years after 1958 Israel's manufactured exports increased greatly in importance, but in 1958 they were a relatively small proportion of net domestic supplies for the sectors included in Table VIII.2. Exports were 10% of net domestic supplies in rubber, chemicals, and products and were 6% or less in all other sectors.

14. Pack suggests that there was excessive import substitution (from a purely economic viewpoint; there may have been good noneconomic reasons, such as defense) in food processing, chemicals, and, perhaps, textiles. Howard Pack, Structural Change and Economic Policy in Israel, New Haven: Yale University Press, 1971, pp. 80-81.

15. All calculations from data in JDS, The National Accounts, 1959-1965, p. 66; and JDS, The National Accounts, 1959-1966, p. 78.

16. See Salih M. Jadallah, "The Phosphate Industry in Jordan," unpublished M.B.A. dissertation, Department of Business Administration, American University of Beirut, Beirut, Lebanon, 1965. Jadallah's thesis is particularly concerned with the high costs of transporting Jordanian phosphate and the weaknesses of the efforts to market it abroad.

17. If estimated East Bank value added in mining and manufacturing (from Table V.3) is deflated by the Amman consumer price index, then value added in real terms declined slightly

between 1967 and 1971. The industrial production index of principal industries was 13.6% higher in 1971 than in 1966 (CBJ, Ninth Annual Report, 1972, p. 11). This constitutes an average annual growth rate of 2.6%, but production in principal industries may have expanded faster than production in other industries.

18. See, for example, Thomas H. Miner and Associates, Inc., Industrial Survey of Jordan, 2 vols., for United Nations Industrial Development Organization, Chicago, Ill., 1973, pp. 71-74.

19. Calculated from Table V.3, p. 99, above.

20. CBJ, Monthly Statistical Bulletin, 13 (April 1977), Table 45.

21. Data on tonnage and value of phosphate exports are from JDS, External Trade Statistics, various years; and JDS, External Trade Statistics and Shipping Activity in Aqaba Port, quarterly, various issues. The price is measured by unit value, i.e., total value of phosphate exports divided by the total tonnage of phosphates exported.

22. NPC, Five Year Plan, p. 70.

23. Calculated from ibid., pp. 109, 122.

24. Ibid., pp. 117, 339. The plan's assumption about phosphate prices is calculated from its forecasts of 1980 export value and volume.

25. W. D. Scott and Company Pty. Ltd., Development Prospects for Manufacturing Industry in Jordan, draft final report, 1976.

26. This section draws heavily upon personal interviews in Jordan. I am particularly indebted to Dr. Hashem Dabbas, Ghalib Arafat, Ziyad Annab, Tawfiq Battarsi, Wadei J. Halasa, Kamel Abu-Jaber, and Ali Dajani.

27. This ministry was known as the Ministry of National Economy until 1974. The acronym MIC will be used consistently here to refer to this ministry under either of its titles.

28. Most other imports also require an import license (generally granted automatically), but import licensing for industrial equipment is a distinct process in which the application is subject to greater scrutiny by the MIC.

29. Between 1967 and 1976 customs revenues as a proportion of the value of imports (less three major duty-free import groups: live animals, wheat and wheat flour, and crude oil) ranged from 10% to 18%, with the higher ratios in 1967-1970 (calculated from data in CBJ, Monthly Statistical Bulletin, various issues).

30. When a domestic firm which had a monopoly over competitive imports was judged by the government to have been failing to supply adequately the domestic market, the government allowed others temporarily to import the monopolized products.

31. Of many studies the most influential probably has been Ian Little, Tibor Scitovsky, and Maurice Scott, Industry

239

and Trade in Some Developing Countries: A Comparative Study, London: Oxford University Press, 1970. Quantitative restrictions not only give extra windfall gains to individuals and may lead to corruption, but they often lend themselves to higher levels of protection because the degree of protection is less evident than under a tariff. See NPC, Three Year Development Plan, p. 112.

32. For a policy statement on the use of tariffs over direct controls see ibid., p. 118.

33. Jordan Times, July 11, 1976, p. 2.

34. Legally, any product's price may be regulated, but it is very rare (though not unknown) for the prices of products not highly protected by government measures to be controlled.

35. In some instances (cement and petroleum products for a time after 1973) the regulated domestic price was held below the price in other countries and had to be maintained by forbidding exports.

36. If the domestic industry is competitive, any increase in the tariff beyond the point at which the price of imported goods equals the price at which domestic supply and demand intersect has no effect on domestic price or quantity. But if the domestic industry is monopolistic, an increase in the tariff beyond the point at which the price of the imported good equals average total cost (assuming this is above marginal cost) will increase the domestic price and monopoly profits (until the tariff raises the price to the level at which the monopolist would set it in the absence of any foreign competition).

37. Investments in poultry, tourist hotels and busses, and sea transport were also eligible for exemptions under the same law. Industry was by far the most important recipient of exemptions under the law. For a three year period ending in October 1975, industry accounted for over 80% (whether measured by number or by amount of capital) of the projects granted exemption under the law (from unpublished sources, MIC).

38. The law allowed considerable discretion in the exemptions that could be awarded to an Economic Project, but in practice the exemptions given to an Economic Project have been the same for all Economic Projects. I am indebted to Ghalib Arafat of the Encouragement of Investment Office in the MIC for help in understanding the law as it is actually carried out.

39. I have interviewed five present or past participants in the process of awarding the exemptions. Their responses in separate interviews were generally quite consistent with each other.

40. In the three years ending in October 1975 the average project granted Economic Project status had a capital of J.D. 47 thousand while the average project receiving the

status of Approved Economic Project had a capital of J.D. 220 thousand (from unpublished sources, MIC).

41. See Chapter 9 below.

42. Zeid Jawdat Sha'sha'a, "The Mixed Industrial Sector in Jordan," unpublished M.B.A. thesis, Department of Business Administration, American University of Beirut, 1969, pp. 44-45, 49-56. In one case the government accepted shares in lieu of payment from a financially pressed company against which the government had won a court suit (ibid., p. 47).

43. Jordan Budget Department, Budget Law for the Fiscal Year 1976 [Amman, 1976], appended schedule B.

44. Sha'sha'a, pp. 71-75.

45. See ibid., passim.

46. On the IDB and some of its problems at the time of its inception see Michael A. Barnard, Industrial Development Bank: A Report on the History, Formation and Operations, 2 vols., report prepared for U.S. Agency for International Development, Washington, D.C., 1965.

47. Actual dividends paid were 6% until 1971, when they were raised to 7%, and in 1974 to 7.5%.

48. IDB, Eleventh Annual Report, 1975 (Arabic), Exhibit A (after p. 29).

49. Ibid., pp. 25, 28, and Exhibit A.

50. IDB, Industrial Development Bank (1965-1975), Amman, n.d., p. 9.

51. With additional service charges both the IDB and the commercial bank interest rate would be about one percentage point higher.

52. According to the IDB, there did not appear to be a significant excess demand for IDB loans over its supply. Of course, this is not an easy matter to determine, since it is also affected by the application procedures and creditworthiness criteria adopted by the lender.

53. In 1975 90% of amounts coming due were collected (IDB, Eleventh Annual Report, p. 26). In the politically troubled earlier years repayment on time was at a considerably lower rate, but most of the overdue sums ultimately were collected.

54. During 1965-74 only 16% of the total amount of loans approved went in loans of less than J.D. 25,000 (about $70-75 thousand). IDB, Industrial Development Bank (1965-1975), p. 8.

55. The maximum amount is J.D. 2,000 and the maximum term is 10 years. The loans are limited to the purchase of machinery and tools. Eligible firms are those employing five persons or less and producing manually or with simple tools and machines. Some services establishments, such as blacksmiths and car repair shops, are eligible.

56. United Nations Economic and Social Office in Beirut (UNESOB), Studies on Development Problems in Selected Countries of the Middle East, 1973, New York: United Nations, 1974, p. 40.

57. The IDB receives the names of recipients of industrial investment licenses from the MIC and of touristic investment licenses from the Ministry of Tourism and Antiquities. It then contacts the licensees to inform them of its services.

58. All calculations are from data in CBJ, Monthly Statistical Bulletin, various issues.

59. For a good analysis see "Institutional Framework of the Arab Common Market," in UNESOB, Studies on Development Problems in Selected Countries of the Middle East, 1972, New York: United Nations, 1973, pp. 1-11.

60. It was not intended to establish common tariffs on all imports from outside the union. The union was to be a free trade area, rather than a customs union. However, on intermediate materials and capital goods which were used by competitors in Jordan and Syria, tariff unification was sought so that neither country's producers would have an unjustified advantage over competitors in the other country.

61. Since tariffs have relatively little effect on imports when imports are controlled by the government, the integration agreements have provided for increased Syrian imports from Jordan by several special provisions, including minimum amounts to be purchased by Syrian state agencies and provisions permitting importation by private entities in Syria subject to prior notification of, and acquiescence by, the state trading agency.

62. During 1972-75 30% of electric energy generated in the East Bank was generated by manufacturing industries. JDS, Statistical Yearbook, 1975, p. 194.

63. Planned projects include construction of a thermal power station near the petroleum refinery, electrification of outlying areas, integration with Syria's electricity grid, and establishment of a hydroelectric power station at the Maqarin Dam being constructed on the Yarmouk River. See NPC, Five Year Plan, pp. 387-421.

9
Development Planning

1. EARLY DEVELOPMENT PLANS

    The first official published development plan
for Jordan was the Five Year Plan for 1962-67
issued by the Jordan Development Board (JDB).
Partly because of a lack of aggregative economic
data, the plan was limited to proposals for government investment projects and fiscal and administrative reforms, without much attempt to design an
overall strategy or to make aggregative projections
for the economy as a whole. On an aggregative
level, the primary effort of the plan was to ensure
consistency between projected development expenditures and their sources of financing. On the basis
of the assumption that the absolute level of annual
budget support aid would remain at 1961-62 levels
throughout the plan period, the plan forecast an
average annual GNP growth rate of 8% and a reduction
in the balance of trade deficit.[1]
    Less than two years after the publication of the
Five Year Plan in 1961, the JDB decided to revise
it. The result was a completely new plan document:
the Seven Year Plan for 1964-70. Reasonably reliable national accounts estimates first became
available about 1961. The Seven Year Plan was the
first plan to make use of national accounts data
and consequently the first to present integrated
aggregative forecasts for the plan period. It was
an ambitious planning effort, both in its aggregative forecasts and in project presentation and proposals for fiscal and administrative reform.
    The stated reason for abandonment of the 1962-
1967 plan and adoption of the Seven Year Plan was
a change in the expected magnitude of future budget
support aid. The Five Year Plan's assumption of a
constant level of budget support aid was believed to

have been overoptimistic, and large reductions came to be expected. The effect of these revised expectations was to raise "reduction of the foreign deficit" to top priority status, at least nominally. However, it is difficult to perceive the concrete effect of this shift in priorities upon the microeconomic aspects of the Plan.[2] In the aggregative projections also, the effect of the assumed reduction in budget support was not so significant as might be expected, because the plan assumed a very large increase in "development grants" and foreign borrowing to compensate for the assumed reduction in budget support aid. However, while budget support aid is unrestricted as to use, development grants and loans generally are given to finance specific projects. Perhaps then the major reason why the expected reduction in budget support aid necessitated the preparation of a new plan may have been the need to present more project proposals in order to secure the necessary financing.

The Seven Year Plan forecast an average increase in real GNP between 1964 and 1970 of 6.1% per year--somewhat lower than the rate that had prevailed in the preceding years. Although the plan did not specify the expected growth rate for all sectors, it can be deduced that the mining, tourism, and construction sectors were expected to be among the fastest-growing sectors, while the government sector was expected to grow slowly. The plan projected 4.7% average annual growth in agricultural output and 6.7% for manufacturing value added.[3] In view of the rapid growth rate of manufacturing prior to 1964 and the considerable scope that existed for further industrialization the latter projection was exceedingly conservative.

According to the plan, gross domestic investment was to rise sharply from 13.8% of GNP in 1964 to 25.3% in 1967, after which it would decline gradually to 18.7% in 1970.[4] This pattern was primarily due to scheduled investments in the Yarmouk irrigation project. The 1964-70 gross aggregate ICOR implied by the projections of the Seven Year Plan was 3.4--significantly higher than it had been in preceding years. Even if we exclude investment in the capital-intensive Yarmouk project, whose contribution to increased output was not to occur until after the plan period, the ICOR would be 3.1 --still somewhat above Jordan's prior experience. As previously observed,[5] the plan seriously underestimated probable investment in manufacturing and dwellings. If better estimates for these sectors were used, the ICOR might have been 10-20% higher.

The Seven Year Plan projected a striking rise in gross domestic saving from virtually zero in 1964 to about 15% of GNP in 1970. The projected improvement in savings was the consequence of optimistic, but reasonable, assumptions about government saving and implausibly optimistic assumptions about private saving. To achieve the improvement in government saving, the plan assumed a sufficient relaxation of tensions in the Middle East that annual defense expenditures could be held constant, and a rapid increase in government domestic revenue from administrative reforms, new taxes, and increased tax rates proposed in the plan. According to the plan, gross private saving was to increase from 10.9% of disposable income in 1964 to 19.7% in 1970. To achieve this increase required an average annual increase in real per capita private consumption of about 1%, compared to a historical rate over 3%. The implied marginal propensity to consume was only .59--well below the historical rate for Jordan and the level in other countries.[6]

Kanaan[7] pointed out a major accounting inconsistency in the Seven Year Plan's projections of the private sector and the foreign accounts. He observed that not all of private saving was accounted for by private investment or private lending to government. Indeed, the discrepancy was very large and accounted for about 35% of total private saving over the 1964-70 period as a whole. There was a corresponding discrepancy in the foreign accounts, manifesting itself in projected foreign borrowing well below foreign borrowing recorded in the private and government accounts. One might be tempted to deduce from this apparent projected surplus of saving and foreign exchange savings that the plan understated the scope for additional investment or for reducing foreign aid. However, since the underlying estimates were reached by unrealistic projections of saving (and hence of consumer goods imports), the plan's projections appear to have been on balance overly optimistic about the prospects for decreasing dependence on foreign aid by 1970.

In conclusion, the Seven Year Plan appears to have been somewhat schizophrenic in its aggregative projections. The planners' projections for government revenues and expenditures, while optimistic, were not unreasonable from the vantage point of

1964. However, from external evidence the projections for the private sector appear to have been pretty much an afterthought. The projections of private consumption, saving, and investment were highly implausible. In effect, the Seven Year Plan for 1964-70 was fundamentally a long-term government investment budget, of which its aggregative economic projections were not an integral part. This is not a serious evil, especially in an open, free-enterprise economy such as Jordan's, in which the private sector is inherently difficult to predict. Development plans of this nature probably are the norm in LDCs, and usually with reason.

For almost five years after the 1967 Middle East war economic development policy was not carried out in a systematic manner. To the degree that development policy existed at all, it was conducted on an ad hoc, improvisatory basis. It is difficult to imagine anything different in view of the enormous uncertainties at the time--about a Middle East settlement, return of the West Bank, and civil war with the Palestinian commando forces. After the defeat of the Palestinian forces in Jordan and the end of hopes for an early Middle East peace, the National Planning Council (NPC), successor to the JDB, was charged with the preparation of a short-term plan to oversee the recovery of the economy and lay the groundwork for subsequent longer-term development planning.

The Three Year Plan for 1973-75 was essentially an interim program to bridge the gap between the period of policy improvisation in the early postwar years and the resumption of systematic development policy-making. The plan projected an average annual growth in GDP at factor cost of 8%, with the most rapid growth to be in the sectors of electricity and water, mining and manufacturing, and construction.[8] From the vantage point of 1972, this seemingly ambitious objective was achievable because not all the growth would have to come from an increase in productive capacity; some growth was possible from increased use of underutilized capacity. The Three Year Plan projected a large, but plausible, increase in the rate of investment during the plan period over the depressed levels of 1967-72.[9] Inexplicably, it projected a decline from 1973 to 1975 in both the absolute and relative levels of government fixed investment.[10] It would have been more reasonable to project an increase in public investment, as projects designed and prepared early in the plan period were undertaken later in the period, which in fact is what happened.

The Three Year Plan made projections of saving, investment, sectoral investment and growth, and international transactions for 1973-75. Since they were based on highly untrustworthy national accounts data for the combined East and West Banks, they do not warrant extended consideration. The projected growth rates were not seriously implausible in the light of Jordan's previous experience and circumstances at the time. In terms of projected growth, the Three Year Plan probably was more sensible than the Seven Year Plan--the most substantial planning effort to that time.[11] In terms of its overall strategy and expectations, the Three Year Plan broke little new ground,[12] as befits a plan whose purpose was essentially transitional.

Striking changes occurred during 1973-75 that could not have been foreseen when the Three Year Plan was drawn up: the oil price revolution, acceleration of world inflation, a great increase in aid available to Jordan, enhanced employment prospects for Jordanians abroad, and a boom in world phosphate prices. Under such circumstances there would be no reason to expect any plan for this period to be accurate in its projections or to be carried out as planned. Given the weaknesses of national accounts data (compounded by the problem of deflating them for very high rates of inflation), it is not possible to say even in retrospect how close the plan's projections were to what actually happened. It appears that the projection of 8% average annual real GDP growth probably was not terribly wide of the mark if allowance is made for the poor crop year in 1975.

Although actual 1973-75 government investment expenditure in current prices roughly equalled the amount projected by the Three Year Plan,[13] a substantial fraction of the projects and measures proposed in the plan were not realized during the plan period. Because of rapid inflation after 1972, actual public expenditures in current dinars would have had to be much greater than the original planned levels for the public expenditure program to have been executed on schedule. Although there is no single unambiguous measure of such things, by most counts less than two-thirds of the planned projects were carried out within the plan period. Major undertakings, such as the Zarka River project, the ceramics factory, and the glass factory, fell behind schedule and were not to be completed until after the plan period.

A variety of circumstances contributed to the failure of the Three Year Plan to be fully realized. In part, the plan was overambitious, failing to allow sufficient time for project formulation and preparation. The 1973 Middle East war, delays in receiving equipment and inflation in their costs due to worldwide and regional influences, shortages of trained manpower attracted by employment opportunities in newly enriched oil-producing countries of the region all were unpredictable elements outside Jordan's control contributing to delays and cost overruns in planned projects. Weaknesses in the NPC's handling of project preparation and implementation also played a role.[14] Given the special circumstances of the Three Year Plan period, perhaps no great significance should be attached to the failure of the plan to be realized on schedule. Its fundamental purpose was to achieve a transition to systematic development planning after the interruptions of war, partition, and civil war, and this it achieved.

2. THE FIVE YEAR PLAN FOR 1976-80

When the Five Year Plan for 1976-80 was prepared in 1975, Jordan's economic and diplomatic position had vastly changed from the time of preparing the 1973-75 plan. Unutilized industrial capacity was no longer significant. Concern about unemployment in 1972 had given way to worries about manpower bottlenecks by 1975. The civil war in Lebanon and especially the enrichment of neighboring countries by the oil-price revolution both appeared to offer opportunities for Jordan to expand its foreign earnings. Most significant of all, by 1975 Jordan had access to a continuing flow of foreign grants and loans that was vast in relation to its small economy. These developments inevitably had a substantial influence on the shaping of the Five Year Plan.

In assessing the Five Year Plan it must be realized that the quantitative projections of the plan are not of much significance for their precise numerical values. In combination with other presentations in the plan, they may be helpful as broad qualitative indicators of development strategies, but they have too many limitations to be useful quantitative indicators. As will subsequently be evident, some of the projections are highly implausible. Furthermore, the national accounts data on which they were based are not very accurate, and the projections are complicated by the problem of inflation.[15] Because there had been no recent, sustained experience of truly normal development conditions in the East Bank, there was little basis on which to extrapolate projections for the future. The free-enterprise nature of the economy and its susceptibility to external influences make it inherently difficult to predict in the most favorable circumstances. Some of the quantitative estimates in the plan were recognized as obsolete in the short time between the preparation of the plan and its official release, most important of which was the plan's extremely optimistic projection of future phosphate exports.[16]

Table IX.1 indicates the sectoral pattern of East Bank growth and investment projected for the plan period. While the average annual rate of growth in real GDP at factor cost shown there is 11.9%, the projected growth in GNP is somewhat lower (11.5%) because of the lower growth rates of indirect taxes and net factor income from abroad.[17] Even by the standard of rapid growth achieved by Jordan in the decade and a half preceding the 1967 Middle East war, this is a strikingly high rate, particularly since there was little unutilized industrial capacity in 1975 to provide "easy" growth in industrial output, as there was during 1972-75. From Table IX.1 it is evident that the sector of mining and manufacturing is the key to the rapid growth projected for GDP as a whole, as its growth accounts for nearly a half of the expected overall growth. To achieve this required a 26.2% average annual growth in industrial value added, which is much too high to be credible. Such a rate is far above Jordan's past experience or normal experience in other LDCs. It is partly predicated upon growth in phosphate exports which was recognized to be overoptimistic by the time the plan was officially released.[18] Since some planned industrial projects (most importantly, the potash plant) were not scheduled to begin production until after the plan period and others (such as the ambitious chemical fertilizer plant) were not unlikely to fall behind schedule, the rapid industrial growth rate projected was doubly unrealistic. For the same reason, and also because of the capital-intensive character of planned industrial projects, the gross ICOR in industry implied for the plan period may be low.

TABLE XI.1. SECTORAL PROJECTIONS OF THE FIVE YEAR PLAN FOR 1976-80

	Average Annual 1975-80 Growth Rate (percent per year)	Share in GDP 1975 (percent)	Share in GDP 1980 (percent)	Share in Total Growth of GDP 1975-80 (percent)	Share in Total Investment 1976-80 (percent)	Gross ICOR 1976-80
Agriculture	7.0	10.3	8.3	5.5	14.7	9.3
Mining and Manufacturing	26.2	15.5	28.3	45.4	30.0	2.3
Water and Electricity	17.1	1.7	2.2	2.8	8.9	11.3
Transport and Communications	10.6	9.0	8.5	7.8	18.3	8.2
Trade	7.2	19.0	15.4	10.6	0.5	0.2
Ownership of Dwellings	12.0	5.9	5.9	6.0	10.8	6.4
Others	7.4	38.6	31.5	22.0	16.8	2.7
TOTAL	11.9	100.0	100.0	100.0	100.0	3.5

Source: NPC, Five Year Plan, pp. 109, 122, 292, 681.

NOTES

All figures here are derived from projections in constant-price dinars. Investments in irrigation are included in the agricultural sector.

It is clear that the growth in GDP projected by
the plan is overstated because the projected growth
in mining and manufacturing is overstated. The
effect is substantial. For illustration only, if
the annual growth of mining and manufacturing value
added were reduced from 26.2% to 15%--still an extremely high rate--that alone would reduce the
annual growth rate of GDP from 11.9% to 9.4%. In
turn, a lower projected GDP growth rate implies
lower growth for sectors whose growth usually is
closely linked to that of the economy as a whole,
such as trade, transport, and some services. Finally, the 7% growth rate for agriculture--quite high
compared with most LDCs--can be considered a plausible projection only if it is assumed that 1980 will
be a normal rainfall year, and then much of the
growth between 1975, a poor rainfall year, and
1980 would be due simply to the weather differences. This is reasonable, but it should be recognized that this, and not a 7% annual growth in
agricultural productive capacity, accounts for much
of the projected 7% annual growth in agricultural
output. To project a 7% annual growth rate of
agricultural productive capacity during 1975-80
would be overoptimistic, since important projected
investments in agriculture, the Maqarin Dam and related projects, would not contribute to output until after the plan period and since major advances
in dryland agriculture require changes with a substantial gestation period.
    In conclusion, the projected growth rate is
clearly too high. Jordan could reasonably expect
to achieve 7-8% average annual growth in constant-
price GDP during the plan period, which would be
comparable to the admirable rate sustained in the
years preceding the 1967 war. Subsequent analysis,
particularly of the manpower question, will give
further reason to believe that the growth rate in
the plan is overstated. Because of the major projects expected to come to fruition in the early
1980s, a somewhat higher average growth rate (perhaps 8-9%) might be hoped for over the longer
period, 1975-85.
    Despite the weaknesses of the plan's growth pro-
jections in numerical terms, Table IX.1 gives an
indication of the overall strategy of the Five Year
Plan, which is reflected in other aspects of the
plan as well. Investment was to be heavily concentrated on agriculture and especially industry.
Implicit in Table IX.1 is another critical characteristic of the plan: It is a high investment plan.

251

This is implied by the fairly high aggegrate ICOR, even though the projected ICORs for industry, trade, and dwellings appear to be underestimates.[19] Over the plan period gross domestic investment was scheduled to average 32.3% of GDP at market prices--compared to about 18% for Jordan in 1959-66 and for the typical country at a comparable level of income per head. The plan projected investment to rise between 1975 and 1977 and then to fall steadily to 1980, both in proportion to GDP and (surprisingly) in absolute terms. Investment was to rise from 28.5% of GDP in 1975 to 42.2% in 1977, declining to 21.9% in 1980. Such a pattern could easily overtax the administrative capacities and manpower supplies of public and private investing institutions in the years of peak investment, but--largely for this very reason--this pattern was unlikely to be implemented.[20]

Not only was the development strategy of the Five Year Plan a high-investment strategy, but (probably related to this) it was something of a big-projects strategy. As Table IX.2 shows, only eight projects (five in the industrial sector) accounted for almost a third of projected investment during the plan period. The definition of what constitutes a project cannot be precise; by a slightly more expansive definition large projects (over J.D. 20 million) would make up over 40% of total planned investment.[21]

It is not difficult to imagine why planners chose a high-investment, big-projects strategy for the Five Year Plan. Obviously, the ready availability of foreign assistance prompted the high-investment approach. The plan projected foreign aid and loans during 1976-80 equal to 86.3% of gross domestic investment during the same period.[22] The emphasis on large projects probably has several sources. Some of Jordan's best investment opportunities probably did lie in large projects, some of which (particularly the Maqarin Dam and related parts of the Yarmouk project) had been planned for years. In addition, it may be easier to attract foreign financing for a few large projects than for many small ones. Finally, the selection of a high-investment strategy also influenced the choice of a big-project strategy. Very high levels of investment threaten to exceed the administrative-technical capabilities of a developing economy, and the prospect is particularly likely in a country like Jordan, where booming demand has drained skilled talent from government employment to employment in

TABLE IX.2. MAJOR INVESTMENT PROJECTS IN THE FIVE YEAR
PLAN FOR 1976-80

		Planned Investment (J.D. million)	Share in Total Plan Investment (percent)
1.	Maqarin Dam	25.35	3.3
2.	Phosphate Expansion	24.00	3.1
3.	Petroleum Refinery Expansion	39.00	5.1
4.	Chemical Fertilizer Industry	61.00	8.0
5.	Potash Extraction	25.00	3.3
6.	Cement Factory in Southern Jordon	21.30	2.8
7.	Central Thermal Power Station at Zarka	21.89	2.9
8.	Amman International Airport	25.50	3.3
	TOTAL for Eight Projects	243.04	31.8

NOTES

Source: NPC, Five Year Plan, pp. 122, 267, 355, 420, 495.

Total plan investment was J.D. 765 million.

the private sector and abroad. The selection of
large, "enclave" projects, with a substantial input
from foreign contractors and skilled labor, is
partly an attempt to avert such a bottleneck.[23]
     According to the plan, domestic savings, both
private and government, were to increase sharply
over the course of the plan period. As a result,
the reliance on foreign assistance was to be much
reduced by 1980. The plan's projection of private
saving implied a marginal propensity to save of .32
out of private disposable income; i.e., a marginal
propensity to consume of .68. This marginal propensity to consume is very low by comparison with
other countries or by historical standards for Jordan.[24] Since an acceleration in the rate of growth
may increase the saving rate, the plan's low marginal propensity to consume could be justified if
its optimistic growth targets were met,[25] but as
suggested previously, that appears unlikely. As a
practical matter, the question is not of importance,
since the national accounts estimates of private
saving for postwar Jordan are highly unreliable in
any event. The significance of this demonstration
is as another illustration of the Five Year Plan's
highly optimistic nature.
     Projections of government receipts and outlays
may be somewhat more meaningful than aggregate projections of consumption, saving, and investment, because the basic data for the former, while they have
serious limitations, are significantly more reliable. Equally important, government receipts and
expenditures are more operational instruments of
development planning, since policy makers generally
can exert more influence over them. And although
Jordan adheres to a generally free-enterprise philosophy, the government budget is of strategic importance because--thanks to high levels of foreign aid
receipts--it is extremely large in relation to the
economy (equal to more than half of GNP at the beginning of the plan period, as shown in Tables IX.3
and IX.4).
     As Table IX.3 indicates, the plan projected a
marked decline in the relative importance of government outlays over the course of the plan period,
primarily due to slow growth in government investment and government expenditures on defense and
public security. Deceleration in the growth of
the defense establishment, which grew rapidly
immediately after the 1967 Middle East war,
was not an unreasonable forecast, but is always

TABLE IX.3. PROJECTED GOVERNMENT OUTLAYS OF THE FIVE YEAR PLAN FOR 1976-80

	Share in GNP (percent)			Average Annual Growth Rate, 1976-80 (percent per year)
	1975	1977	1980	
Total Current Expenditures	36.7	33.7	30.8	7.6
Central Government	35.3	32.4	29.7	7.7
Defense and Public Security	14.9	13.1	11.4	5.5
Other	20.4	19.4	18.3	9.1
Municipalities	1.4	1.3	1.1	7.0
Gross Capital Formation	14.4	18.1	9.9	3.5
Loans and Grants to Private Sector	4.9	6.7	3.2	2.1
Debt Repayment	2.7	2.7	2.4	8.4
TOTAL	58.7	61.3	46.2	6.3

Source: NPC, Five Year Plan, pp. 109, 112, 114.

255

subject to possible events beyond Jordan's control. The projected share of government outlays in GNP does not fall continuously, but increases from 1975 to 1977 and falls thereafter, due to the heavy concentration of planned investment around 1977.

Both government investment and government loans and grants to the private sector (partly related to private investment) were projected to reach their peaks in 1977. This pattern of planned investment, which was noted previously, was unlikely to be fulfilled. By projecting a pattern in which 1980 investment is low, the plan makes it appear that government expenditures, and hence the reliance on foreign assistance, would be greatly reduced by the end of the plan period.

The clustering of planned investment in the middle of the plan is reflected also in the pattern of planned government receipts shown in Table IX.4. As a proportion of total projected government receipts, foreign financing (grants, technical assistance, and loans) rises from 46% in 1975 to 51% in 1977, then falls precipitously to 27% in 1980. Over the period 1975-80 government current domestic revenues were to rise from about 24% of GNP--already quite high compared to prewar Jordan-- to 36% of GNP. The boom in the world phosphate market, which peaked around 1975, was largely responsible for the comparatively high level of government current domestic revenues in 1975, through the export tax on phosphates, corporate profit tax on the phosphate company, and profits on the government's shareholdings in the phosphate company. The rapid projected growth in central government domestic revenues was predicated upon rapid growth and continued high prices for phosphate exports, the plan's projections of which were recognized to be overoptimistic before the plan was officially inaugurated. Therefore, the growth rates projected for current domestic revenue of the central government must be considered overly high.

Total tax revenue as a percentage of GNP was projected to rise only slightly (from 13.3% to 13.8%) between 1975 and 1980, with a decrease in the percentage for indirect tax revenue being slightly more than offset by an increase for direct taxes. Plan proposals for increasing direct tax revenue were mainly in general terms, except for a proposed tax on capital gains from the sale of real estate. Almost all of the projected increase in the share of government current domestic revenues in GNP is attributable to the projected

TABLE IX.4. PROJECTED GOVERNMENT RECEIPTS OF THE FIVE YEAR PLAN FOR 1976-80

	Share in GNP (percent)			Average Annual Growth Rate, 1976-80 (percent per year)
	1975	1977	1980	
Total Current Domestic Revenues	23.9	26.5	30.0	16.6
Central Government	21.7	24.0	27.1	16.5
Direct Taxes	2.4	2.7	3.9	22.7
Indirect Taxes	10.9	10.1	9.9	9.5
Property and Investment Income	5.7	8.6	10.9	26.9
Other	2.7	2.5	2.4	18.4
Municipalities	2.2	2.5	2.8	17.6
Foreign Grants and Technical Assistance	20.1	13.7	10.4	-2.3
Foreign Loans	6.8	17.1	1.9	-13.7
Domestic Borrowing	7.9	4.0	3.9	-2.9
TOTAL	58.7	61.3	46.2	6.3

Source: NPC, Five Year Plan, pp. 109, 111, 113.

increase in property and investment income (mainly earnings on government shareholdings and profits of the CBJ). The plan projected property and investment income to more than triple between 1975 and 1980,[26] a highly questionable forecast in view of the scaled-down forecasts for phosphate sales. Partly because of exceptional increases in foreign aid and phosphate receipts, the CBJ's holdings of foreign currency reserves increased sharply between 1974 and 1975, leading to an increase in CBJ profits of 32%. It was neither likely nor desirable that Jordan should increase its foreign currency holdings at a comparable rate over the course of the plan.

Although not evident in quantitative projections, several other important strategies are embodied in the plan. One strategy, strong promotion of cooperative societies, primarily in agriculture, has been noted in Chapter 7. Another new emphasis in the plan is on measures to promote the development of modern financial instruments and institutions in an effort to increase and mobilize savings and to channel them to productive investments. Among the plan's proposals are a variety of measures to promote financial "liberalization," as advocated by economists such as McKinnon and Shaw.[27] These include increasing interest rates on bank loans and deposits, encouraging specialized credit institutions (such as the ACC, IDB, and Housing Bank) to attract deposits and issue bonds at competitive interest rates, increased sale of government bonds to the public, and the establishment of a domestic financial market. Other plan proposals, however, run directly counter to the policy recommendations of the financial liberalization school. These include credit ceilings on bank loans to some sectors and incentives to induce bank lending to others.[28] Another principal strategy in the Five Year Plan is a strong emphasis on vocational education. This is one aspect of a broader issue with crucial implications for development during the plan period and beyond. That is the manpower question, covered in the next section.

3. THE PROBLEM OF MANPOWER

In prewar development plans the issue of manpower was essentially one of creating jobs to reduce unemployment. In the late 1960s policy makers began to take an interest in planning education and training programs in accordance with expected future demands for different categories of skills. In 1969 the NPC established a Manpower Planning Section to incorporate manpower planning into general development planning. In the 1973-75 plan attempts were made to identify future demands in seven broad skill categories using conventional manpower forecasting techniques. These techniques generally have had only modest success in most countries in which they were used. Partly as a result of the manpower forecasting exercise, the plan stressed the need for expanding vocational training. For the labor force taken as a whole, the concern of the 1973-75 plan, like the prewar plans, was with increasing employment opportunities.

By the time the Five Year Plan for 1976-80 was formally inaugurated in June 1976, the primary manpower question was no longer one of providing employment opportunities, but the possibility that manpower shortages might prevent the achievement of the plan's growth goals. By then, all signs pointed to conditions of tightness in Jordanian labor markets. At this point, three different manpower problems raised their heads: (1) whether the growth projections of the Five Year Plan were consistent with the increase in the total labor force to be expected over the plan period, (2) the possibility of shortages in some important skill categories, and (3) the loss of skilled personnel in government administration to employment abroad and in the Jordanian private sector. The plan recognized the last two issues, but gave little acknowledgement to the first one.[29] However, in a paper prepared after the plan was completed, Jordanian government manpower specialists, using standard manpower forecasting techniques, forecast a balance between aggregate supply and demand for labor consistent with the achievement of the growth goals of the plan.[30] It will be argued here that their forecast embodied highly implausible assumptions and that more plausible ones would suggest that labor force growth during the plan period would be inadequate to support the ambitious growth goals of the plan.

The Ghawi-Masri study concluded that the aggregate demand for labor in 1980 would only slightly exceed labor supply in that year if the plan were fulfilled, but the major probable sources of bias in their estimation all tend to understate future labor demand or overstate future labor supply. They assumed fairly high rates of growth in labor productivity over the plan period.[31] More important, 43% of their estimated labor force was not allocated to any sector when they made their projections. As a result, their projections implicitly assumed zero growth in the demand for this unaccounted-for labor over the plan period. Using the Ghawi-Masri assumptions about labor productivity increases, I estimated the increased demand for labor implied by the plan growth projections using my estimate of 1974-75 sectoral employment from Table VI.2, p. 112, above. The implied growth in labor demand was 8.1% per year, compared to 4.4% in the Ghawi-Masri study.[32] Since unemployment in 1974-75 was low and since the population of working age was increasing at about 3% per year, the plan projections appear to imply a gross inconsistency between future labor supply and demand.

A variety of factors may cause the labor force to grow at a different rate from the population of working age. For example, increased school attendance by persons of working age would cause the labor force to grow more slowly than the population of working age, whereas an increase in labor force participation rates would have the opposite effect. The only serious possibility for accelerating the growth rate of the labor force significantly above that of the working-age population would be a substantial increase in labor force participation rates of Jordanian women. The Ghawi-Masri study assumed extremely high labor force participation rates for women reaching working age or completing their schooling between 1976 and 1980: 80-90%.[33] Only a sudden revolution in behavior patterns could bring about such a change. In Jordan in 1961 women in the nonagricultural labor force equalled 3.4% of the total number of women 15-64. For the East Bank in 1974 the corresponding figure was 7.0%.[34] The lower percentage of the population on farms in the East Bank in 1974 may account for much of this apparent increase. Even if all of the increase were due to increased female labor force participation by women, the 1974 rates were far below the assumptions in the Ghawi-Masri study.[35] Even if 30% of all women reaching age 15 between 1976 and 1980 entered the labor force and the number of women other ages in the labor force were unchanged, the labor force would grow at only 5% per year.[36]

In conclusion, even when generous allowance is made for the uncertainties of forecasting and the weaknesses in labor force data, there seems little doubt that the growth forecasts of the Five Year Plan for 1976-80 were inconsistent with the labor force likely to be available at the end of the plan.

As it stands, the plan projections suggest an increase in aggregate demand for labor of at least 7-8% per year and in aggregate supply of no more than 4-5% per year. Only large net in-migration, a great increase in female labor force participation, or remarkable increases in average labor productivity could reverse this conclusion.

The first plan to emphasize vocational education was the Three Year Plan for 1973-75, which planned to expand enrollment in first-year vocational secondary school classes from 8.4% to 15% of all first-year secondary school enrollments over the course of the plan and to 30% by 1980.[37] The projected expansion in enrollments was achieved for 1972-75, over which time total vocational school enrollments increased at an average annual rate of 32% from a rather small base.[38] In the Three Year Plan the primary justification for promoting vocational education was the prospect of high unemployment among school leavers from the academic, nonvocational stream.

On a different justification, the Five Year Plan for 1976-80 presented an ambitious plan for doubling the size of the established vocational education system (a continuation of an objective already enunciated in the preceding plan) and for establishing a large, new "National Training Scheme" to provide intensive, short-term "crash courses" of vocational training and apprenticeship. In the new context of aggregate labor shortages the rationale was no longer the danger of a surplus of academically trained workers, but the possibility that a shortage of technically skilled labor would be a bottleneck in plan fulfillment. The Five Year Plan projected that 7,500 persons would pass through the new system of short courses. Combined, these two programs would enroll very roughly a quarter of all Jordanians expected to enter the labor force (either at home or abroad) during 1976-80.[39]

The major innovation in the plan's program for vocational education, the National Training Scheme, was justified by some of its proponents as a temporary expedient to meet an exceptional situation until longer-term adjustments could be made. Others saw advantages in the greater flexibility of short courses that might justify their existence on a long-term basis. The scheme was to be implemented by establishing a Labour Vocational Training Corporation with a board of directors composed of government, business, and labor representatives.

Its activities would be financed by funds from the government budget, foreign assistance, and compulsory contributions from companies. Companies would be given incentives to establish in-plant training centers by the crediting of their expenditures against their liability for contributions to the Labour Vocational Training Corporation.

The ambitious program for vocational education in the Five Year Plan was justified largely on the basis of impressionistic evidence of shortages of technical skills. However, the market for low-skill labor was also tight, and the shortages of skilled labor may simply have been a manifestation of an overheated economy with an excess demand for labor of all kinds. And even if there existed a skilled labor bottleneck, it is not clear whether a crash program to expand formal vocational education was the most effective means to deal with it. A cost-benefit evaluation of industrial secondary vocational schools before the 1967 war was carried out in a thoughtful and thorough analysis by al-Bukhari.[40] He found that although secondary industrial schools were very expensive per student compared with general secondary schools, the graduates of secondary industrial schools were only slightly, if at all, preferred by employers over general secondary school graduates and that the job-specific parts of their training frequently were unutilized when they were employed. Most job-specific training took place within the employing establishment in Jordan. The study suggested that the educational system concentrate on providing generally educated and trainable graduates rather than specifically trained graduates.

The point is not that vocational education for Jordan today has been proven uneconomical. Al-Bukhari's study has been outdated by changes in the economy and in the vocational education system.[41] What his study does indicate is that the desirability of a large program in vocational education cannot be taken for granted. That the demand for places in Jordanian vocational schools exceeded the supply has sometimes been taken as proof of the need for expanded vocational education. However, since government, not only the student, paid a significant part of the cost of vocational education, high demand for places was not proof of positive net benefits to society as a whole. An integral part of Jordan's ambitious vocational education program must be a systematic evaluation as it progresses. The Five Year Plan contains no indication

of the need for evaluation. Programs to promote
vocational education cannot be halted to await the
completion of a scholarly study of their effectiveness, but they should be seen as tentative and ex-
ploratory, subject to revision or even abandonment,
as evidence of their effects becomes available.

The third aspect of the manpower problem--the
drain of manpower from government service--was recognized by the government and planners. Improved
opportunities in the private sector and abroad,
combined with the lagging of civil service salaries
behind inflation, led to the departure of numerous
able civil servants. While some of this realloca-
tion of employment toward improved opportunities
elsewhere probably is desirable, most impressions
were that the outflow was too great, especially if
the government was to implement an ambitious development plan. Accordingly, the Five Year Plan
proposed improvements in the pay, fringe benefits,
and working conditions of government workers.

4. PLAN EXECUTION

The real substance of a development plan does
not lie in its aggregative projections for the economy. This is particularly true of contemporary
Jordan, for which inadequacies of data and susceptibility to unpredictable external influences make
most quantitative projections of very limited
value. What significance those projections do
have is as one indication of the broad strategy
planners apparently intend to pursue. The heart
of a development plan lies in its proposals for
specific projects and policy measures and their
implementation. Major projects and measures proposed in the Five Year Plan have been touched upon
both in this chapter and in relevant sections of
preceding chapters.

It is not rare in LDCs for a planning agency
and the development plan it promulgates to have
almost no influence on actual decisions which
affect development. However, in Jordan it is evident that the NPC has had the potential for considerable influence over development decisions,
through its role in negotiating and administering
foreign aid for projects in the development plans.[42]
Of course, on aid-supported projects the NPC influence is shared in some part with aid donors and
Jordanian ministries or other agencies undertaking
the projects. The JDB, predecessor of the NPC,
concentrated most of its efforts on negotiating and

administering foreign-assisted projects. Between 1971 and 1973 the JDB was transformed into an NPC with ostensibly greater responsibility for formulating, executing, and monitoring the progress of national development plans. Nevertheless, its role of negotiating and administering foreign-assisted projects remained the NPC's biggest concern and one elevated in importance by great increases in aid availability after 1973.

Both the Jordanian government and outside observers judged the implementation procedures for the 1973-75 Three Year Plan to have been highly unsuccessful. For each project in the Three Year Plan the concerned government agency was to appoint a project manager, assisted by a project team, to monitor and report on its progress. The information was then to be passed on to one of nine sectoral or four special committees, from whence it would proceed to a steering committee composed of ministers, other high officials, and private representatives, under the chairmanship of the prime minister. This cumbersome system apparently foundered because of its heavy demands on the time of high officials and reliance on project managers who were sometimes poorly trained in follow-up procedures and not always familiar with the project from its inception.[43] The Five Year Plan proposed improvements in plan implementation procedures, but in fairly general terms.[44]

The performance of the NPC during the Three Year Plan period and in the formulation of the Five Year Plan gave indications of serious weaknesses in the operation of the NPC that called into question its ability to adequately administer the ambitious plan for 1976-80. The NPC played only a limited role in the preparation of the Five Year Plan itself. The failure to complete much of the Three Year Plan on schedule provided another indication, although the NPC's organizational weaknesses could be considered only one of several elements contributing to that outcome.

An American management consulting firm diagnosed the failings of the NPC as poor personnel policies arising from a seriously over-centralized management style.[45] The failure of top NPC management to delegate authority and delineate responsibilities sapped the morale and performance of the NPC staff. At the same time that top management was overburdened, qualified staff at lower levels were often underutilized. Its poor personnel policies hindered the NPC's efforts to attract and

264

retain the most qualified personnel or to identify staff members who were performing poorly. This in turn may have aggravated the tendency of top management to assume excessive responsibilities.

Since government expenditure is a crucial instrument of development policy, and especially so in Jordan, a planning agency such as the NPC can influence development policy largely to the extent that it influences the actual allocation of government expenditures. The Jordanian budget is divided into two virtually unrelated sections. Part Two consists of aid-assisted projects negotiated through the NPC.[46] It is a self-contained budget, whose budgeted outlays could only be expended to the extent that corresponding foreign assistance was received. On this part of the budget, the NPC inevitably exerted significant influence.

Part One of the Jordanian budget includes all budgeted receipts and expenditures not in Part Two. This includes both current and capital expenditures within and outside the development plan. The NPC did not directly control most of the expenditures in any of the categories of Part One, and even its indirect influence on this part of the budget appears to have been fairly modest. The NPC's influence on the budget was less than it might have been, partly because junior and inexperienced staff often were assigned to the analysis of proposed project budgets.[47] The leading role in budget preparation has rested with the Budget Department of the Ministry of Finance.

The Budget Department was established in 1962 and in the succeeding decade and a half achieved improvements in budget preparation and presentation, but the change was very gradual. Even by the end of that period, the Budget Department's function was largely one of bookkeeping for purposes of accountability. Although modest progress had been made toward a program and activity classification of budget expenditures, budget procedures and documentation still did not lend themselves very well to analytical evaluation of budget decisions. The heavy emphasis on accountability in the budget preparation and review processes led to the multiplication of detailed rules for the transfer of allotted appropriations, which minimized the room for discretion by the ministries and led them to overstate their requirements in an effort to achieve some discretionary financial slack. Budget appropriations for a particular ministry involved negotiations between representatives of the ministry and Budget Department examiners, with the final decisions frequently at higher levels, not rarely by the Council of Ministers. At all stages of the process, relatively little analytical information was available and subjective judgments tended to predominate.[48]

In conclusion, more effective plan execution requires improvements in the planning organization itself, in procedures for monitoring the progress of planned projects, and in the budgeting process. It requires measures to strengthen the linkages between plans and annual government budgets, which have always been somewhat tenuous.[49] To keep these problems in perspective, it should be realized that they are all characteristic of LDCs. In particular, the problems of linking plans to budgets and of establishing effective budget procedures are almost universal in LDCs, and solutions are likely to be achieved only by gradual improvements.[50] Of course, the ubiquity of the problems does not warrant disregarding them. To the degree that Jordan continues to set highly ambitious development goals, the need to alleviate the weaknesses in plan execution becomes ever more pressing.

5. CONCLUSION

The Five Year Plan for 1976-80 seems clearly overoptimistic in its aggregative economic projections and, a little less certainly, overambitious in its investment program. But pragmatically, do these weaknesses in the plan document threaten any concrete harm to Jordan's development effort? I suggest that overoptimism in aggregative projections is unlikely to have any more serious consequences than mild embarrassment for the planners. Overambition in the investment program has more serious dangers, but most are avoidable.

The primary function of aggregative projections in development plans is to serve as a check on the implications of the plan. If a plan implies that future foreign exchange outlays will exceed available foreign exchange, future investment will exceed available investible resources, or government outlays will exceed funds available to the government, a warning signal is sent up to revise the plan. Had the projections for the Five Year Plan period been based on less optimistic assumptions about such things as private saving, the government budget, and foreign earnings, they would have revealed some such imbalances as an implication of the high planned growth rate. However for Jordan, in contrast to other LDCs where plan projections have a more prominent role, the errors introduced by faulty assumptions of this nature are dwarfed by other likely sources of error in forecasting. In particular, foreign aid receipts, which so predominate in the Jordanian economy, are highly unpredictable. A large percentage error in predicting government tax revenue may be erased by a small percentage variation in foreign aid receipts. To put it bluntly, it makes little practical difference how accurate the aggregate projections for the economy are.[51]

While the optimistic aggregative projections for the economy have some significance as indicators of planners' strategies, they do not directly affect policy actions. However, the apparently overambitious investment program does represent a specific program of action and therefore poses concrete risks. The danger is that in trying to do too much, planners will waste investment funds in hasty implementation of poorly prepared projects for which the needed complementary resources, particularly administrative and technical skills, are lacking. Undeniably, when the availability of foreign aid increases greatly, as it did in Jordan, it is inevitable and, to a point, desirable that some relaxation of standards in project design and implementation take place in order to achieve a high volume of investment. When aid became more available after 1973, the NPC increased its efforts to solicit and negotiate additional aid somewhat at the expense of efficient project design and implementation. Such a trade-off is valid; the danger lies in pushing it too far. Excessive short-run expediency threatens longer term difficulties, for example, if aid donors become disillusioned by ineffective aid utilization, or if slack project preparation and execution procedures become embedded in the government's bureaucratic structure, from which they cannot readily be removed even if aid becomes scarce again in the future.

While the ambitious nature of the Five Year Plan poses some dangers, the fact that it, like all plans everywhere, cannot be carried out precisely as conceived may be its salvation. The plan is being modified as it progresses. It seems probable that the overambition of the plan will be resolved primarily by stretching it out. Projects, some of which were planned to be completed on very tight

schedules, will simply fall behind schedule, as was
common during the Three Year Plan period. No development plan is a literal, binding prescription
for development policy, and in the case of Jordan's
Five Year Plan for 1976-80 it is particularly fortunate that this is the case.

NOTES

1. Jordan Development Board (JDB), Five Year Program for
Economic Development, 1962-1967, n.p., 1961, pp. 15-16. The
World Bank mission that visited Jordan in 1955 published a
detailed report, but lacking national accounting data, it
concentrated upon proposals for feasible projects and government reforms. It did not have official status as a development plan, but undoubtedly influenced development policy.

2. Perhaps it simply made those preparing project proposals more conscious of the need to find projects that saved
foreign exchange. It definitely did not manifest itself in
a changed "shadow price" for foreign exchange, since accounting prices different from market prices or expected market
prices have not been used in project analysis in Jordan.

3. JDB, Seven Year Program, pp. 34, 147, 202.

4. Ibid., pp. 34, 44.

5. See p. 39.

6. All figures in this paragraph calculated from JDB,
Seven Year Program, pp. 34-36, 43.

7. Taher H. Kanaan, "Projection of Jordan's Foreign
Trade 1970, 1975," UNCTAD Projections Section, n.d., n.p.
(mimeographed), pp. 52-54.

8. NPC, Three Year Development Plan, p. 24. The economic projections of the plan were all in terms of the combined East and West Banks, since official national accounts
statistics for the East Bank alone did not exist at the time
the plan was prepared. Of course, investment projects and
policy measures proposed in the plan were for the East Bank
only.

9. Gross fixed investment was to rise from 15.6% of GDP
at market prices during 1967-72 to 20.9% during 1973-75
(ibid., pp. 47-48).

10. Ibid., p. 48.

11. For example, the marginal propensity to consume for
1972-75 implied by the Three Year Plan was .82 (ibid., p. 30).
While optimistically low, this estimate was much more plausible than the Seven Year Plan's estimate of .59.

12. The Three Year Plan did identify an additional development objective not in previous plans: the regional distribution of the gains from development (ibid., p. 15), sub-

sequently reiterated in the Five Year Plan for 1976-80. This arose from increasing concern about the concentration of population and wealth in the Amman region. Because this concern was relatively new, there was little indication of it in the concrete measures proposed by the plan.

13. Over the three years of the plan period, public sector investment was projected to be J.D. 99.6 million (ibid., p. 34). Actual gross fixed government investment for 1973-75 has been estimated at J.D. 98.3 million. CBJ, Monthly Statistical Bulletin, 13 (June 1977), Table 41.

14. See the discussion in section 4 below.

15. All plan projections are ostensibly in constant dinar prices. In most respects this, and not current-price estimation, is the appropriate procedure. However, it does mean that the plan does not project the actual magnitudes of financial flows, such as foreign grants and loans, but only their constant-price values, on the questionable, but probably unavoidable, implicit assumption that the constant-price values are invariant to the level of inflation.

16. Also, the estimates of expenditures on some plan projects would require substantial upward revision.

17. The plan projected net factor income from abroad to grow at less than 11% annually in constant prices. Since the 1972-75 rate of increase had been 65% annually in current prices, the plan's estimate seems unduly pessimistic.

18. Assuming that value added in phosphate remains about half the value of total sales, the growth of phosphate exports projected by the plan accounts by itself for 17% of the total projected 1975-80 growth in GDP at factor cost (calculated from NPC, Five Year Plan, pp. 109-17). If there were no growth in phosphate value added, the growth rate of GDP at factor cost would be reduced from 11.9% to 10.2%, other things equal.

19. For comparison with previous estimates of Jordan's ICOR, the appropriate aggregate ICOR for the plan is 3.2, derived using GDP at market prices. The figure of 3.5 in Table IX.1 is for GDP at factor cost. In either case, the plan ICOR is significantly above that of prewar Jordan.

20. Ibid., p. 110. (Investment in aircraft by the national airline is not included in any of the plan's projections of investment). This projected timing of investment, which probably seriously understates investment at the end of the plan, makes some measures of progress during the plan period look excessively favorable. In particular, the expected reduction in dependence on foreign aid is overstated. Understating investment at the end of the plan period makes it appear that at that time there would be less demand for imports of capital goods and less need for foreign-supplied financing for investment.

21. Other projects directly connected to the Maqarin Dam, such as extension of irrigation canals, could be included as

part of the same project. Also, there are three major and one minor projects in the expansion of Aqaba port facilities, which might be considered essentially a single project.

22. The category of foreign aid and loans includes current transfers, loans, and technical assistance to the government from abroad and net foreign loans and contributions to the private sector on capital account, from ibid., pp. 113, 116, 119.

23. This point was made explicitly by one of the principal designers of the plan at the conference in Amman which officially introduced the plan in June 1976.

24. Plan projection computed from ibid., p. 115. Estimates of the marginal propensity to consume in Jordan are handicapped by the poor quality data available, but it probably was about .9. See Akram M. Steitieh, "Consumption Patterns of Wage Earners in Jordan," Amman: Economic Research Department, Royal Scientific Society, 1974. For other countries see Houthakker, p. 219.

25. Raymond F. Mikesell and James E. Zinser, "The Nature of the Savings Function in Developing Countries: A Survey of the Theoretical and Empirical Literature," Journal of Economic Literature, 11 (March 1973), 10. The coefficients found in the studies cited there are of a size that could account for much of the increase in the average private saving rate projected for Jordan between 1975 and 1980.

26. All projections are in constant prices. In current prices the implied increase would be four- or five-fold between 1975 and 1980.

27. See Ronald I. McKinnon, Money and Capital in Economic Development, Washington: Brookings Institution, 1973; and Edward S. Shaw, Financial Deepening in Economic Development, New York: Oxford University Press, 1973.

28. See NPC, Five Year Plan, Ch. 3.

29. The Five Year Plan again placed "achievement of the highest possible level of employment" on its list of development objectives (NPC, Five Year Plan, p. 52).

30. [Salem O. Ghawi and Munthar Masri], "Labour Force in Jordan," [Amman], Jordan Development Conference No. 76/5, 1976 (mimeographed).

31. E.g., 7% in mining and manufacturing and 3.5% in agriculture.

32. Both of these estimates are for the increase in net demand for labor, i.e., the increase in the total size of the labor force required. This equals new entrants into the labor force minus withdrawals from the labor force. Increase in the gross demand for labor (i.e., new entrants) would be somewhat greater.

33. They implicitly assumed that 30% of female school leavers at higher educational levels and 10% at lower educational levels do not enter the domestic Jordanian labor force. These percentages include both women who do not seek work and

270

women who are employed abroad. The same percentages were used for male school leavers. I am grateful to the authors for explaining to me this assumption, which is not made explicit in their paper.

34. JDS, First Census, vol. II, pp. 3, 10; JDS, Multi-Purpose Household Survey, 1974, pp. 47, 183-84.

35. When an average rate is rising, the corresponding marginal rate will be above the average. Using some very rough assumptions to link the 1961 Jordanian female labor force participation rate to the 1974 East Bank female labor force participation rate, I computed a net marginal rate of labor force participation among females 15-64 of 12%. This implies that a net increase of 100 in the number of women 15-64 induced a net increase of 12 in the number of women in the labor force. While the assumptions and data used are very rough, the point is that this percentage is nowhere near the rate assumed in the Ghawi-Masri study and even a very substantial error in the estimate would not change that result.

36. The calculation is based on the additional assumptions that the male labor force grows at 3% per year, that women constituted 10% of the labor force in 1975, and that the number of females 9-14 in 1975 was equal to 45% of the number in the total labor force during 1975. All these assumptions are in line with the rather limited information we have on these matters.

37. NPC, Three Year Development Plan, pp. 219-23, 270-73.

38. NPC, Five Year Plan, p. 550; and unpublished sources, Jordan Ministry of Education.

40. Najati Mohammed Amin al-Bukhari, Issues in Occupational Education and Training: A Case Study in Jordan, Stanford, California: Stanford University, 1968.

41. For example, the industrial schools studied by al-Bukhari offered only seven specializations. By the mid-1970s the vocational education system in Jordan offered a much wider choice of specialization.

42. The largest part of foreign aid is "budget support" aid, which is not linked to any specific project. It is used to finance the general government current budget and is not administered by the NPC.

43. [Ahmad Mango], "Implementation and Follow-Up of Five Year Plan 1976-1980," [Amman], Jordan Development Conference No. 76/2, 1976 (mimeographed), pp. 1-3.

44. Ibid., pp. 3-6; and NPC, Five Year Plan, pp. 104-6.

45. McKinsey and Company, Inc., "Revitalizing the National Planning Council," n.p., 1976. My personal observations of the NPC during 1976 and interviews with persons both within and outside the Jordan government tend to support the conclusions of this study.

46. A minor part of foreign civilian project assistance has gone directly to the concerned ministry or government agency and has not been included in the government budget.

271

47. Ibid., pp. 2-3.

48. The government budgetary process in Jordan has been the subject of numerous studies over the years. Among them are Gordon V. Potter, A Five Year Plan of Budget and Planning Improvement, Amman: USAID/Jordan, 1966; Naim Husni Dahmash, "The Role of Budgeting in National Economic Planning in Developing Countries with Emphasis on Jordan," unpublished Ph.D. thesis in accounting, University of Illinois at Urbana-Champaign, 1973; Adnan Hassan El-Hindi, "Reforms in Jordan's Budget System," unpublished Ph.D. thesis, Department of Economics, Syracuse University, Syracuse, N.Y., 1976; and three unpublished master's theses submitted to the American University of Beirut: Husayn Harrim, "Government Budgetary Process in Jordan," 1968; Rima Faiq Halazun, "Fiscal Policy and Economic Development in Jordan," 1968; and Wasfi Mahmoud Osman, "Major Problems of Government Budgeting and Planning: An Appraisal of Jordan's Experience (1948-1968)," 1969.

49. For example, in the government budget for 1976, prepared at about the same time as the Five Year Plan, the forecast of 1976 government expenditures was significantly below the corresponding plan projection for current expenditures and above it for capital expenditures. Cf. Jordan Budget Department, Budget Law for the Fiscal Year 1976, Schedule No. 2; and NPC, Five Year Plan, Annexes 4 and 5.

50. See Albert Waterston, Development Planning: Lessons of Experience, Baltimore: Johns Hopkins, 1965, especially Chs. 7-9. For an interesting analysis of the failings of development planning in LDCs, stressing political and decision-making processes, see Tony Killick, "The Possibilities of Development Planning," Oxford Economic Papers, n.s. 28 (July 1976), 161-84.

51. This conclusion is reinforced by the fact that Jordan enjoys considerable leeway for error from its relatively large holdings of foreign reserves and from fairly sizable government deposits with domestic banks. It is further reinforced by the likelihood that some foreign aid donations may respond to changes in the Jordanian economy in a deliberately compensating manner.

10
Conclusion: A Look Ahead

1. RETROSPECTIVE

According to most statistical estimates, Jordan in the years preceding the 1967 Middle East war appeared to be one of the outstanding "success stories" of economic growth among the less developed countries of the world. However, because of limitations in the economic data available, it was not easy to accept this conclusion with full confidence. A primary goal of Part 1 of this study is to bring statistical evidence--including estimates of total product measured, for the first time, in constant prices and estimates of the sectoral allocation of investment--to bear on the question of the pace and nature of Jordan's prewar economic growth. The new evidence does not contradict the generally favorable impression of Jordan's prewar development performance, but it does place the conclusions on a firmer footing and helps to spell out more clearly the dimensions of postwar growth.

Between 1959 and 1966 real domestic product grew at an average annual rate in the neighborhood of 7%. Data for the 1950s are less reliable, but they suggest a growth rate that was equally high, or perhaps modestly higher. While growth of around 7% per year is lower than erroneous estimates of around 10% that have commonly been cited, it represents an outstanding performance in comparison with most other LDCs. Prewar growth was rapid enough to reduce substantially the high unemployment rate that prevailed in the early 1950s.

Since Jordan's rapid prewar output growth was achieved with an investment rate that was only about average for an LDC, it appears that Jordan was able to make comparatively effective use of its available resources. This also is indicated by two rough measures: the relatively low level of Jordan's ICOR, which suggests effective use of investment, and the relatively high residual, or growth in total factor productivity, which suggests effective use of increases in labor and capital combined. They also suggest that Jordan's superior growth record could not be attributed solely to its relatively large aid receipts.

Compared to most other economies at Jordan's level of development, economic activity in prewar Jordan was heavily concentrated in the services sector. More than half of the difference between Jordan and the typical LDC in the relative size of the services sector was accounted for by Jordan's relatively large import surplus. Other, lesser, causes of services concentration included Jordan's heavy defense burden, comparative advantage in tourism, and the historical heritage of what might loosely be called a structural disequilibrium in manufacturing. Although poor data and erratic changes in the postwar years limit any attempt at measurement, it is evident that services concentration characterized the postwar East Bank economy as it had prewar Jordan and that the import surplus and defense burden were at least as important causes as they were in prewar Jordan.

Might there be a connection between the concentration of Jordan's economy in the services sector and its superior growth performance in the prewar years? According to Ginor,[1] an import surplus which permits an LDC to shift resources to services production permits a higher level of domestic production, since LDCs typically have a comparative advantage in the production of services not traded internationally. Hence, a large (relative to total product) import surplus causes a high level of GDP. However, for the import surplus to contribute to a higher growth rate of GDP, it must be rising in relative size. During 1959-66 there was a distinct decline in the size of the import surplus relative to GDP. The data for the 1950s are much less satisfactory, but they do suggest a generally upward trend in the import surplus relative to GDP. Therefore, Jordan's import surplus, through its effect on services concentration, may have contributed somewhat to the high GDP growth rate of the 1950s. However, Jordan's outstanding growth performance during 1959-66 was achieved in spite of, not because of, this effect.

Part 2 of this study surveyed the overall pattern of the postwar East Bank economy and its

development. The many weaknesses and gaps in statistical information seriously limit any attempts
at analysis. Even the size of postwar East Bank
population is not precisely known, and the growth
of real output can only be guessed at. It appears
that the growth of real gross domestic product between 1967 and 1975 was modest and barely kept up
with the growth of population over the same period.
Considering the circumstances, it is difficult not
to consider this an achievement. Real national
product may have grown as much as several percentage points faster than real domestic product because of large increases in remittances from Jordanians employed abroad.

In important respects the East Bank economy of
the mid-1970s was similar to that of Jordan a decade
earlier. The general pattern of industrial production and merchandise exports was broadly similar; the
greatest change--in the value of phosphate exports--
was largely fortuitous and temporary. No major
changes seem to have occurred in the financing of
total domestic investment nor (except for phosphate
royalties) in the system of raising domestic revenue for government. Although the agriculture sector declined in relative importance between 1967
and 1975, in absolute terms it was little changed.
The lack of development in agriculture was partly
due to the interruption in agricultural development
policy and investment caused by the years of strife
from 1967 to 1971 and partly due to weaknesses in
development policy, particularly in dryland grain
production.

Among the most conspicuous differences between
the East Bank economy of the mid-1970s and the
Jordanian economy of a decade earlier were the much
higher aid levels in the later years and, partly as
a consequence, the greater relative size of total
domestic investment, government spending, and military employment. While the share of the military
in total employment was increasing, agriculture's
share was declining. In the event of a Middle East
peace settlement permitting a reduction in Jordan's
defense efforts, the large share of defense in
total employment could represent both an opportunity
and a problem: the opportunity to alleviate the manpower shortages implied by Jordan's ambitious goals
for development (see Chapter 9, section 3) and the
problem of assimilating military manpower into appropriate civilian employment.

Chapters 7-9 surveyed three critical areas of
development policy: agriculture, industry, and

275

development planning. It is easy to draw a false impression of Jordan's economic policy from a superficial examination of measures used. Jordan has investment, import, and foreign exchange licensing. It has controls on exports and imports of agricultural products. It has had price controls on some important commodities, sometimes combined with export restrictions. On the face of it, such measures suggest a highly controlled economy, but in practice the degree of control has not been great. Especially in recent years, licensing measures had little effect because licenses were granted readily. Restrictions on agricultural imports tended to be applied when there was little motive to import anyway, and similarly for exports. The most substantial restraints on prices were applied temporarily only.

Despite appearances, the fundamental strategy has been one of free enterprise. Nonetheless, the government's role has been significant. Most important, large foreign aid receipts have permitted the government to have a great impact through government expenditures and to some degree, through its provision of finance (including equity capital) to private enterprise.

In prewar Jordan agricultural production increased substantially, with the major impetus coming from irrigation and livestock production. In the East Bank between 1967 and 1975 there was no discernible growth in agricultural output, partly because military and civil conflict during 1967-71 temporarily halted the development of irrigated areas.

The promotion of irrigated agriculture has been the primary element in the government's strategy for agricultural development. The rationale is that Jordan is endowed with a unique irrigable area of high potential in the Jordan Valley and it is in irrigated agriculture that the international community offers some of the best opportunities for borrowing and adapting new technologies. Development of new irrigated areas is critical to the success of the government's plans for agriculture, but important problems must be overcome, such as the need to settle additional farmers in the East Jordan Valley.

Throughout much of the prewar and postwar periods there was no discernible trend in dryland crop production. In the prewar and early postwar periods this might partly be blamed on the lack of government effort to promote this sector. However,

by the mid-1970s intensified government efforts in
this area might have been expected to show results.
They did not, partly because policies to promote
farmer adoption of new techniques did not deal
adequately with the problem of adapting techniques
to local conditions and partly because wheat price
policies made it temporarily unprofitable to adopt
new techniques. The 1976-80 plan placed heavy
emphasis on improving the delivery of new techniques to the farmer, particularly through the
agricultural cooperatives, but improved adaptive
research probably merited the greater emphasis.

Significant further development of livestock
production (aside from poultry) appears to require
a long, slow process involving major changes in
land-use practices. Short-term government policy
in the 1976-80 plan called for promotion of egg
production and dairy cattle, but the improvement of
sheep and goat production, not as much emphasized
in the plan, may offer better prospects. Land tenure, agricultural extension, marketing, and credit
offered some opportunities for improvement, but
probably none has constituted a critical bottleneck to agricultural growth.

The greater part of the growth of Jordan's
industrial sector occurred between 1959 and 1966,
fueled by increased phosphate exports, increased
domestic demand as incomes rose, and especially by
the substitution of domestic production for imports. For the industrial sector, relatively underdeveloped in 1959, the level of import substitution
achieved by 1966 was fairly typical of LDCs at comparable levels of income, although--as comparison
with Israel indicates--the limits of ultimately
feasible import substitution were not approached.
In the aftermath of the 1967 war little industrial
development occurred and by 1974 the industrial
structure of the East Bank was little different
from that of the East Bank of Jordan as a whole on
the eve of the war. The major difference was a
transitory one: the temporarily very high world
prices received for Jordan's exports of phosphates.
At the time that the new Five Year Development Plan
for 1976-80 was presented in 1976, the significance of the industrial sector still lay mainly in
its future potential, rather than its quite limited
current development.

Although Jordan adheres to a fundamentally
free-enterprise philosophy, in its industrial policy
this has been combined with a certain paternalism
and administrative discretion that may be most

277

appropriate for an industry in its embryo stage and
lacking sophisticated entrepreneurship. Restrictive investment licensing of new competitors,
tariff protection, and direct restrictions on imports tended to insulate established domestic firms
from competition, but in the early and mid-1970s
the government moved toward policies promoting
greater competition. As the economy and its industry matures, these measures are likely to proceed
further. Likewise, as industry matures, some highly discretionary measures of industrial promotion
may become less attractive.

After a postwar hiatus during which there was
essentially no systematic development policy-
making, the Three Year Plan for 1973-75 was inaugurated. Although many of its objectives were
not achieved on schedule due to its overambitious
nature, weaknesses in plan implementation, and a
variety of unforeseeable events, it did achieve
its primary purpose of restoring a systematic approach to development policy. The succeeding Five
Year Plan for 1976-80 adopted a high-investment,
big-project strategy predicated on expected foreign
aid receipts that were extremely large in relation
to the size of the economy. The extraordinarily
high growth of domestic product projected by the
Five Year Plan hinged on a projected growth in
mining and manufacturing value added that was
highly implausible. The future manpower requirements implied by the plan also indicated that the
projections were overoptimistic. However, because
of the circumstances of the Jordanian economy, the
practical consequences of overoptimism in the development plan are not likely to be nearly as
serious as they might be in most other LDCs.

Plan execution in Jordan has been plagued by
the usual array of problems common to LDCs: over-
centralization of authority and other poor management practices in the planning agency, a lack of
connection between development plans and government budgets, and weak procedures of budget analysis
and control. One of Jordan's problems is not typical: increased inefficiency in project implementation as foreign aid becomes so readily available
that planners' efforts are diverted from using resources most efficiently to attracting more foreign-
supplied resources. It is a problem other LDCs
might envy, but it is nonetheless a genuine problem
with potentially serious long-run dangers.

2. FUTURE PROSPECTS

a. No Political Changes Assumed

Jordan absorbed with striking resiliency a series of shocks in the late 1960s and early 1970s. Subsequently, it was the beneficiary of a variety of fortuitous external events, including great increases in foreign assistance, earnings of Jordanians employed abroad, and phosphate export earnings. By the mid-1970s the East Bank was a booming economy, healthy in some respects, but it was also an embryonic, fragile one, still subject to changes in Middle East economic and political conditions and highly vulnerable in the event of a substantial, sustained reduction in foreign aid. Behind the prosperity of the mid-1970s the two most important factors must have been increases in foreign aid and in remittances from Jordanians employed abroad. An uncompensated reversal of these trends could readily snuff out the boom. A country with a quarter of its labor force in the (largely aid-financed) armed forces and with foreign aid receipts equal to more than a quarter of the value of its GNP must consider its prosperity somewhat contingent. This vulnerability of the economy would be accentuated by adherence to the high-investment, aid-dependent strategy chosen by the designers of the 1976-80 plan to take advantage of the increase in Jordan's access to foreign aid.

In the absence of political disruption and major cutbacks in foreign aid, there appears to be little reason why the East Bank economy could not achieve over the medium term a rate of growth comparable to that of prewar Jordan. There exist promising investment opportunities, including further development of irrigated agriculture in the Jordan Valley and of tourism in the Aqaba Port area, expansion of phosphate output, and new manufacturing industries serving the home market and perhaps exporting to nearby oil-producing countries. The economy faces some new problems not existing in prewar years, particularly the possibility of manpower shortages, but it also has some new opportunities. Success will depend partly on development policy decisions to be made in the future, some of which were intimated in Chapters 7-9.

Numerical projections of Jordan's medium- or long-term economic prospects are of negligible

value. They would be highly contingent upon unpredictable future events, such as future aid availability and political and economic developments in
neighboring countries. In a small country still as
underdeveloped as Jordan is, a single major investment could have a significant effect on the
overall structure of production, trade, and employment. An economy whose structure is already
fleshed out has a degree of momentum, and therefore predictability, in its future growth that a
country like Jordan lacks.

One common approach to long-term projections
is through the balance of payments, examining how
Jordan could increase foreign earnings or decrease
foreign payments sufficiently to achieve independence of foreign aid. This approach has some, but
limited, value, if two dangers can be avoided.

First, an emphasis on achieving independence
of foreign aid easily leads to the view of a given
gap between foreign earnings and payments, which
constitutes a requirement for foreign aid. In
other words, the line of causation is seen as running strictly from the foreign trade gap to the
aid necessary to finance it. The tendency is to
overlook the line of causation in the opposite
direction. The availability of foreign aid can
generate, or increase, a gap between imports and
exports; indeed, for the financial aid flow to increase the real resources available to the domestic
economy of the recipient, it must do so. In Jordan's case, this second direction of causation
cannot be ignored. In part, the reason there is
such a large trade gap for foreign aid to finance
is that there is so much aid available to finance
it. The availability of aid increases the trade
gap through such things as expenditures by government and other aid recipients in Jordan, the
effect of foreign aid receipts on the domestic
money supply, and liberalizing of import restrictions permitted by the availability of foreign exchange. When the trade gap is seen in this light,
as partly a desirable consequence of aid availability, it may not seem so impossible for Jordan to
achieve independence of foreign aid in the long run.

The second danger lies in the tendency to
place the burden of proof on the achievement of
independence, i.e., to require identification of
the specific sources of increased foreign earnings
or decreased foreign expenditures. This also tends
to exaggerate the difficulty of achieving independence of foreign aid. It is the well-rewarded job

of successful entrepreneurs to identify specific opportunities for earning or saving foreign exchange. We can deal only in generalities.

There appears to be much scope for saving foreign exchange by further import substitution. For the manufacturing sector this point was made in section 1 of Chapter 8 above. In agriculture Jordan continues to import large quantities of wheat and meat for which it could in time substitute domestic production.

Jordan's exports of goods have been mainly primary products, including phosphates, fruits, and vegetables.[2] Significant expansion of phosphate production is feasible and has been scheduled in the 1976-80 plan, but greater marketing efforts may be required. Fruit and vegetable output would be greatly increased by the planned development of irrigated areas in the Jordan Valley, a process that would not be complete until around the end of the century. The unique characteristics of the area give Jordan a seasonal comparative advantage. As fruit and vegetable supplies increase, problems of marketing abroad may become more serious, particularly if the limits to the demand in neighboring Arab oil-producing states are reached.[3] There are some possibilities for developing new primary product exports, particularly potash and other minerals from the Dead Sea.

Up to the mid-1970s Jordan's exports of manufactured products were of very modest importance and were scattered among a variety of goods. For the immediate future one planned new industry, the fertilizer plant using Jordanian phosphate, offers the prospect of significant expansion of manufactured exports. The prospects for increasing exports of other manufactures are enhanced by the rapidly growing markets in nearby Arab countries and by the Jordanian government's measures promoting greater competition in domestic industry.

Before 1967 Jordan's major hope for increased foreign exchange earnings lay in tourism. Tourism then was a significant source of foreign earnings, and its potential had not nearly been tapped. For the postwar East Bank without Jerusalem and the rest of the West Bank, tourism offers foreign earnings opportunities which are not negligible, but the prospects do not approach what could have been anticipated without the loss of the West Bank.

The annual number of non-Jordanian Arab and other foreign arrivals to Jordan reached a peak in 1966, declined to 1972, and subsequently rose

281

steadily. In 1975 for the first time the total sur-
passed the 1966 level and by 1976 it was 72% above
it. The total number increased 50% between 1975
and 1976. Part of the 1975-76 increase must have
been due to the civil war in Lebanon at that time.
Almost all the increase of 1976 over 1966 was in
Arab visitors, whose number more than doubled,
while the number of other visitors increased only
a little more than a quarter.[4] Jordanian border
statistics do not differentiate between tourists
and other visitors, so that, e.g., truck drivers,
businessmen, and travellers in transit are counted
along with tourists. In fact, only a small fraction
of the visitors enumerated can have been tourists
properly speaking. In 1975 half of all visitors
were from Syria or Turkey.[5] The great majority of
the Syrian visitors must have been in Jordan for
business or personal reasons unconnected with
tourism. Many of the Turkish visitors were travelers in transit on pilgrimage to the Moslem holy
cities of Mecca and Medinah; they were often too
poor to afford air travel and can have spent but
little in Jordan.

In the mid-1970s Jordan attracted an increased
number of tourists, including tourists on their way
to the West Bank and Israel, summer visitors from
Saudi Arabia and Persian Gulf states, and winter
visitors to Aqaba. By permitting tourists to pass
over the Jordan River to the West Bank, Jordan
was able to attract foreign tourist groups, but
the average stay in Jordan must have been brief,
often only a day or two. The increasing number of
vacationers from Saudi Arabia and the Persian Gulf
was the result not only of rising incomes in the
oil states, but also because competitive loca-
tions--the West Bank and Lebanon--were inaccessible
or unattractive to these travelers. Political and
economic recovery in Lebanon or a Middle East
peace settlement restoring the access of Arab visitors to the West Bank could cut greatly into the
East Bank's tourism earnings from this source. The
beaches and warm winter climate around Aqaba should
continue to attract winter visitors. Development
of Aqaba port and industry there could diminish its
attractiveness somewhat, but newer tourism developments will be located at a greater distance from the
developed area. The one imponderable in the future
of Jordan's tourism is the possible effect of a
Middle East peace agreement which admitted visitors
from Israel. Conceivably, a great many Israelis
and visitors to Israel might be attracted. The

number of such visitors, their length of stay, and
their expenditure in Jordan are all beyond estimation, but it is possible the numbers could be quite
large.

In conclusion, the Jordan economy would appear
to have reasonable long-run prospects for adjusting
its foreign earnings and expenditures to achieve
ultimate independence of foreign aid. In the
short run Jordan could adapt its balance of payments in the event of a significant, but not total,
reduction in foreign aid, just as it adapted to a
large increase in foreign aid; in this event, Jordan's substantial foreign reserves would ease the
transition. However, complete independence of
foreign aid is necessarily a long-run proposition.
The Jordan economy has adapted itself to relatively
large aid inflows extending over a quarter century,
e.g., in the large weight of the services sector in
the country's economic structure. The sudden complete cessation of aid would likely entail extreme
economic, and possibly political, dislocation.

Over the long term, say several decades, Jordan's dependence on foreign aid to achieve balance
in its foreign accounts could be eliminated by the
steady expansion of import-substituting and ex-
change-earning activities along a broad front.
Barring remarkable and unanticipated discoveries
of exportable minerals, no single source of foreign
earnings offers the prospect by itself of replacing
aid in Jordan's foreign accounts. The nearest
possibility to such a deus ex machina would appear
to be remittances from Jordanians abroad, which
have increased strikingly. Yet these are highly
contingent on the continued economic strength of
neighboring Arab oil countries and on political
attitudes there. The host countries are likely to
limit growth in the number of expatriate workers
for political and social reasons, and in time
citizens of the host countries may develop the
skills to replace some foreign workers. The necessity of adjusting the balance of payments gradually
along a broad front if independence of aid is to
be achieved means that almost the entire spectrum
of government economic policies will play a role, including exchange rate policy, agricultural research
and investment, development of tourist attractions,
and policies to promote competitiveness in industry.

b. Political Settlement Assumed

Quantitative projections of the Jordanian

economy under alternative assumptions about a Middle
East peace settlement would be even more fanciful
than quantitative projections assuming no political
change. We can, however, outline some general
propositions that might shape one's thinking about
the economic implications of alternative political
settlements. While possible political settlements
may vary in details, there really are only two
major dimensions relevant to the economic status
of Jordan: the political status of territories
occupied by Israel in 1967 and the post-settlement
relationships between Israel and the Arab countries. The most likely alternatives in the first
dimension are either placing the greater part of
the Occupied Territories under Jordanian sovereignty, perhaps in a federated status, or the creation
of an independent Palestinian state. In the second
dimension the primary relevant alternatives involve
varying forms of economic cooperation between
Israel and Arab states, such as the opening of
trade or even preferential trading agreements,
lowered barriers to international movement of capital and labor, and cooperation in matters such as
transportation, tourism, industrial projects, and
agriculture.

The postwar economy of the Occupied Territories has been reviewed elsewhere and will only
be sketched here.[6] Constant-price GNP in both the
West Bank and Gaza grew at an average 14% per year
between 1968 and 1975.[7] Some of this growth represents simply recovery from the dislocations of
war and its aftermath, but this can be only a
modest part of the total. The primary driving
force in the growth was increased employment in
Israel of residents of the Occupied Territories,
who commuted from their homes. This accounted
directly for about a third of the growth of GNP
and indirectly probably for a significant part of
the remaining growth. Because the most rapid
growth was in earnings "abroad" (i.e., in Israel),
the growth of GDP for the territories was perceptibly less than the growth in their GNP, but it
was still substantial. Most of the employment in
Israel was in construction and to a lesser degree
in agriculture. Although training programs, mainly
in basic construction skills, were instituted in
the Occupied Territories, the overall training
effect of employment in Israel must have been
modest because of the concentration of employment
at the low-skill end of the employment spectrum.
Growth in employment in Israel was accompanied by

falling unemployment rates and rising labor force participation rates among residents of the Occupied Territories. By the mid-1970s these sources of increasing employment were greatly diminished, so that further expansion of nonresident employment in Israel would be more directly at the expense of the labor supply available for economic activity in the Occupied Territories themselves.

Over the postwar period to 1975 the changes in the economic structure of the Occupied Territories themselves were quite modest considering the substantial growth in incomes during that time. In the West Bank there was no perceptible change in the share of agriculture and industry in total product. The share of construction (primarily residential) increased, presumably in consequence of higher incomes, and the share of services declined. Compared to the prewar period the decline in the share of services must have been quite large because of the cessation of services supplied to the Jordanian army and to Arab tourists in the West Bank. The Gaza Strip economy, because it was less developed initially than the West Bank, experienced greater structural changes in the postwar period. The share of industry in domestic product increased significantly from a miniscule base, promoted partly by the establishment of Israeli-owned firms in the Erez industrial estate in Gaza near the Israeli border. Aside from this modest development of small-scale industry, there was little investment by Israelis in the industry of the Occupied Territories because of obvious political uncertainties. In Gaza, as in the West Bank, the share of construction in domestic product expanded significantly while the share of services declined.

Investment in the Occupied Territories was not of the size or character to produce significant structural change. One consequence of the Israel government's policy of minimal intervention in the Occupied Territories was that public investment remained low. Private investment by Israelis in the Occupied Territories, outside of Jewish settlements there, was discouraged by political uncertainties. Private fixed investment in the territories by their residents increased greatly between 1968 and 1975, but a large fraction (nearly two-thirds in 1975[8]) was in residential construction. Private investment in industry may have been discouraged by competition from Israeli producers in some sectors, but the high Israeli tariffs on many products might have encouraged investment in other industrial

sectors. More discouraging may have been the lack
of organized financial institutions. West Bank
branches of banks with head offices in Jordan remained closed, while Israeli branches in the territories attracted few deposits. Hence, there was
virtually no banking system in the territories.

The primary postwar development in the agricultural sector of the Occupied Territories was
the significant reduction in numbers employed while
the total output was not only maintained, but at
least modestly increased. Hence, agricultural productivity per worker in agriculture rose substantially. Workers were drawn from farm work in the
territories by improved employment opportunities
elsewhere, mainly in Israel. It is not clear how
much of the resulting rise in agricultural output
per worker is due to increases in hours worked per
worker, to the withdrawal of marginal, low-produc-
tivity farmers and farms from production, to new
cropping patterns, and to advances in production
techniques. There was some transfer of knowledge
of new agricultural technologies from Israel to the
territories, including the use of plastic covers in
vegetable cultivation, new plant varieties, and improved irrigation practices. There were some
shifts in the pattern of output (notably, the reduced importance of melons), but overall the pattern
was not greatly changed. In view of this and the
continuing low share of purchased inputs in total
farm production, it appears that there was no great
structural or technological change in the agriculture of the Occupied Territories; the sharp reduction in the number of workers employed was the only
major change.[9]

Not surprisingly, the foreign trade of the
Occupied Territories was reoriented toward Israel in
the years after 1967 as a result of the elimination
of trade barriers between them and the imposition
of Israeli tariff schedules on the territories' imports from areas outside Israel. In 1975 65% of the
territories' export trade and over 90% of their import trade was with Israel. About 85% of the West
Banks' exports to Israel were of industrial goods,
a substantial portion of which were produced under
subcontracting with Israeli firms.[10] Industrial
exports were around half of Gaza's exports to
Israel and subcontracting played a role there also.
Since Israeli tariff levels were generally higher
than those that were applied in the territories before 1967, there is a presupposition that imposition of Israeli tariff schedules on the imports of

the Occupied Territories from the outside world may on balance have harmed them, as higher-priced goods from Israel displaced imports from the outside world.[11] However, other developments, such as the expansion of subcontracting, may at least partly have counterbalanced that effect.

From this cursory review of postwar developments in the economy of the Occupied Territories, one paramount point is suggested: The occupation of the territories has not so changed their economies that economic considerations represent a significant obstacle to the conclusion of a peace settlement that is mutually acceptable on political grounds. While the occupation has brought numerous economic links between Israel and the Occupied Territories, these links could, if necessary in the greater interests of a peace settlement, be disentangled without drastic economic effect or could be maintained under a variety of alternative settlement arrangements. Further, the structure of economic activity and the capital stock within the Occupied Territories has not been greatly changed during a decade of occupation. Consequently, any political settlement that was feasible from a purely economic standpoint before 1967 should be comparably acceptable in economic terms in the late 1970s. Finally, any economic implications of a peace settlement will be small compared to the volume of aid potentially available to implement a Middle East political settlement. To put it bluntly, the economies of the Occupied Territories are so small that economic dislocations resulting from a peace settlement could readily be set aright by sums of foreign aid money that donors would consider trivial in the context of a Middle East peace settlement.

The employment in Israel of residents of the Occupied Territories is perhaps the most significant economic link between the two areas. Almost a third of the labor force of the Occupied Territories was employed in Israel during 1973-75.[12] This employment has increased the wage rates of low-skilled workers from the Occupied Territories both working in Israel and in the territories. In the process, it presumably has reduced the inequality of income among residents of the territories. The severing of this link will have significant economic costs for the Occupied Territories. Simply because the Israeli economy is much larger than that of the Occupied Territories, the relative costs to Israel would be less, but not negligible.

Since the economic benefits from employment in

Israel of residents of the Occupied Territories are mutual, there is an economic motive for maintaining the link after a political settlement. However, a continued large flow of workers does represent a pressure point that might endanger the permanence of a Middle East peace settlement. For the early post-settlement years when the foundations of peaceful coexistence are being established, it might be necessary to reduce the size of the worker flow to minimize this vulnerability.

If employment of Occupied Territories' residents in Israel were to be discontinued, there are factors that would attenuate the severity of the impact on the territories. Since their employment in Israel is largely in low-skill occupations, the workers have not acquired highly specialized skills that could be used only in Israel and not elsewhere. Many of the skills used in Israel, especially fairly general construction skills, could readily be exploited in the Occupied Territories themselves. Whatever the post-settlement political status of the Occupied Territories, a Middle East peace settlement is likely to be followed by an inflow of financial assistance to the territories (which under the occupation have received negligible net government resource transfers, either from Israel or other countries) and an increase in the demand for labor, especially in construction projects.

The second primary economic link between Israel and the Occupied Territories is the exchange of goods and services. It is not plausible that existing trade arrangements would be maintained intact following a Middle East settlement. Whether the Occupied Territories were to become independent or be federated with the East Bank, they would most certainly be withdrawn from the Israeli tariff area and placed within another. Taken by itself, it is unlikely to be very harmful to the Occupied Territories and it may well be beneficial for them to be withdrawn from behind the high Israeli tariff wall. The Israeli economy probably would be hurt somewhat from the loss of the captive market in the Occupied Territories, but because it is large in relation to the economy of the Occupied Territories, the relative size of the loss could not be too great. In 1974/75 exports from Israel to the Occupied Territories were less than 10% of total Israeli exports and only about 3% of Israel's GNP. [13] Of course, the value of the loss to Israel would be much less than this, being only the difference between the price received on sales to the Occupied

Territories and the returns that could be received in alternative uses of the same resources.

In the event of a political settlement some preferential trading arrangements between Israel and Jordan or a Palestinian state would be conceivable, but they would probably be of modest scope. A customs union arrangement seems improbable. Israel would not wish to change its tariff structure drastically for the sake of greater trade with much smaller economies, so that a union would have to have a tariff structure similar to Israel's. Such a tariff structure would be inappropriate for the much less industrialized economies of the East Bank or the Occupied Territories. Also, the Palestine-Jordan state(s) would probably desire tariff protection for some domestic industries against competition from Israel. The latter consideration would be an obstacle to a free trade area arrangement as well as to a customs union. There remains only the possibility of a limited amount of preferential tariff concessions. One important possibility for a mutually beneficial trade agreement would be arrangements to permit the continuation of subcontracting by Israeli firms to firms in Arab territories.

Other forms of post-settlement cooperation between Israel and the Palestine-Jordan state(s) could be important. Transit rights through Israel to the Mediterranean are one obvious possibility. If Gaza were joined to the West Bank or Jordan, transit rights between the areas would be virtually a logical necessity. But transit rights from the West Bank to the Mediterranean through an Israeli port is another possibility of potentially mutual benefit. Before 1967 foreign goods reached the West Bank either via the port of Beirut and trucking through Lebanon, Syria, and Jordan or via the port of Aqaba and a long road trip through Jordan. Transit rights through Israel could save greatly on transport costs. An important reason for the greater development of the East Bank before 1967 was its superior location on Jordan's transport connections with foreign countries. Transit rights would shift the balance considerably in favor of the West Bank, which would become the most economic location for some industries either exporting to the West or making heavy use of imported inputs.

Other forms of cooperation and interaction are conjectural. They include cooperation in projects in areas such as transportation, communications, industry, and agriculture. In tourism cooperation or spillover effects could allow both the West and East Banks to attract both Israeli tourists and tourists from among travelers to Israel. Peace in the area could attract more foreign investment to the West Bank, where it has been negligible, and the East Bank as well. Investment by Israelis is a possibility, although political sensitivities may require that it develop only gradually.

One possible outcome of a Middle East peace settlement is an independent Palestinian state, composed either of the West Bank alone or the West Bank and Gaza combined. In either case, the resulting state would be small, although the population of a combined West Bank-Gaza state would roughly equal that of Jordan at its creation after the 1948-49 Arab-Israeli War. It would not be generously endowed with natural resources. It would have some attraction to tourists from developed countries, but without the return of East Jerusalem the potential would be modest. It would draw summer visitors from oil-rich Arab states as the West Bank did to a limited extent before 1967.

The economic issue of a Palestinian state is sometimes formulated in terms of "viability," a term that has never been given a useful meaning. It has never been specified what is expected to happen to a country that is economically not "viable." It might be poor, or develop only slowly, or rely on foreign aid, but there are undeniably "viable" economies that fall into some or all of these categories. Instead of pursuing this rather sterile approach, the discussion here will focus on the constraints on economic development policy that its position and small size would impose on a prospective Palestinian state, whose government is assumed to seek economic development.

The small size, underdeveloped economy, and prospective sources of income of a Palestinian state would considerably limit the range of discretionary economic policy choices open to a government seriously seeking development. A large, diversified economy has some leeway to choose a greater or lesser involvement in the international economy, because many of the gains from specialization in activities of comparative advantage can be realized from internal trade. A Palestinian state (and, for that matter, the Jordanian state, with or without the West Bank) must be heavily engaged with the international economy to achieve economic development. In consequence, its use of tariff policy and other protective measures will be constrained within a limited range. The small size and openness of a Palestinian state implies that optimal economic policy will set limits to the degree of discretionary flexibility in monetary and exchange-rate policy. The economic theory of optimum currency areas and monetary integration suggests (though it does not prove) that a fixed exchange rate and a passive monetary policy that accommodates to the balance of payments may be most appropriate for a small, open economy. For the most part, this has been the arrangement in Jordan.

One of the major sources of foreign exchange receipts that might be expected by a future Palestinian state would be remittances and investments by Palestinians employed abroad. The danger of frightening away or otherwise discouraging these international flows would exert another constraint on the economic policy choices of a Palestinian government, restraining measures such as heavy taxation, low ceilings on interest rates, and unstable monetary policy. A Palestinian state might also be constrained by the need to satisfy foreign aid donors, although the political spectrum of prospective donors--from Libya to the U.S. to Saudi Arabia--is so broad that a wide range of policies may be compatible with at least some prospective donor.

Small size and economic circumstances put practical limits on the use of some economic policy measures in both Jordan and a possible Palestinian state. The most important area of economic policy over which a Palestinian state would have wide discretionary latitude that it might not have if federated with Jordan is government expenditure. On the presumption that a post-settlement Palestinian state would receive relatively ample foreign aid, the control of government expenditure would take on considerable quantitative importance. Of course, insofar as aid donors attach conditions to their aid, the latitude for discretion in government spending will be narrowed. If the West Bank were to be federated with Jordan, conceivably there might be constitutional arrangements or stipulations in foreign aid grants so that the West Bank could be assured control over government expenditures not greatly less than what it might have as a separate state.

Perhaps the greatest potential economic effect of a Middle East peace settlement on the economy of the East Bank is the possibility of reducing Jordan's very large defense establishment. If peace

291

allowed Jordan to reduce its relative defense burden to the level typical of other LDCs, Jordan could reduce its armed forces by more than two-thirds. However, it may not be possible--at least for a long period--to achieve the requisite degree of mutual trust, not only between Jordan and Israel, but also between Jordan and neighboring Arab states. Because military forces may be shifted from one border to another, tensions elsewhere in the Middle East may inhibit disarmament in the front-line states of the Arab-Israeli conflict. For example, if Saudi Arabia maintained a substantial military capability to offset Iranian military strength, Israel might feel obliged to retain a large military force to defend against the Saudis, in turn influencing Jordan to maintain a substantial defense capability.

For political reasons post-settlement disarmament in the front-line states of the Arab-Israeli conflict probably would have to be gradual. This may be fortunate for Jordan from an economic standpoint. If the Jordanian armed forces were cut to, say, a third of their pre-settlement size, this would require redeployment of 15-20% of the total Jordanian labor force. Such a redeployment could only be done effectively if it were done fairly gradually. The tight labor markets that have prevailed in Jordan and Arab oil countries since about 1974 would ease the adjustment. The reduction in the defense burden could release substantial resources to be used for government development expenditures, but this depends on how foreign aid--some of which has been granted explicitly to support Jordan's military expenditures-- would be adjusted as Jordan's armed forces declined in size.

Whether after a Middle East settlement the West Bank, and possibly Gaza, were joined to Jordan or became an independent Palestinian state, the outcome probably would not have a profound impact on the East Bank economy, although there would certainly be noticeable effects. On the assumption that Jordan and the Palestinian state remained relatively open to international trade, which is rational policy for such small economies, trade between them might not be much less than if they were part of a single state. If a Middle East settlement allowed the West Bank to retain East Jerusalem, which seems extremely unlikely, then the acquisition of the West Bank might make a substantial net contribution to Jordan's foreign receipts, for in addition to tourism receipts there would be receipts of remittances and investment funds from West Bank Palestinians employed abroad. In the absence of the great tourist potential of East Jerusalem, there is little reason to think that the West Bank's net contribution to Jordan's balance of payments would be very great either positively or negatively.

If there can be any conclusion emerging from this analysis, it is the primacy of political, as opposed to economic, considerations in the shaping of a Middle East peace settlement. Given the malleability of the very simple economies of the East Bank and the Occupied Territories and the volume of aid resources potentially available to make a Middle East settlement successful, any likely settlement that is mutually acceptable in political terms can be made to work tolerably well in economic terms. Middle East peace negotiators do not require a battery of economic studies as a prerequisite to reaching a settlement of the Middle East conflict.

NOTES

1. Ginor, passim.

2. Olive oil, although the output of an industrial process of sorts, is best classified as a primary product export.

3. On exporting agricultural products see Haim Ben Shahar, Eitan Berglas, Yair Mundlak, and Ezra Sadan, "Economic Structure and Development Prospects of the West Bank and the Gaza Strip, Report R-839-FF, The Rand Corporation, Santa Monica, California, 1971, pp. 57-62, 145-52.

4. CBJ, Monthly Statistical Bulletin, various issues.

5. Jordan Ministry of Tourism and Antiquities, unpublished.

6. Among the most useful sources on the economics of the Occupied Territories are Ben Shahar et al.; Arie Bregman, Economic Growth in the Administered Areas, 1968-1973, Jerusalem: Bank of Israel, 1974; idem, The Economy of the Administered Areas, 1974-1975, Jerusalem: Bank of Israel, 1976; Abba Lerner and Haim Ben-Shahar, The Economics of Efficiency and Growth: Lessons from Israel and the West Bank, Cambridge, Mass.: Ballinger Publishing Company, 1975, Chapters 23-24; and Brian Van Arkadie, Benefits and Burdens: A Report on the West Bank and Gaza Strip Economies since 1967. New York: Carnegie Endowment for International Peace, 1977. The outline here draws primarily on these sources, especially those by Bregman and Van Arkadie.

7. Bregman, The Economy..., 1974-1975, p. 8. Note that all statistics on the Occupied Territories exclude East Jerusalem.

8. Calculated from ibid., pp. 20, 45, on the assumption that the share in total construction area of residential construction equals the corresponding share for value.

9. This is the conclusion of Van Arkadie, pp. 127-35.

10. Bregman, The Economy..., 1974-1975, pp. 50-51.

11. See Van Arkadie, pp. 48-49, 88-95.

12. Bregman, The Economy..., 1974-1975, p. 24.

13. Ibid., p. 55; and Israel Central Bureau of Statistics, Monthly Bulletin of Statistics, 28 (August 1977), 17. Here I exclude from Israeli exports purchases of services in Israel by workers from the Occupied Territories.

Appendix: Prewar Economic Statistics

1. TOTAL PRODUCT

a. <u>The Official Estimates for 1959-66</u>

As do most less developed countries, Jordan compiled estimates of GDP basically from estimates of value added in the various industrial sectors of the economy. For some sectors, these were based on estimates of production and intermediate costs; for others, on estimates of factor incomes. While there also exist GDP estimates by expenditure and (since 1965) by income, these are not independently derived, but depend upon the value added estimates. Therefore, to evaluate the methods of estimating GDP, it is appropriate to examine the estimates of value added sector by sector.

Estimates of the value of crop production were derived from statistics of acreage planted and crop production per acre. During the prewar period these acreage and yield statistics were derived from subjective estimates, mainly by local agricultural officers. This method has been widely used in LDCs. This approach is obviously much less reliable than one based on accurate farm accounts or on crop-cutting on a sampling basis. Hence, a fairly high margin of error must be attached to estimates of output and value added in crop production during this period. But while the probability of random error is high, there is no evident source of systematic bias in the growth rate.

The value of production in the livestock sector has never been estimated in a very satisfactory way. Estimates of the changes in livestock numbers were based on subjective evaluations by veterinary extension agents and are not considered very reliable. Data on production of such products as milk, wool, eggs, and poultry were rough estimates based upon scanty data. Statistics of the value of meat production from sheep, goats, cattle, and camels were arrived at by estimating the number of animals slaughtered, subtracting the number imported, and adding the number exported. The basic

information on the number of animals slaughtered was provided
by records of the number slaughtered in abbatoirs in the
cities and in refugee camps. However, many slaughterings took
place elsewhere. (Only about half the population lived in the
cities and refugee camps.) The JDS made a rough approximation
of these unrecorded slaughterings, but the method used evidently overstates their rate of growth. According to my own
rough estimates of this bias, it overstates by about one percentage point the average annual 1959-66 growth rate of the
value of production of meat and animal products and by about
0.1 percentage point the corresponding growth rate of GDP.
Because of the speculative nature of these estimates no explicit adjustment was made in the GDP estimates used in this
study.

In contrast to the estimates for the agricultural sector, statistics of production and value added for the mining
and manufacturing sector should be quite reliable, for they
have been based upon extensive annual surveys. The estimates
of mining and manufacturing value added in 1959 were derived
from a complete industrial census for that year. Data for
subsequent years were derived from annual surveys which involved complete enumeration of all large firms and sample
surveys of small firms. Jordan's statistics for the mining
and manufacturing sector undoubtedly compared very favorably
with other LDCs, which often rely upon censuses at long
intervals and sometimes are forced to omit altogether any
sampling of small establishments.

The likeliest sources of error in estimating mining
and manufacturing value added are the largely unavoidable
ones familiar to LDCs: inadequacy or nonexistence of records, particularly in smaller establishments; fear of di-
vulging to a government agency information which might affect
one's tax status; and a general preference for secrecy.
However, the largest firms, which dominated the mining and
manufacturing sector in terms of value added, including the
oil refinery, phosphate mining company, cement company,
vegetable oil refinery, and tannery, all had government participation in their ownership and management. Since their
operations were not concealed from the government in any case,
there was little reason for them not to cooperate with the
industrial surveys.

In estimating economic activity in wholesale and retail
trade, the JDS combined rough estimates of average trade
margins on a wide variety of domestically produced and imported goods with estimates of the volume of sales of domestic
and imported goods. The estimates are subject to the possibility of substantial error, a problem Jordan shares with
many other LDCs. The likely source of greatest error is trade
in agricultural products, both because trade in domestically
produced agricultural products accounted for a very large
share of earnings in the trade sector and because sizable

errors in the estimation of agricultural production are not terribly unlikely. Although the estimates for any one year are subject to a substantial degree of uncertainty, there is no strong reason to presume long-term growth rates are likely to be biased in one direction.

In the transport sector revenue estimates were based upon informal questioning of operators and a considerable amount of subjective judgement. Hence, the estimates of value added must be rough ones. Furthermore, the growth rate may be systematically understated. The JDS estimates of value added in road passenger transport essentially assumed constant productivity per vehicle over the period. Yet since this was a time of much road building and improvement, one would expect some rise in productivity per vehicle over time.

As with other LDCs, Jordan was able to utilize budget documents and other public accounts to derive reasonably satisfactory estimates of value added in public administration and defense. However, there is one special failing of the Jordanian estimates: The JDS was supplied with figures for total expenditures in defense, but not with the breakdown of defense expenditures between value added and intermediate items. Consequently, it was forced to assume value added in defense to be a constant proportion of total defense expenditures (with a rough adjustment for years in which purchases of military supplies were extraordinarily high).

JDS estimates of value added in the construction sector are not particularly reliable, but there does not appear to be any strong bias of the growth rate. The methodology of the JDS construction estimates is comparable to that of most other LDCs. Estimates of value added in the ownership of dwellings are always highly conjectural, particularly in LDCs, and Jordan was no exception.[1] Value added in services was composed of components of varying degrees of reliability: Statistics of government and UNRWA expenditures on wages and salaries in education and health are probably fairly reliable, while estimates for professional services, domestic servants, hotels,and restaurants are subject to large margins of error.

b. Porter's Estimates for 1954-59

The estimates by Porter of 1954-59 GNP must be considered less reliable than the JDS estimates for 1959-66. Porter's estimates of value added in agriculture and in public administration and defense are similar in methodology and quality of source to the corresponding JDS estimates for later years; hence, these are probably only slightly less reliable.

Porter's estimates for 1954-58 in manufacturing, construction, and transport are extrapolations from 1959 values largely in proportion to trends in the imports of major inputs. Value added in trade was extrapolated on the basis of trends in estimated consumption (not very reliable itself) and the trends in import values of fuels, motor vehicles and parts, and building materials. Estimates of value added in ownership of dwellings and other services involve similar approximations. For all these sectors Porter's estimates of 1954-58 value added must be considered very much inferior to the corresponding ones made for 1959-66 by the JDS.

The Porter estimates appear to overstate significantly the rate of growth in the transport sector. To derive 1954-58 value added in transport, he extrapolates backward from 1959 according to changes in imports of gasoline and diesel fuel. Since value added in transport comprises only the services of "public vehicles" (i.e., commercial carriers, which excludes cars for personal use as well as vehicles operated by the government, by farmers, and by firms outside the transport sector, such as mines and factories), Porter's procedure would be valid only if value added by public vehicles grew at a rate similar to that of nonpublic vehicles. However, the growth in public vehicles appears to have been much slower.[2] As per capita incomes grow, people switch from riding buses or taxis to driving their own cars. Also, as industry develops, larger firms arise, operating their own trucks rather than purchasing trucking services from transport companies. A rough estimate of this factor suggests that the transport growth rate estimated by Porter may be as much as four times as large as the true rate.

Since the Porter GNP estimates for 1954-59 are comparable in methodology with estimates for 1959 and later years by the JDS, the two series may be linked together. However, it would be a serious error to link the two simply by combining the Porter estimates for 1954-58 and the JDS estimates for 1959-66. The JDS figure for 1959 GNP is significantly larger than the Porter estimate, partly because of greater coverage (unrecorded livestock slaughter, unlicensed construction) in the JDS estimates and partly because of other adjustments to the data.[3] To combine Porter's unadjusted estimates for 1954-58 with the JDS estimates for later years, as several studies have done, would be to exaggerate the rate of growth as the increased coverage between 1958 and 1959 would then be treated as a growth in income. In this study the 1954-58 estimates have been adjusted to make them comparable in coverage to the estimates for later years.

2. INVESTMENT AND SAVING

In most respects the methods used to make the official estimates of 1959-66 investment in Jordan were comparable to those common in other LDCs. The JDS used the production, or commodity-flow, approach, based upon estimates of the domestic production and importation of capital goods. This, rather than the alternative expenditure approach, is most commonly

298

used in LDCs.

Generally, investment statistics of LDCs ignore, or at least seriously understate, own-account investment by farmers in such things as terracing land, digging wells and irrigation ditches, and developing orchards and vineyards. Jordan is no exception. The JDS did make an estimate of private construction on farms, but this was a small fraction of total investment and neglected such important items as terracing and tree planting. It seems clear that private farm investment was understated in Jordan. Perhaps the underestimate was not as serious in Jordan as in other LDCs because the relative importance of agriculture was less in Jordan than in other countries at a similar level of economic development. But, on the other hand, terracing and tree planting may have been exceptionally important in Jordan, given its hilly terrain and the rapid expansion of citrus production experienced prior to the 1967 war.

LDC estimates of the value of changes in stocks or inventories generally are incomplete in coverage and not very accurate. Jordan's national accounts share this deficiency. Estimates of annual changes in livestock herds were made by the extension staff of the Veterinary Department of the Ministry of Agriculture. Being based largely upon judgement, the results cannot be very accurate. Estimates of changes of stocks of wheat and wheat flour were based on a rough approximation which produced a long-run average estimate of zero. No account was taken of most other stock changes, such as in traders' inventories, and increases in such stocks presumably were recorded as consumption.

It seems certain that inventory investment was underestimated in Jordan, but inventory investment is underestimated in most LDCs, because the national accounts of most LDCs record inventory change of only a few commodities. Data presented by Hooley from a small sample of countries suggest that countries (like Jordan) recording inventory change in only a few commodities (probably the majority of LDCs) may understate total investment by 15-20%.[4]

While the most serious problems mentioned above are those common to most LDC economic accounts, two important problems are particular to Jordan. The first is that the official national accounts estimates of investment omitted capital expenditure on imported aircraft by the national airline. While the precise magnitude of the omission is unavailable, it appears to have been on the order of 5% of gross domestic investment. Because of the somewhat speculative nature of this figure, where relevant two alternatives are presented in this study: one excluding and one including a 5% adjustment for unrecorded investment in aircraft.

In the national accounts the JDS included a "statistical discrepancy" as part of inventory investment. This statistical discrepancy represented the difference between gross

domestic investment and its financing (domestic saving plus
net resources supplied from abroad). However, the direct estimate of domestic investment is most certainly more accurate
than the estimate of resources available for domestic investment, or at least of the private saving component, which can
have but little claim to accuracy. It seems more reasonable
to work with figures of gross domestic investment that exclude
the extremely dubious estimate of statistical discrepancy,
and this adjustment to the official estimates of investment
is used here.

This adjustment to the official estimates of investment
implies a corresponding adjustment to the official estimates
of saving. Essentially, I transfer the statistical discrepancy from the statistically more reliable item, investment,
to the statistically less reliable one, private saving. The
JDS computed private saving as a residual from its estimates
of private disposable income and private consumption expenditure. The JDS estimate of private consumption expenditure
cannot be considered very reliable, as it was derived from an
analysis based upon judgement and approximation. For each
class of goods and services, this analysis divided the total
available quantity (imports plus domestic production) among
its possible uses (private consumption, government consumption, investment, intermediate uses, exports) by methods
which were only rough approximations. The approach taken here
is to estimate private saving as a residual from estimates of
gross domestic investment, the deficit on foreign current
account, and government (dis-) saving, items likely to be more
accurately estimated than private consumption and disposable
income.

The JDS distinguished two types of foreign aid received
by the government: current transfers and capital transfers.
Current transfers to government, according to the JDS classification, were grants (in one case, a loan) unrestricted as
to use, frequently termed budget support. Other transfers
to government, all of which were in some formalistic way tied
to capital formation in Jordan, were classified as capital
transfers. Current transfers were treated in a manner similar
to current domestic revenues of the government, whereas capital transfers were treated as financing the government deficit.

The rationale for distinguishing between current and
capital transfers is that it is possible to identify certain
types of transfers which finance consumption--current trans-
fers--and to distinguish them from transfers which finance
investment--capital transfers. This is a fallacy. It represents an attempt to give economic significance to a legal or
administrative distinction. There is no practical way to
determine what economic activity each particular foreign
transfer finances. Even if a transfer were specified legally
to be for the financing of a particular project, that project

300

might have been undertaken even in the absence of the transfer, so that some other activity was in fact the consequence of the transfer. In this study all foreign transfers to government are treated as capital transfers to government, which means that all such transfers are treated as foreign-supplied saving financing the government deficit. This treatment has been customary in aggregative development models. Since the JDS classified most foreign transfers to government as current transfers, this change in treatment has a large effect on the measurement of foreign and domestic contributions to the financing of development.

Foreign transfers to households are affected by an error in the JDS estimates of the balance of payments. The error lies in the treatment of payments by UNRWA, other UN agencies, and other charitable institutions for the services of Jordanians employed locally (e.g., as school teachers by UNRWA). The national accounts recorded these payments as export of services. This is surely incorrect, for the services were "consumed" by Jordanians, not foreigners. The payments properly should be recorded not as exports, but as transfer payments from abroad to private households. In the national accounts balance of payments estimates, I therefore reduced services exports and increased transfers to households by the same amount, equal to payments for services by UNRWA, other UN agencies, and other charitable institutions. All balance of payments and foreign aid estimates for 1959-66 used in this study embody this correction. Since my correction involves a change in the export figure, the maintenance of the national income accounting identity, $Y=C+I+G+X-M$, requires a corresponding adjustment elsewhere. However, there exists no corresponding identifiable error in the other terms of the identity.[5] Therefore, in some tables presented here the usual accounting identities do not hold precisely.[6]

NOTES

1. The area of private building construction classified according to type of building material primarily used, was derived from annual records of building permits issued. Estimates of the area of unlicensed construction were based upon a survey conducted in 1965. To these figures was applied a rough estimate of average cost per square meter derived from informal inquiries among building contractors. Government construction was taken from the public accounts and from information supplied directly to the JDS by government agencies. These methods obviously embody a sizable margin of error.

2. From the JDS Economic Section I have obtained data on vehicles registered in Jordan each year from 1961 to 1966. The average annual growth rates between 1961 and 1966 were 2.0% for public buses, 4.5% for public taxis, and 3.6% for public trucks. Only the services of these three categories

301

are counted as part of transport value added. The growth rates for the categories not included in the transport sector were 16.2% for private cars, 19.3% for private trucks, 9.1% for government vehicles, and 13.3% for vehicles belonging to other organizations (such as UNRWA).

3. While the first JDS estimate for 1959 was identical with Porter's estimate, subsequent revisions of the JDS estimates (mainly expanding coverage) produced a sizable discrepancy between the two estimates.

4. Richard W. Hooley, "The Measurement of Capital Formation in Underdeveloped Countries," Review of Economics and Statistics, 49 (May 1967), 199-200.

5. The JDS correctly recorded the services of Jordanians employed by UNRWA, etc., as domestic production on the production side of the national accounts and as private consumption on the expenditure side.

6. There is a second reason why some accounting identities do not hold precisely here: my adjustment of the statistical discrepancy, moving it from the estimate of investment to the estimate of private saving.

Bibliography

1. Burhan Abu Howayej, "Factors Affecting Delinquency in Repayment of Agricultural Institutional Loans in Jordan," unpublished M.S. thesis, Department of Agricultural Economics, American University of Beirut, Beirut, Lebanon, 1970.
2. Ahmad Abu-Shaikha, "Land Tenure in Jordan: A Case Study of the Beni-Hassan Area," unpublished M.S. thesis, Department of Agricultural Economics, American University of Beirut, Beirut, Lebanon, 1971.
3. Najati Mohammed Amin al-Bukhari, Issues in Occupational Education and Training: A Case Study in Jordan, Stanford, California: Stanford International Development Education Center, Stanford University, 1968.
4. Oddvar Aresvik, The Agricultural Development of Jordan, New York: Praeger, 1976.
5. Odd Aukrust, "Factors of Economic Development: A Review of Recent Research," Productivity Measurement Review, 40 (February 1965), 6-22.
6. Hisham Awartani, "Progress Appraisal of the East Ghor Rural Development Project," Cooperative Institute, Jordan Cooperative Organization, Amman, 1968.
7. Abdul Wahhab Jamil Awwad, "Agricultural Production and Income in the East Ghor Irrigation Project: Pre and Post-Canal," Amman: United States Agency for International Development, 1967.
8. Gabriel Baer, "Land Tenure in the Hashemite Kingdom of Jordan, Land Economics, 33 (August 1957), 187-97.
9. Bela Balassa, "Patterns of Industrial Growth: Comment," American Economic Review, 51 (June 1961), 394-97.
10. Pranab K. Bardhan, "Size, Productivity and Returns to Scale: An Analysis of Farm-Level Data in Indian Agriculture," Journal of Political Economy, 81 (November/December 1973), 1370-86.
11. Pranab K. Bardhan and T. N. Srinivasan, "Cropsharing Tenancy in Agriculture: A Theoretical and Empirical Analysis," American Economic Review, 61 (March 1971), 48-64.

303

12. Shawki Barghouti, "The Role of Agricultural Cooperatives in Improving Wheat Production in Jordan," working draft, The Ford Foundation, Amman, 1976 (typescript).

13. Michael A. Barnard, Industrial Development Bank: A Report on the History, Formation and Operations, 2 vols., report prepared for the U.S. Agency for International Development, Washington, D.C., 1965.

14. Solon L. Barraclough and Arthur L. Domike, "Agrarian Structure in Seven Latin American Countries," in Charles T. Nisbet, ed., Latin America: Problems in Economic Development, New York: The Free Press, 1969.

15. James Baster, "The Economic Problems of Jordan," International Affairs, 31 (January 1955), 26-35.

16. Yoram Ben-Porath and Emanuel Marx, "Some Sociological and Economic Aspects of Refugee Camps on the West Bank," Santa Monica, Calif.: The Rand Corporation, Report R-835-FF, 1971.

17. Haim Ben Shahar, Eitan Berglas, Yair Mundlak, and Ezra Sadan, "Economic Structure and Development Prospects of the West Bank and the Gaza Strip," Santa Monica, Calif.: The Rand Corporation, Report R-839-FF, 1971.

18. Jagdish N. Bhagwati, Amount and Sharing of Aid, Washington: Overseas Development Council, 1970.

19. Samuel Bowles, Planning Educational Systems for Economic Growth, Cambridge, Mass.: Harvard University Press, 1969.

20. _____, "Sources of Growth in the Greek Economy, 1951-1961," Economic Development Report No. 27, Project for Quantitative Research in Economic Development and Development Advisory Service, Center for International Affairs, Harvard University, Cambridge, Mass., 1967 (revision, mimeographed).

21. Arie Bregman, Economic Growth in the Administered Areas, 1968-1973, Jerusalem: Bank of Israel, 1975.

22. _____, The Economy of the Administered Areas, 1974-1975, Jerusalem: Bank of Israel, 1976.

23. Michael Bruno, Interdependence, Resource Use and Structural Change in Israel, Jerusalem: Bank of Israel, 1962.

24. Henry J. Bruton, "Productivity Growth in Latin America," American Economic Review, 57 (December 1967), 1099-1116.

25. D. R. Campbell, "Jordan: The Economics of Survival," International Journal, 23 (Winter 1967-68), 109-23.

26. Central Bank of Jordan (CBJ), Annual Report, Amman.

27. _____, Monthly Statistical Bulletin, Amman.

28. Hollis B. Chenery, "Patterns of Industrial Growth," American Economic Review, 50 (September 1960), 624-54.

29. Hollis B. Chenery and Alan M. Strout, "Foreign Assistance and Economic Development," American Economic Review, 56 (September 1966, Part I), 679-733.

30. Hollis B. Chenery and Moises Syrquin, Patterns of Development, 1950-1970, London: Oxford University Press, 1975.

31. Hollis B. Chenery and Lance Taylor, "Development Patterns: Among Countries and Over Time," Review of Economics and Statistics, 50 (November 1968), 391-416.

32. Stephen N. S. Cheung, "Private Property Rights and Share-cropping," Journal of Political Economy, 76 (November-December 1968), 1107-22.

33. _____, The Theory of Share Tenancy, Chicago: University of Chicago Press, 1969.

34. Marion Clawson, Hans H. Landsberg, and Lyle T. Alexander, The Agricultural Potential of the Middle East, New York: American Elsevier, 1971.

35. William R. Cline, Economic Consequences of a Land Reform in Brazil, Amsterdam: North-Holland, 1970.

36. Adnan Dabbas, "Lending Procedures Followed by the Institutional and Non-Institutional Sources of Credit in the Balqa District of Jordan," unpublished M.S. thesis, Department of Agricultural Economics, American University of Beirut, Beirut, Lebanon, 1973.

37. Naim Husni Dahmash, "The Role of Budgeting in National Economic Planning in Developing Countries with Emphasis on Jordan," unpublished Ph.D. thesis in accounting, University of Illinois at Urbana-Champaign, 1973.

38. Mazen Dajani, "Economic Development with Unlimited Supplies of Labour: The Jordanian Case, 1948-1968," unpublished M.A. thesis, Graduate Program of Development Administration, American University of Beirut, Beirut, Lebanon, 1969.

39. N. Dajani, "Employment, Occupations and Income of Palestinian Refugees in Jordan," n.p., [1954], (mimeographed).

40. _____, The Israeli Aggression: Economic Impact, Amman, 1967.

41. Edward F. Denison, The Sources of Economic Growth in the United States and the Alternatives Before Us, New York: Committee for Economic Development, 1962.

42. Padma Desai, "Alternative Measures of Import Substitution," Oxford Economic Papers, n.s. 21 (November 1969), 312-24.

43. Evsey D. Domar, "On the Measurement of Technological Change," Economic Journal, 71 (December 1961), 709-29.

44. Fahd Mahmud El-Hamawi, "Structure, Conduct and Performance of the Amman Organized Wholesale Fruit and Vegetable Market," unpublished M.S. thesis, Department of Agricultural Economics, American University of Beirut, Beirut, Lebanon, 1971.

45. Adnan Hassan El-Hindi, "Reforms in Jordan's Budget System," unpublished Ph.D. thesis, Department of Economics, Syracuse University, Syracuse, N.Y., 1976.

46. Mohamed Haitham Mahmoud El-Hurani, "Economic Analysis of the Development of the Wheat Subsector of Jordan," unpublished Ph.D. thesis, Department of Economics, Iowa State University, Ames, Iowa, 1975.

47. A. M. El-Zoobi, Socio-Economic Survey of the Operator Far-

305

mers in the Three Pilot Areas of the Project, FAO/Dry-
land Farming Project, Socio-Economic Series No. 8,
Karak, Jordan, 1973.

48. Robert E. Evenson and Yoav Kislev, Agricultural Research
and Productivity, New Haven, Conn.: Yale University
Press, 1975.

49. Lawrence L. Ewing and Robert C. Sellers, The Reference
Handbook of the Armed Forces of the World, 1966, Washington, 1966.

50. FAO Mediterranean Development Project, Jordan County Report, Rome: Food and Agriculture Organization of the
United Nations, 1967.

51. FMC International, S.A., Executive Summary: Integrated
Dairy-Beef Complex, Jordan, presented to National Planning Council, Amman, 1975.

52. A. L. Gaathon, Economic Productivity in Israel, New York:
Praeger, 1971.

53. Andreas S. Gerakis, "Pegging to the SDR," Finance and Development, 13 (March 1976), 35-38.

54. [Salem O. Ghawi and Munthar Masri], "Labour Force in Jordan," [Amman], Jordan Development Conference No. 76/5,
1976 (mimeographed).

55. Fanny Ginor, "The Impact of Capital Imports on the Structure of Developing Countries," Kyklos, 22 (1969-Fasc. 1),
104-21.

56. Norman Goetze and David P. Moore, "Constraints on Adoption
of Improved Wheat Production Practices in Jordan," in
Jordan Wheat Research and Production.

57. Carl H. Gotsch, "Wheat Price Policy and the Demand for Im-
proved Technology in Jordan's Rainfed Agriculture,"
Discussion Paper No. 2, Studies of Dryland Agriculture,
The Ford Foundation, Amman, 1976.

58. Great Britain Naval Intelligence Division, Palestine and
Transjordan, Geographical Handbook Series, London: Oxford University Press, 1943.

59. Brook A. Greene, "Mexipak Wheat Performance in Lebanon,
1970-71," Middle East Journal, 28 (Autumn 1974), 437-40.

60. Rima Faiq Halazun, "Fiscal Policy and Economic Development
in Jordan," unpublished M.A. thesis, American University
of Beirut, Beirut, Lebanon, 1968.

61. Leonard Haldorson, "Availability of Goods and Services for
Improved Wheat Production in Jordan," in Jordan Wheat
Research and Production.

62. Nadav Halevi and Ruth Klinov-Malul, The Economic Development of Israel, New York: Praeger, 1968.

63. Frederick Harbison and Charles A. Myers, Education, Manpower and Economic Growth: Strategies of Human Resource
Development, New York: McGraw Hill, 1964.

64. Husayn Harrim, "Government Budgetary Process in Jordan,"
unpublished M.A. thesis, Department of Political Studies
and Public Administration, American University of

Beirut, Beirut, Lebanon, 1968.

65. Yujiro Hayami and Vernon W. Ruttan, Agricultural Development: An International Perspective, Baltimore: Johns Hopkins, 1971.

66. Jared E. Hazleton, "The Impact of the East Ghor Canal Project on Land Consolidation, Distribution and Tenure," Royal Scientific Society, Economic Research Department, Amman, 1974.

67. Jared E. Hazleton and G. E. Khoury, "Monetary Analysis of Balance of Payments Surpluses and Deficits: A Review," Amman: Royal Scientific Society, 1974.

68. Z. Y. Hershlag, Introduction to the Modern Economic History of the Middle East, Leiden: E. J. Brill, 1964.

69. Sa'id B. Himadeh, ed., Economic Organization of Palestine, Beirut: American University of Beirut, 1938.

70. Harley H. Hinrichs, A General Theory of Tax Structure Change During Economic Development, Cambridge, Mass.: Harvard University Law School, 1966.

71. P. M. Holt, Egypt and the Fertile Crescent, 1516-1922: A Political History, Ithaca, N.Y.: Cornell University Press, 1966.

72. Richard W. Hooley, "The Measurement of Capital Formation in Underdeveloped Countries," Review of Economics and Statistics, 49 (May 1967), 199-208.

73. David Horowitz and Rita Hinden, Economic Survey of Palestine, Tel Aviv: Economic Research Institute of the Jewish Agency for Palestine, 1946.

74. H. S. Houthakker, "On Some Determinatns of Saving in Developed and Under-Developed Countries," in E. A. G. Robinson, ed., Problems in Economic Development, London: Macmillan, 1965, pp. 212-24.

75. John D. Hyslop, "The Dryland Subsector of Jordanian Agriculture: A Review," Agriculture Division, USAID, Amman, Jordan, 1976 (mimeographed).

76. Industrial Development Bank (IDB), Annual Report, Amman.

77. _____, Industrial Development Bank (1965-1975), Amman, n.d.

78. [International] Institute for Strategic Studies, The Military Balance, London, annual.

79. International Bank for Reconstruction and Development (IBRD), The Economic Development of Jordan, Baltimore: Johns Hopkins, 1957.

80. International Labour Office, Yearbook of Labour Statistics, Geneva, 1966.

81. International Monetary Fund, International Financial Statistics, Washington, monthly.

82. Israel Central Bureau of Statistics, Monthly Bulletin of Statistics, Jerusalem.

83. _____, Monthly Statistics of the Administered Territories, Jerusalem.

84. _____, Quarterly Statistics of the Administered Terri-

tories, Jerusalem.

85. _____, Statistical Abstract of Israel, Jerusalem, annual.

86. Maurice B. Issi, "Socio-Economic Aspects of the Wadi Dhuleil Area of Jordan, 1973-1974," Economic Research Department, Royal Scientific Society, Amman, 1975.

87. Salih M. Jadallah, "The Phosphate Industry in Jordan," unpublished M.B.A. dissertation, Department of Business Administration, American University of Beirut, Beirut, Lebanon, 1965.

88. Jordan Budget Department, Budget Law for the Fiscal Year 1976, [Amman, 1976].

89. Jordan Department of Statistics (JDS), The Agricultural Sample Survey in the Ghors, 1974, Amman, 1975.

90. _____, Agricultural Statistical Yearbook and Agricultural Sample Survey, 1974, Amman, 1975.

91. _____, Agricultural Statistical Yearbook and Some Results of the Agricultural Census, 1975, Amman, 1976.

92. _____, Amman and Zarka Consumer Price Index and Civil Servants Price Index, Amman, monthly.

93. _____, Analysis of the Population Statistics of Jordan, prepared by the demographic section under the direction of Dr. Hilde Wander, vol. I, Amman, 1966.

94. _____, Consumer Price Index for Amman, Zarqa, Irbid, Aqaba and Civil Servants, Amman, monthly.

95. _____, The East Jordan Valley: A Social and Economic Survey, Amman, 1961.

96. _____, External Trade Statistics, Amman, annual.

97. _____, External Trade Statistics and Shipping Activity in Aqaba Port, Amman, quarterly.

98. _____, Family Expenditures and Cost of Living Index for Civil Servants, 1968, Amman, 1968.

99. _____, First Census of Population and Housing, 18 November 1961, 4 vols., Amman, 1964.

100. _____, Jordanian Students in the Third Level of Education, 1969/1970, Amman, 1971.

102. _____, Multi-Purpose Household Survey, January-April 1972, Amman, 1974.

103. _____, Multi-Purpose Household Survey, January-April 1974, Amman, 1976.

104. _____, The National Accounts, Amman, annual.

105. _____, Population and Labor Force in the Agriculture Sector, 1967, Amman, 1968.

106. _____, Population Census and Internal Migration for Amman, Jerusalem, Zarqa, Ruseifa, Irbid and Aqaba, 1967, Amman, n.d.

107. _____, Social and Economic Survey of the East Jordan Valley, 1973, Amman, 1973.

108. _____, Statistical Yearbook, Amman, annual.

109. Jordan Development Board (JDB), Five Year Program for Economic Development, 1962-1967, n.p., 1961.

110. _____, Seven Year Program for Economic Development, 1964-1970, Amman, n.d.

111. Jordan Ministry of Education, Annual Report for School Year 1959-1960, Amman (Arabic).

112. _____, Yearbook of Educational Statistics for the Year 1966-1967, Amman.

113. _____, The Statistical Yearbook of Education 1973-1974, Amman.

114. Jordan River and Tributaries Regional Corporation (JRTRC), Jordan Valley Project: Agro- and Socio-Economic Study, Final Report, Dar al-Handasah, Beirut, and Netherlands Engineering Consultants, The Hague, 1969.

115. Jordan Times, English language daily, Amman.

116. Jordan Valley Commission (JVC), Jordan Valley Development Plan, 1975-1982, n.p., 1975.

117. _____, Jordan Valley Social Development Program: A Supplement to the Jordan Valley Rehabilitation Plan, n.p., 1974.

118. _____, Summary: Jordan Valley Development Plan, 1975-1982, Amman, 1976.

119. Jordan Wheat Research and Production, final report of contract AID/sa-C-1024 between Agency for International Development and Oregon State University, 1976.

120. Taher H. Kanaan, "Projection of Jordan's Foreign Trade 1970, 1975," UNCTAD Projections Section, n.p., n.d. (mimeographed).

121. Wael Kanaan and Yousef Attieh, Jordan: Agricultural Development, Jordan Ministry of Culture and Information, Amman: Jordan Press Foundation, 1974.

122. Jack Kattan, Factors Affecting Demand Deposits in Jordan, Amman: Central Bank of Jordan, 1974.

123. John W. Kendrick, Productivity Trends in the United States, Princeton, N.J.: Princeton University Press, 1961.

124. Tony Killick, "The Possibilities of Development Planning," Oxford Economic Papers, n.s. 28 (July 1976), 161-84.

125. Ernest J. Kirsch, "Report to the Government of Jordan on Dryland Farming Extension Programs in the Irbid Project Area," draft UNDP/FAO Project JOR/75/011, Amman, 1975 (mimeographed).

126. A. Konikoff, Transjordan: An Economic Survey, Jerusalem: Economic Research Institute of the Jewish Agency for Palestine, 1946.

127. Simon Kuznets, Economic Growth of Nations: Total Output and Production Structure, Cambridge, Mass.: Harvard University Press, 1971.

128. _____, Modern Economic Growth: Rate, Structure, and Spread, New Haven, Conn.: Yale University Press, 1966.

129. _____, "Quantitative Aspects of the Economic Growth of Nations: II. Industrial Distribution of National Product and Labor Force," Economic Development and Cultural Change, 5 (July 1957, supplement).

130. _____, "Quantitative Aspects of the Economic Growth of
Nations: V. Capital Formation Proportions: International
Comparisons for Recent Years," Economic Development and
Cultural Change, 8 (July 1960, Part II).

131. _____, "Quantitative Aspects of the Economic Growth of
Nations: VII. The Share and Structure of Consumption,"
Economic Development and Cultural Change, 10 (January
1962, Part II).

132. _____, "Quantitative Aspects of the Economic Growth of
Nations: IX. Level and Structure of Foreign Trade: Comparisons of Recent Years," Economic Development and Cultural Change, 13 (October 1964, Part II).

133. Uma Lele, The Design of Rural Development: Lessons from
Africa, Baltimore: Johns Hopkins, 1975.

134. _____, "The Roles of Credit and Marketing in Agricul-
tural Development," in Nurul Islam, ed., Agricultural
Policy in Developing Countries, New York: John Wiley &
Sons, 1974, pp. 413-41.

135. Abba Lerner and Haim Ben-Shahar, The Economics of Efficiency and Growth: Lessons from Israel and the West Bank,
Cambridge, Mass.: Ballinger, 1975.

136. William Libbey and Franklin Hoskins, The Jordan Valley
and Petra, London, 1905.

137. Ian Little, Tibor Scitovsky, and Maurice Scott, Industry
and Trade in Some Developing Countries: A Comparative
Study, London: Oxford University Press, 1970.

138. Joergen R. Lotz, "Patterns of Government Spending in Developing Countries," The Manchester School of Economic
and Social Studies, 38 (June 1970), 119-44.

139. Jørgen R. Lotz and Elliott R. Morss, "Measuring 'Tax
Effort' of Developing Countries," International Monetary
Fund Staff Papers, 14 (November 1967), 478-97.

140. Robert Mabro, "Employment and Wages in Dual Agriculture,"
Oxford Economic Papers, n.s. 23 (November 1971), 401-17.

141. Ronald I. McKinnon, Money and Capital in Economic Development, Washington: Brookings Institution, 1973.

142. McKinsey and Company, Inc., "Revitalizing the National
Planning Council, n.p., 1976.

143. [Ahmad Mango], "Implementation and Follow-up of Five-Year
Plan 1976-1980," [Amman], Jordan Development Conference
no. 76/2, 1976 (mimeographed).

144. Michel Isa Marto, An Econometric Money Supply Model for
Jordan, Amman: Royal Scientific Society, 1974.

145. _____, A Money Supply Model: Jordan, Amman: Central
Bank of Jordan, 1974.

146. Michael P. Mazur, "Economic Development of Jordan," in
Charles A. Cooper and Sidney S. Alexander, eds., Econo-
mic Development and Population Growth in the Middle East,
New York: American Elsevier, 1972, pp. 211-79.

147. _____, "The Economic Development of Jordan," unpublished Ph.D. thesis, Department of Economics, Massa-

chusetts Institute of Technology, Cambridge, Mass., 1972.

148. Raymond F. Mikesell and James E. Zinser, "The Nature of the Savings Function in Developing Countries: A Survey of the Theoretical and Empirical Literature," Journal of Economic Literature, 11 (March 1973), 1-26.

149. Thomas H. Miner & Associates, Inc., Industrial Survey of Jordan, 2 vols., for United Nations Industrial Development Organization, Chicago, Ill., 1973.

150. Ministry of Social Affairs, Social Survey of Amman, 1960, Amman, n.d.

151. David P. Moore, "Soil Fertility Research on Wheat in Jordan," in Jordan Wheat Research and Production.

152. Robert R. Nathan, Oscar Gass, and Daniel Creamer, Palestine: Problem and Promise, Washington: Public Affairs Press, 1946.

153. "The National Income of Jordan, 1952-1954," prepared by the Economic Research Institute of the American University of Beirut under the direction of Albert Y. Badre with the cooperation of the JDS, n.d. (unpublished typescript).

154. National Planning Council (NPC), Five Year Plan for Economic and Social Development, 1976-1980, [Amman, 1976], mimeographed version.

155. _____, Three Year Development Plan, 1973-1975, n.p., n.d.

156. Hanna S. Odeh, Economic Development of Jordan, 1954-1971, Amman: Ministry of Culture and Information, 1972.

157. Gur Ofer, The Service Industries in a Developing Economy: Israel as a Case Study, New York: Praeger, 1967.

158. Wasfi Mahmoud Osman, "Major Problems of Government Budgeting and Planning: An Appraisal of Jordan's Experience (1948-1968)," unpublished M.A. thesis, Graduate Program of Development Administration, American University of Beirut, Beirut, Lebanon, 1969.

159. Howard Pack, Structural Change and Economic Policy in Israel, New Haven, Conn.: Yale University Press, 1971.

160. Raphael Patai, The Kingdom of Jordan, Princeton, N.J.: Princeton University Press, 1958.

161. _____, "On Culture Contact and Its Working in Modern Palestine," American Anthropological Association Memoir Series No. 67, American Anthropologist (new series), 49 (October 1947).

162. Paul Grounds Phillips, The Hashemite Kingdom of Jordan: Prolegomena to a Technical Assistance Program, Chicago: University of Chicago, 1954.

163. R. S. Porter, "Economic Survey of Jordan," Beirut: British Middle East Office, 1953 (mimeographed).

164. _____, "Economic Trends in Jordan, 1954-1959," Middle East Development Division, British Embassy, Beirut, Lebanon, 1961 (Mimeographed).

165. _____, "The Movement of Palestine Funds to Jordan,

1948-1952," Beirut: British Middle East Office, n.d. (mimeographed).

166. Gordon V. Potter, A Five Year Plan of Budget and Planning Improvement, Amman: USAID/Jordan, 1966.

167. F. Qushair and J. Hyslop, "Brief Analysis of Feedgrain Requirements for Livestock and Poultry Industry in Jordan," [Amman], USAID/Jordan, 1975 (typescript).

168. Joseph D. Reid, Jr., "Sharecropping and Agricultural Uncertainty," Economic Development and Cultural Change, 24 (April 1976), 549-76.

169. "Report on the Social Survey of Amman, Jordan," in United Nations Economic and Social Office in Beirut (UNESOB), Studies on Social Development in the Middle East, 1969, New York: United Nations, 1970, pp. 19-88.

170. E. B. Rice, Extension in the Andes: An Evaluation of Official U.S. Assistance to Agricultural Extension Services in Central and South America, Cambridge, Mass.: The MIT Press, 1974.

171. Hanna Rizk, Summary of Findings and Conclusions of the National Fertility Sample Survey, Amman: Jordan Department of Statistics, 1972.

172. James A. Roumasset, Rice and Risk: Decision Making Among Low Income Farmers, Amsterdam: North-Holland, 1976.

173. Royal Scientific Society (RSS), Economic Research Department, "Agro-Economic Aspects of Tenancy in the East Jordan Valley, 1975," Amman, 1975.

174. Yusif A. Sayigh, "Economic Implications of UNRWA Operations in Jordan, Syria, and Lebanon," unpublished M.A. thesis, Department of Economics, American University of Beirut, Beirut, Lebanon, 1952.

175. W. E. Schmisseur, "Economic Evaluation of Dryland Wheat Technologies Introduced in Jordan," in Jordan Wheat Research and Production.

176. Theodore W. Schultz, Transforming Traditional Agriculture, New Haven, Conn.: Yale University Press, 1964.

177. W. D. Scott and Company Pty. Ltd., "Development Prospects for Manufacturing Industry in Jordan," draft final report, 1976.

178. Zeid Jawdat Sha'sha'a, "The Mixed Industrial Sector in Jordan," unpublished M.B.A. thesis, Department of Business Administration, American University of Beirut, Beirut, Lebanon, 1969.

179. Edward S. Shaw, Financial Deepening in Economic Development, New York: Oxford University Press, 1973.

180. Frederic C. Shorter, "The Application of Development Hypotheses in Middle Eastern Studies," Economic Development and Cultural Change, 14 (April 1966), 340-54.

181. Benjamin Shwadran, Jordan: A State of Tension, New York: Council for Middle Eastern Affairs Press, 1959.

182. Robert M. Solow, "Technical Change and the Aggregate Production Function," Review of Economics and Statistics,

39 (August 1957), 312-20.

183. Akram M. Steitieh, "Consumption Patterns of Wage Earners in Jordan," Economic Research Department, Royal Scientific Society, Amman, 1974.

184. Thomas Stickley and Marwan Hayek, Small Farmer Credit in Jordan: A Country Program Paper on the Agricultural Credit Corporation of Jordan, Faculty of Agricultural Sciences, American University of Beirut, Beirut, Lebanon, 1972.

185. Systems Research Corporation, Area Handbook for the Hashemite Kingdom of Jordan, Washington: U.S. Government Printing Office, 1969.

186. Abdul Rahman S. Tukan, "The Implications of Achieving Fiscal Independence for Jordan," unpublished Ph.D. thesis, Department of Economics, Vanderbilt University, Nashville, Tennessee, 1967.

187. Umayya Salah Tukan, An Analysis of Central Banking in Jordan, Amman: Central Bank of Jordan, 1974.

188. United Nations, Report of the Commissioner-General of the United Nations Relief and Works Agency for Palestine Refugees in the Near East, 1 July 1965 - 30 June 1966, New York, 1966.

189. United Nations Conciliation Commission for Palestine, Final Report of the United Nations Economic Survey Mission for the Middle East, 2 vols., Lake Success, N.Y., 1949.

190. United Nations Department of Economic and Social Affairs, A Study of Industrial Growth, New York, 1963.

191. _____, World Economic Survey, 1967, New York, 1968.

192. _____, World Economic Survey, 1969-1970, New York, 1971.

193. _____, Statistical Office, Yearbook of International Trade Statistics, 1974, vol. I, New York, 1975.

194. United Nations Development Program (UNDP)-FAO, "Dryland Farming: A Socioeconomic Study with Special Reference to Land Tenure Problems in Abu-Naseir and Mubis Villages, Baq'a Valley," report prepared for the government of Jordan, Rome, 1970.

195. United Nations Economic Commission for Europe, Economic Survey of Europe in 1961: Part 2. Some Factors in Economic Growth in Europe in the 1950s, Geneva, 1964.

196. United Nations Economic and Social Office in Beirut (UNESOB), Studies on Development Problems in Selected Countries of the Middle East, 1972, New York, 1973.

197. _____, Studies on Development Problems in Selected Countries of the Middle East, 1973, New York, 1974.

198. United Nations Relief and Works Agency for Palestine Refugees in the Near East (UNRWA), UNRWA Reviews, Information Paper no. 6, Beirut, 1962.

199. Brian Van Arkadie, Benefits and Burdens: A Report on the

West Bank and Gaza Strip Economies Since 1967, New
York: Carnegie Endowment for International Peace, 1977.

200. P. J. Vatikiotis, Politics and the Military in Jordan: A
Study of the Arab Legion, 1921-1957, London: Frank Cass,
1967.

201. Richard J. Ward, "Foreign Aid and the Moral of Compulsory
Imports (The Case of Jordan)," Indian Journal of Economics, 45 (January 1965), 267-76.

202. Doreen Warriner, Land Reform and Development in the
Middle East, 2nd ed., London: Oxford University Press,
1962.

203. _____, Land Reform in Principle and Practice, London:
Oxford University Press, 1969.

204. Albert Waterston, Development Planning: Lessons of Experience, Baltimore: Johns Hopkins, 1965.

205. Jeffrey G. Williamson, "Dimensions of Postwar Phillipine
Economic Progress," Quarterly Journal of Economics, 83
(February 1969), 93-109.

206. Eugene P. Winter, "Wheat Research and Extension Program
in Jordan: Phase II," in Jordan Wheat Research and Production.

207. Yarmuk-Jordan Valley Project, Master Plan Report, Michael
Baker, Jr., Inc., Rochester, Pa., and Harza Engineering
Co., Chicago, Ill., 1955.

For Product Safety Concerns and Information please contact our EU representative GPSR@taylorandfrancis.com Taylor & Francis Verlag GmbH, Kaufingerstraße 24, 80331 München, Germany

Printed and bound by CPI Group (UK) Ltd, Croydon, CR0 4YY

08/05/2025

01864366-0014